VARIEGATED PLANTS

VARIEGATED PLANTS

A GARDENER'S INDEX TO PATTERNED FOLIAGE

•

SUSAN CONDER
and
ANDREW LAWSON

CASSELL

To the unfading memory of Andrew David Steiner, an
exceptional man

Cassell Publishers Limited
Villiers House, 41/47 Strand, London WC2N 5JE

First published 1994

British Library Cataloguing in Publication Data
A catalogue record for this book is available from the British Library

ISBN 0 304 34113 4

Conceived and produced by Gardenhouse Editions
15 Grafton Square, London SW4 0DQ

Editors: Judy Martin and Louisa McDonnell
Art Director: Lorraine Johnson
Design: Hammond Hammond
Horticultural consultant: Barbara Haynes
Index: Dorothy Frame

Typesetting and Artwork: BMD Graphics Ltd, Hemel Hempstead, Herts
Origination: Daylight Colour Art, Singapore
Printed and bound by Kyodo Printing Co Pte Ltd, Singapore

Overleaf: A deep border at Denmans, Sussex.

CONTENTS

INTRODUCTION

The ornamental value of leaves, as distinct from the more strident attraction of flowers (whose job, after all, is to seduce pollinators through colour, form and fragrance) has long been recognized. The acanthus leaf of Corinthian-style architecture; the vine, ivy and holly leaves of Gothic carvings; the willow leaves of William Morris designs; and the Victorian mania for collecting and growing unusual foliage plants, are just a few examples.

After a temporary eclipse in the first half of this century the popularity of ornamental foliage has gone from strength to strength, as a foil to flowers and as a feature in its own right. Variegated plants have taken the lion's share of this appreciation. With two or more colours per leaf, they have special appeal – two (or more!) for the price of one, so to speak — an offer that's especially hard to refuse where gardening space is limited. The number of variegated plants is increasing all the time as breeders respond to popular demand and especially attractive cultivars quickly become international 'stars', available far beyond their country of origin.

THE VARIEGATED PALETTE

Variegated foliage provides a wonderfully rich source of raw material for creative gardening. It includes the whole spectrum of greens, ranging from the clear hues of children's crayons to smoky grey-greens; acid yellow greens; cool, milky greens; and intense blue-greens. Although green is often not considered as a colour that 'counts' in the garden, once the subtle contrast and composition that occurs within a green and white or green and yellow variegated leaf and the assemblage of leaves on the plant are fully appreciated, the plants can be juxtaposed in the garden to maximum effect.

As well as greens, variegated foliage also offers white, pure yellows, oranges, reds and purples; shades and tints of cream, beige, pink, salmon, apricot, mauve, russet, scarlet, burgundy and crimson – that can equal the brightest flower. Leaf colour, however, is longer lasting than the longest-lasting flower, ranging from a few weeks, for seasonal flushes, to six months or more if deciduous, year-round if evergreen.

And as well as bicoloured forms, there are tricolours and multicolours, such as *Tovara virginiana* 'Painter's Palette' and *Ajuga reptans* 'Burgundy Glow'.

VARIEGATED FORMS

Variegated and variety share the same Latin root, *varius*, meaning various. The number of various forms that variegation can take is overwhelming – a testament to nature's creativity, ingenuity or simply randomness. Each type of variegation has its admirers and detractors, but all have their uses in the garden.

CONTRASTING EDGING

Orderly, contrasting leaf edging – often yellow or white margins around a central green or grey area, or the reverse – emphasizes the leaf shape, whether bold and solid or intricate and lacy. As leaves are generally symmetrical, margins that closely follow the edge take on an elegant, geometric, formal quality. Variegated hollies such as *Ilex aquifolium* 'Argentea Marginata' and 'Golden King'; hostas such as *Hosta crispula* and *Hosta decorata decorata*; and old-fashioned, tricolour zonal pelargoniums, with their concentric rings of colour, like hundreds of bull's-eyes seen *en masse*, are all examples.

Edgings can also be irregular, broadly striking margins, as in the variegated Canary Island ivy, *Hedera canariensis* 'Gloire de Marengo', or *Elaeagnus pungens* 'Maculata', with green edging to a large, central yellow area. Such edging often defines or becomes part of central splashes, and where one stops and another starts is hard to distinguish.

PAINTERLY VARIEGATIONS

Splashes, pointilliste-type speckles and streaks are more painterly aspects of variegation, each leaf a potential abstract artwork in miniature – comparing a single plant's variations from leaf to leaf can be a pleasant hour's exercise in close observation. The Himalayan lilac, *Syringa emodi*, for example, combines an acid green base colour and dark green splashes, in various proportions – some all acid green leaves, except for a tiny blotch; others one-third / two-thirds, others half and half, with the darker central splash often stopping cleanly along the midrib. Certain coleus forms appear intensely multicolour-speckled, as if spray-painted or, the old-fashioned equivalent, speckled with paint flicked from a toothbrush.

CONTRASTING VEINING

Contrasting veining, as in the variegated Japanese honeysuckle, *Lonicera japonica* 'Aureoreticulata', emphasizes the internal leaf structure, like a fascinating map of a river system which, in a sense, it is. When the veining becomes the framework for suffused variations in colour, a marbled effect results, as in the common garden spotted dead-nettle, *Lamium galeobdolon* 'Variegatum'; cyclamen; and *Arum italicum* cultivars.

CONTRASTING STRIPES

Like striped clothing, striped leaves range from visually arresting, visible from across a crowded garden, to an almost imperceptible understatement; and they can emphasize form or contradict it. Stripes are usually longitudinal, parallel to the leaf midrib or edges, as with variegated phormiums, most ornamental grasses and iris, but a few are horizontal, as with *Miscanthus sinensis* 'Zebrinus' and *Scirpus lacustris tabernae-montani* 'Zebrinus'. The stripes can be

bicolour, tricolour or multicolour, and of equal or varying widths.

SHARP VERSUS SOFT

Variegations can be sharply defined or melt, blend or suffuse into one another, like water-colours, creating a whole range of subtle tints and shades. The variegated culinary sage, *Salvia officinalis* 'Tricolor', contains grey-green within a creamy white edge, the whole softly suffused pink and purple in spring. Even seemingly two-toned leaves, such as variegated figwort, *Scrophularia auriculata* 'Variegata', *Hosta ventricosa* 'Aureomacu-lata' and *H. fortunei* 'Albopicta', often have subtle half-tones and quarter-tones, where one colour merges into another.

USING VARIEGATIONS

Successful gardens are often described as 'pretty as a picture', and creating pleasing scenery, with a sense of liveliness, contrast, movement and depth, is the goal of most garden owners. Variegated plants are invaluable in achieving that goal, whatever the particular style or level of formality desired.

Variegations can enliven shade or a dark background or corner and create a feeling of depth and movement, compared to the relative calm or massive two-dimensionality of all green plants, especially seen from a distance. By virtue of contrast, variegated plants also help define adjacent, plain-leaved plants more sharply.

Lumping all variegated plants together in terms of garden use is as unhelpful as lumping all flowering plants together — both cate-gories encompass forest trees and filmy ground cover, plants of subtle beauty and of unabashed crudity, and self-sufficient plants as well as demanding ones. Even more than with plain-leaved plants, the overall form and growth habit of a variegated plant count, since the assemblage of leaves, the pattern of how they overlap, fan out or otherwise relate to one another enormously affect the plant's appearance; single variegated leaves, for example, with appealingly clear markings can look muddled *en masse*, because of a crowded growth habit.

On the whole, variegations that clearly follow or otherwise emphasize the shape of the leaf – the margins of hostas, for example, or the parallel stripes of phormiums – tend to be easier on the eye and more sculptural in effect than random variegations. The larger the leaf and the simpler the shape, the truer this is.

CONSIDERING DISTANCE AND SPACING

One factor to consider when siting variegated plants is the distance from which the plant is seen. Plants with delicate edging, veining or subtle marbling or splashing, are best placed near a path, sitting area or raised bed, where they can be enjoyed up close. If otherwise suitable, container-growing is ideal. The wild garden is also a good setting because here they will not 'jar' with the other plants.

Boldly variegated plants can also be enjoyed up close, but the bolder the varie-gation and the larger the plant or group planting, the further it carries – across the proverbial crowded garden. Plants such as *Elaeagnus pungens* 'Maculata' are natural focal points, pulling the eye towards them, and need thoughtful siting: at the beginning or end of a path, either side of a gate or door, in the corner of a right-angled bed, at the base of a garden statue or ornament, and so on. Placed in the middle of a bed or border, such plants set up a symmetry that can be difficult to deal with and random siting is also usually unsuccessful.

Two or more large, boldly variegated plants or group plantings grown within view of each other both demand attention simul-taneously, and create a sort of tension between them; again, unless you want a formal effect, avoid equidistant spacing. A variegated hedge 'reads' as a continuous feature, but boldly variegated hedges, such as *Ilex aquifolium* 'Golden King', are liable to visually overwhelm nearby mixed

Left: The variegation of Euonymus fortunei 'Emerald 'n' Gold' is shown off to great effect in front of hypericum.

planting, and best suit expanses of lawn.

Using variegated plant mixtures, such as mixed coleus, *en masse* may look restless, although Victorian-style formal bedding of mixed coleus has its admirers, and containerized mixed coleus can be attractive. 'High-key' displays of mixed variegations also tend to suit geometric, architectural settings, such as on or edging a patio, or edging a straight path.

COLOUR POWER

Given a medium-toned or dark background, white is the most eye-catching variegation, visually advancing in the landscape; pastel variegations with a high white content have a similar effect. Pure yellow is almost as powerful as white, while oranges, reds and purples visually recede, the darker they are.

Against a pale background, such as white-painted brickwork, dark variegations show up best, although pastel- or white-variegated plants with a high proportion of dark tones, whether green or another colour, are also effective, while variegations based entirely on subtle, similar dark tones can read as monochromatic against almost any background.

One of the most effective ways of using variegated plants is to pick out one of the colours featured on a variegated leaf and repeat it with adjacent planting to emphasize it: golden variegated balm, for example, next to solid golden feverfew, golden marjoram or golden creeping Jenny.

COLLECTOMANIA

It is easy to suffer from collector's avarice: trying to accumulate one of each variegated form of a genus – an almost impossible task in the case of ivies, hollies or hostas, but still tempting. Designing a garden as a collector's showcase is perfectly valid, with formal beds for each genus, as in botanical gardens. It is hard, however, to combine a collector's mentality with an informal, relaxed layout, especially since small plants tend to be most effective in large groups of a single kind. It

would be better to group similar but botanically different cultivars: a group of various white-edged or white-centred hostas, for example, or yellow-edged or yellow-centred hollies, separated from other groups by visual buffers.

NATURAL AND UNNATURAL

Variegated plants in wild gardens need thoughtful selection and placement. However exotic a plant's origins, a natural appearance is the main criterion for inclusion in a wild garden. Some variegated plants, especially high-contrast tricolour and multi-colour forms featuring purple, red and orange, look unnatural, almost as if designed by art students rather than nature. But white and yellow variegations, from a distance, can mimic dappled sunlight in wild gardens which are often too shady – consider a group of lamiums for example. Informal clumps or drifts of one form or very similar forms of variegated plants work better in a wild setting than small isolated or scattered specimens.

SEASONAL THOUGHTS

Variegated foliage is especially valuable in winter, and may be the only source of garden colour. A few variegated plants such as *Liriope muscari* 'Variegata', *Scrophularia auriculata* 'Variegata', *Arum italicum* 'Pictum' and *A. i.* 'Marmoratum' are at their best then. Certain variegated ivies and ivy-leaved geraniums are suffused with pink or russet in cool weather, and also when young or grown in dry soil conditions. (Colours are also affected by soil acidity: on acid soil, reds and crimsons become vivid; on chalky soils, hues are more muted than fiery.)

Variegated plants such as *Hosta fortunei* 'Albopicta' and golden balm, *Melissa officinalis* 'Variegata', are most striking as new growth unfolds in spring, then fade as the season progresses, while a few, such as *Actinidia kolomikta*, increase in variegation, and co-ordinating adjacent plants to provide interest during the dull periods is a challenge,

which becomes easier with experience. Consider a pink-flowering clematis twining through the actinidia or a purple-leaved sage near the golden balm.

HOW VARIEGATION WORKS

Variegated plants originate naturally as random seedlings, or as sports – mutant variegated shoots on otherwise plain green plants. Some, such as *Abutilon pictum* 'Thompsonii', are virus-induced, in the same way that the streaked colours of 'Bizarre' tulips result from a harmless virus.

In red- or purple-variegated plants, chlorophyll, the green pigment responsible for photosynthesis and vital for non-parasitic plants' survival, is masked by other pigments, anthocyanins. Yellow and white variegations are caused by imperfect or absent chloroplasts, the granule-like plastids within a cell which contain chlorophyll. In a white- or yellow-edged leaf, the green pigment functions normally in the inner layer of leaf cells, but the outer layer lacks chloroplasts, making the edges white, or contains a preliminary version of chlorophyll, protochlorophyll, creating yellow. A yellow- or white-centred leaf, with green edges, has a defective inner layer of leaf cells. The attractive pink, red or russet spring flushes that some variegated leaves have result from anthocyanins protecting the vulnerable new growth from harsh ultraviolet light rays. Autumnal flushes result from an accumulation of sugar in the leaf tissues, caused by a drop in night temperature which triggers the production of anthocyanins and anthoxanthins.

BUYING VARIEGATED PLANTS

Popular variegated plants, such as spotted laurel and variegated dogwoods, are sold at garden centres, garden sections of DIY centres and some high street chain stores. Specialist nurseries offer a wider choice, often through a mail order service. Some are open to the public while others allow visits at specified times – it is best to always telephone first to avoid disappointment.

Local and national horticultural clubs and societies often have plant exchange and seed distribution schemes. Plant stalls at country fairs and charity sales can be a goldmine of rare or old-fashioned variegated plants, but are totally unpredictable and labelling is often rough, or even absent.

Variegated plant names can be a nightmare, with equally eminent authorities giving contradictory information. Confusion occurs because plants get re-classified or renamed while growers and the public continue to use the former, incorrect but still popular name; because two or more cultivars may be identical but have different provenances, each with its own name, a particular problem with ivies and hostas; or because several different strains may be sold under a single cultivar name. Viewing the plant for sale does not always help, since some develop variegation only when mature or late in the growing season. Using a reputable nursery and asking, if in doubt, are the safest approaches. See the Quick Name Guide to Latin plant names on page 17.

GROWING VARIEGATED PLANTS

Variegated plants are often weaker and less floriferous, with smaller and fewer blooms, than their all-green counterparts, but it is a matter of degree. *Vinca major* 'Variegata', for example, is only slightly weaker than the species and still a potential menace; the variegated Norway maple, *Acer platanoides* 'Drummondii', is noticeably slower and weaker than the species; *Phlox paniculata* 'Norah Leigh' needs ongoing cosseting. An exception is the variegated *Daphne odora* 'Aureomarginata', which is hardier.

Shelter is often more important for variegated than for all-green plants, especially thin-leaved, white- and yellow-variegated types, which can brown if exposed to hot sun, wind or extreme cold, thus destroying their ornamental value.

Providing suitable soil, nutrients, temperature and water is as important as for any

Acting as a punctuation mark at the corner of a box-edged bed is Ligustrum ovalifolium 'Aureum', in the potager at Barnsley House, Gloucestershire. To the left is Buxus sempervirens 'Marginata' clipped to form a standard with a sphere at the top and at the base.

A delightful medley of variegation includes in the foreground Hebe × franciscana 'Variegata', Helichrysum petiolare 'Variegatum' and Lamium maculatum with Abutilon pictum 'Thompsonii' to the right; behind these are the grass Phalaris arundinacea 'Picta' and a variegated ivy, with Tropaeolum majus 'Alaska' at the top.

plant. Some variegated plants, such as variegated forms of *Cornus alba* and *Euonymus japonicus*, are enormously tolerant of almost any soil and aspect, including maritime and urban conditions. Others are tricky, and their particular needs are described in the text.

Reversion, the production of all-green shoots on a variegated plant, increases the plant's vigour but can eventually overwhelm the weaker, variegated shoots, and all-green shoots should be cut out as soon as seen. Variegated plants typically liable to revert include the box elder, *Acer negundo* 'Variegatum'; golden privet, *Ligustrum ovalifolium* 'Aureum', and *Buddleia davidii* 'Harlequin'.

Variegated plants bought bare-rooted, as is often the case with mail order firms, should be planted as soon as possible, in the open ground if weather permits, or otherwise in temporary or permanent containers. If the potting compost of containerized plants is dry it should be soaked before planting.

Offspring grown from seed of variegated plants can lack chlorophyll, or lose the variegation and be all green, but some reliably transmit variegation from generation to generation. These include variegated nasturtium, *Tropaeolum majus* 'Alaska', variegated *Barbarea vulgaris*, ornamental brassicas, *Tovara virginiana* 'Painter's Palette', lungworts, lamiums, variegated eryngium and variegated lunaria.

Sports have to be propagated vegetatively. You can lift and divide established herbaceous types in autumn or spring, discarding any old, woody, central portion and replanting the younger, outer sections separately; or take soft, semi-ripe or hardwood cuttings; or remove and pot up plantlets or offsets separately. Variegated trees are often grafted; with multi-stemmed, suckering shrubs, such as variegated cornus and kerria, division or layering is easily done.

SUN OR SHADE

The intensity of leaf colour is affected by the amount of light available. There are exceptions but generally, variegated plants

with glaucous foliage, such as variegated rue and certain hostas, tolerate more sun than all-green kinds. Those with purple, maroon and brown variegations colour most intensely in sun, often becoming dirty green in shade. Yellow-variegated leaves colour best in full sun, although types with thin foliage, such as golden lamium, can scorch. Yellow-variegated ivy, holly and elaeagnus are happy in sun or light shade. White- and cream-variegated leaves, such as variegated apple mint, tend to prefer shade, especially where the soil is dry. With those that are happy in sun or shade, variegation is often sharpest in sun, but if it is combined with dry soil, smaller leaves and more compact growth result.

Height is also affected by light. Golden-striped zebra grass, *Miscanthus sinensis* 'Zebrinus', for example, is brighter in sun, but taller in shade. Lastly, many variegated plants that prefer sun tolerate shade for a few hours a day, and vice versa, so it is not a black and white issue, but more a series of greys. If in doubt, and you have a few extra plants, plant most of them in the recommended light conditions, and one or two in more adventurous positions, assuming the soil is suitable.

VARIEGATED LEAVES IN FLOWER ARRANGING

In spite of its name, flower arranging is as much about the imaginative use of foliage as it is about flowers, and variegated foliage is especially valuable. As well as providing mass, or infill, and contrast in form for flowers, variegation adds an extra sense of movement, whether the graceful, flowing lines of a white-edged hosta leaf; the sharp verticality of a striped phormium leaf; the boldly sculptural quality of a variegated *Fatsia japonica* leaf, or the lively, jumpy quality of *Berberis thunbergii* 'Rose Glow', with its small, pink, white and purple mottled foliage.

In flower arranging, as in the garden, variegated foliage cannot be treated as a single entity, but each plant observed and used to its best advantage. In many cases, assessing individual sprigs or even leaves is sensible: the markings on one cyclamen leaf, for example, may be more attractive than another, for a miniature display. And, as in a garden, amassing many wildly different types of variegated foliage in a single display is not necessarily a good thing, although a restrained display based on variegations of green and white, or green and gold, foliage can be very effective.

The green of a variegated leaf is always valuable as a soothing element, but the non-green variegation, such as white, yellow, orange, pink, red or purple, can pick up and repeat the flower or container colours, or become the sole source of colour. White, yellow and pastel variegations add eye-catching liveliness; dark-coloured variegations add depth and richness. You can play the game both ways: partner white roses with soft green and white variegated *Mentha suaveolens*, for a gentle, subtle effect, or with *Ajuga reptans* 'Burgundy Glow', for startling contrast.

All-foliage displays are currently fashionable, almost as an intellectual exercise, and rosette-forming variegated plants, such as London pride or arabis often take on the role of flowers, forming the central focal point. A cluster of variegated leaf rosettes arranged at the base of tall, narrow leaves or grasses makes an instant modern display. Old-fashioned posies can be enhanced by an encircling ruff of variegated hosta leaves.

Trailing variegated foliage, such as periwinkle, ivy and nasturtium, provides flowing lines to break the sharp horizontality of a container rim and generally 'relax' an arrangement. For large-scale, pedestal arrangements, such as church or wedding displays, they are invaluable. Diagonally impaling a short length of carefully chosen and well-leafed variegated nasturtium stem on an old-fashioned pinholder in a shallow bowl is an instant flower arrangement, elegant and oriental.

A few pertinent notes on conditioning

specific plants are included in the text, and there are many good flower arranging books that give more detailed information. Generally, however, the younger and less mature foliage is, the quicker it wilts when cut. With woody plants, you can nip off the youngest, newest growth – the tips of ivy or uppermost sprigs of elaeagnus, for example – and use the more mature foliage. With annuals and herbaceous perennials, it is simply a question of waiting, although thin-leaved subjects often last longer if submerged in water for several hours or overnight before they are used in a display.

When cutting material from shrubs, you are also pruning, so keep in mind the plant's overall shape. Always cut cleanly back to just above a growth point, whether a leaf, pair of leaves or branch. Cut sparingly from young variegated shrubs, and from slow-growing ones, such as daphnes or dwarf box. Slit or skin, do not crush, the lowest 2.5-5cm (1-2in) of stem of woody material, and with all stems, remove any foliage that would be submerged in the display. Re-cut the stems just before they are inserted in the vase or florist's foam, and add a drop of bleach to the vase water, to keep it odourless and bacteria free.

Certain plants (mainly evergreens) can be successfully preserved for dried flower arrangements by using glycerine. These plants are identified in the text and the method is as follows:

The stems are best collected between midsummer and early autumn when the leaves are fully mature (not soft), but not over-mature. Use freshly-cut stems and re-move the lower 2.5-5cm (1-2in) of bark. Place the stems in a heavy, narrow-necked con-tainer; mix a solution of equal parts glycerine and water and pour 5-8cm (2-3in) into the container. Top up as the mixture becomes absorbed. The stems are ready when the leaves are fully supple with a shiny, leathery surface. The process can take from one to six weeks to be completed – the thicker the leaf the longer it takes.

USING THIS BOOK

The book is divided into seven sections roughly following the divisions made by garden centres, nurseries and seedsmen but, more importantly, the way plants are used by the 'ordinary person'.

ANNUALS AND BIENNIALS includes generally short-lived plants cheap to buy or grow from seed. These are the low-risk, high-adventure plants, ideal for experimenting with in summer displays for formal schemes or in informal clumps in established beds and borders, as well as in any type of container.

TENDER PLANTS includes half-hardy or tender perennials, trees and shrubs, popular for bedding schemes and general summer display in cool temperate climates but also as more permanent planting in frost-free areas. Many are also house or greenhouse plants that benefit from a sunny spell outdoors in the summer, and are ideal patio plants, being instantly portable. As containerized plants, they offer great freedom for experimenting. These often cost more than annuals but are potentially longer-lived, providing pleasure, indoors and out through the seasons.

HERBS features popular culinary herbs, as useful in the kitchen as in the garden. Other variegated garden plants with herbal associations – and it is surprising how many have or once had medicinal, cosmetic or even occult uses – are listed under plant types.

PERENNIALS is the largest section, and features a wide range of variegated, hardy herbaceous and evergreen perennials, from tiny rockery subjects to substantial, back-of-border plants and from all-time favourites to the most recent introductions. Many of these plants perform reliably year after year, whether in the open ground or containers, while others are more challenging. Many can double as low-maintenance ground cover and most can be increased easily by division.

GRASSES reflects the growing interest in these 'architectural' plants which, by virtue

QUICK NAME GUIDE

Specific Linnaean epithets, though Latin, can still give you a rough idea of what a plant looks like and will help to identify it. The following terms, singly or in combination, often occur in variegated plant names.

ALBA, ALBUM, ALBUS:	WHITE
ALBIDA, ALBIDUM, ALBIDUS:	WHITISH
ANGUSTIFOLIA, ANGUSTIFOLIUM, ANGUSTIFOLIUS:	NARROW-LEAVED
ARGENTEO-, ARGENTEA-, ARGENTEUM, ARGENTEUS:	SILVER
ARGOPHYLLA, ARGOPHYLLUM, ARGOPHYLLUS:	SILVER-LEAVED
AURATA, AUREA, AUREUM, AUREUS:	GOLD-HUED, GOLDEN
BICOLOR:	TWO-COLOURED
CANDIDA, CANDIDUM, CANDIDUS:	GLISTENING WHITE
COLORATA, COLORATUM, COLORATUS:	COLOURED
DISCOLOR:	TWO-COLOURED, DIFFERENT-COLOURED
FLAVA, FLAVUM, FLAVUS:	PALE YELLOW
GLAUCA, GLAUCUM, GLAUCUS:	BLUE-GREY
LATIFOLIA, LATIFOLIUM, LATIFOLIUS:	BROAD-LEAVED
LUTEA, LUTEUM, LUTEUS:	YELLOW
MACROPHYLLA, MACROPHYLLUM, MACROPHYLLUS:	LARGE-LEAVED
MACULATA, MACULATUS, MACULATUM:	SPOTTED, BLOTCHED
MARGINATA, MARGINATUS, MARGINATUM:	MARGINED
MICROPHYLLA, MICROPHYLLUM, MICROPHYLLUS:	SMALL-LEAVED
PICTA, PICTUM, PICTUS:	PAINTED
PURPUREA, PURPUREUM, PURPUREUS:	PURPLE
RETICULATA, RETICULATUM, RETICULATUS:	NETLIKE VEINS
ROSEA, ROSEUM, ROSEUS:	ROSE-COLOURED
RUBRA, RUBRUM, RUBRUS:	RED
SANGUINEA, SANGUINEUM, SANGUINEUS:	BLOOD RED
STRIATA, STRIATUM, STRIATUS:	STRIPED
TRICOLOR:	THREE-COLOURED
VARIEGATA, VARIEGATUM, VARIEGATUS:	VARIEGATED
VERSICOLOR:	VARIOUSLY COLOURED OR CHANGING COLOUR

of their verticality and stripes, act as punctuation points in the garden.

CLIMBERS features hardy variegated plants that need support, whether a wall, trellis or the woody framework of nearby trees and shrubs. These range from subtle to 'high impact' plants, whose sheer size and bold leaf patterns can set the tone of a whole garden, whether used vertically, or horizontally, as ground cover.

TREES AND SHRUBS contains the hardy, woody variegated plants that can form the backbone of a garden and provide large-scale bulk. Being costly and long-lived, they are major investments – the bolder the variegations and larger the plant, the more special thought is required in choice and siting!

Next to each entry is an information box stating the botanical family, height, spread, flowering time, aspect, soil type and minimum temperature, as a quick guide to help you assess the suitability of the plant or plants covered for your garden. As with any condensed information encompassing many factors, it is a general guide only, since microclimates within a particular garden and even specific strains of plants themselves are infinitely variable. The height and spread of a plant, for example, will vary according to available light, nutrients and water, as well as exposure and competition from nearby plants. Likewise, frost-hardiness can vary; the same plant grown in an exposed position and heavy, cold, wet winter soil may succumb to a slight frost, but would survive several degrees of frost if grown in shelter and dry, light root conditions. Plants exposed to long, hot, summer temperatures are often more frost-tolerant than those that are not, so hardiness can also vary from year to year.

Some entries contain many plants with such varying requirements that the information boxes would become unwieldy if everything were included. In these cases, plants which are exceptions to the general rule — more frost tender, for example — are noted in the text.

ANNUALS
AND BIENNIALS

TRAYS OR POTS of popular bedding plants are widely available, but with the possible exception of ornamental cabbage and kale, the following plants can only be enjoyed if you order or buy the seeds in good time, sow them and grow them on yourself. Not a difficult task, in view of the returns: unusual, bright splashes of colour or cooling, soothing white; lush tropical focal points, or hard-working ground cover, according to choice.

Although 'temporary' may have negative overtones in gardening, there is a positive side to inherently short-lived plants. They can provide cheap and effective cover for large areas and allow the experimentation, in placing and juxtaposition, that more expensive, long-lived plants do not. With many hardy annuals and biennials, the initial effort is also the last one, since the plants renew themselves by self-seeding, sometimes in unexpected places and with unexpectedly pleasing results.

Amaranthus tricolor

AMARANTHUS TRICOLOR

Family: Amaranthaceae
Height: 60-90cm (2-3ft)
Spread: 60cm (2ft)
Flowering time: Summer
Aspect: Sun
Soil: Rich, fertile

Joseph's coat, much used by Victorians in formal bedding and as a summer greenhouse and conservatory plant, has suffered decades of disfavour. In spite of being one of the most colourful variegated plants, it is still often omitted from gardening books, even ones specifically about decorative foliage. Its dense, fountain-like rosettes of intensely glowing, broad, red leaves, up to 30cm (12in) long and heavily marked in yellow, copper and green, are perhaps thought too crude for the subdued tastes of gardeners in temperate climates. Hybrids include 'Illumination', with scarlet, bronze, yellow, green and orange leaves; and 'Joseph's Coat', similar to the species, but more vigorous.

Amaranthus tricolor, first introduced to the West from India in the sixteenth century, is slightly more tender than the closely related love-lies-bleeding (*A. caudatus*), whose dark red or green, velvety racemes so pleased the Victorian romantic imagination. All are sown under glass in gentle heat in late winter or early spring, hardened off thoroughly in late spring, and planted out after the last frost. They dislike root disturbance.

These plants grow 60-90cm (2-3ft) high,

slightly less across. Growth is most rapid and leaf colour best in rich, fertile soil, shelter and sun. The modest panicles of small red flowers add little and are best pinched out, to keep the plant compact and colourful. The younger, uppermost leaves are the most colourful, creating a poinsettia-like effect.

Though their original use as pot plants is outmoded, they would enhance a mixed border when planted singly or in small tight groups, backed by a large-scale, single-toned plant; one of the purple-leaved cotinus, in the case of 'Illumination', or phlomis or *Senecio* 'Sunshine', in the case of 'Joseph's Coat'.

The leaves wilt quickly when cut, and are unsuitable for flower arranging.

BRASSICA OLERACEA

Family: Cruciferae
Height: 30cm (12in)
Spread: 20-40cm (8-16in)
Flowering time: Non-flowering
Aspect: Sun
Soil: Neutral or alkaline, rich

Like Joseph's coat, the ornamental, or 'flowering', cabbages and kales have never really achieved legitimacy among the gardening establishment. It is understandable, since their dense, round masses are awkward to incorporate into informal planting; each plant is a visual law unto itself. Nonetheless, their colourful, crinkly leaves, lacily frilled or curled in some forms, are striking, and at their best during the colder months, when colour in a garden is limited. So they continue to appear in seed catalogues, and florists and garden centres feature tidy, pot-grown plants for autumn and winter bedding and window boxes, or for display in cool greenhouses or conservatories.

Both ornamental cabbage (*B. o. capitata* vars) and ornamental kale (*B. o. acephala*) are hardy biennials, 20-40cm (8-16in) in diameter. They are grown as annuals, available as seed selections in uniform or mixed colours. Typical variegations include creamy white leaves edged in green, or a pink central heart shading to purple, attractively veined outer leaves. Colour contrast can be clear and crisp or subtle and suffused. Quick-growing F1 hybrids include cabbage 'Cherry Sundae' with crimson and creamy white leaves, and

Brassica oleracea capitata 'Pink Beauty'

kale 'White Peacock' and 'Red Peacock' with delicate, bicoloured heads, green with a white centre, or deep purple with a cyclamen pink centre. 'Pink Beauty' has typical grey-green outer leaves enfolding pale pink and green variegated inner leaves, with the innermost heart pure pink.

Sow in late spring or early summer; the leaves are dull initially, but colour once night temperatures fall to 10°C (50°F), and colours intensify, the colder it gets.

The leaves add a surprisingly exotic touch to cut flower displays, but put a drop of bleach or small piece of charcoal in the vase water to prevent an otherwise overpowering cabbagy smell. Whole heads form the traditional focal point in large, still-life fruit and floral arrangements. Ornamental cabbages and kales are edible, and a single shredded leaf can pep up the appearance of a winter salad.

Top: Brassica oleracea acephala 'White Peacock'

Above: Mixed Brassica oleracea

Above: Lunaria annua
'Variegata Alba' in flower

Right: Euphorbia marginata

Far right: Galactites
tomentosa

EUPHORBIA MARGINATA

Family: Euphorbiaceae
Height: 60cm (2ft)
Spread: 30cm (12in)
Flowering time: Summer
Aspect: Sun or light shade
Soil: Well drained

Snow-on-the-mountain is a hardy annual spurge, North American in origin. It forms an upright, bushy plant, 60cm (2ft) high and less across, of leafy stems; dwarf, more compact seed selections, such as 'Summer Icicle', are available. The soft, oval, greeny-grey leaves are narrowly margined in white, with the upper, smaller leaves and leaf-like bracts becoming heavily striped with white or all-white in summer. These create eye-catching, flower-like rosettes, especially stunning when seen *en masse*. The actual flowers are insignificant, and are followed by hairy, round seed pods.

An easy plant for sun or light shade, it thrives in any well-drained soil. Where happy, it self-seeds, coming true from seed, replacing itself annually. It is potentially invasive, but it can also be temperamental, and annual reseeding may be necessary. Sow in spring, *in situ*, or in autumn in mild districts. Colour contrast is strongest in sun.

Snow-on-the-mountain is a superb foliage 'filler' in cut flower displays, or in all-foliage arrangements. Like all euphorbias, it exudes a milky sap when cut; sear the cut ends over a flame or dip briefly in boiling water to stop the flow. The sap is an irritant, so handle the stems carefully and wash your hands afterwards.

GALACTITES TOMENTOSA

Family: Compositae
Height: 45-60cm (18-24in)
Spread: 15-20cm (6-8in)
Flowering time: Summer
Aspect: Full sun
Soil: Well drained, ordinary or poor

This rare annual or biennial thistle has grey-green, spiny leaves with midribs and veins heavily marked in white. The leaves form a compact rosette 15-20cm (6-8in) across and the flower stem grows 45-60cm (18-24in) high, bearing mauve thistles in summer. The plant is best suited to a hot, dry position and ordinary poor soil with excellent drainage. It self-seeds freely.

LUNARIA ANNUA 'VARIEGATA'

Family: Cruciferae
Height: 75cm (30in)
Spread: 30cm (12in)
Flowering time: Late spring
Aspect: Light shade
Soil: No special requirements

Honesty, moonwort, silver dollar, money plant, satin flower – this old-fashioned biennial's common names mostly refer to its silvery, oval, flat inner seedcases, much used in dried flower displays. The generic name also refers to its seedcases, although its current specific name, *annua*, is less informative than its former one, *biennis*.

The variegated form has typical dense basal rosettes and leafy stems, 75cm (30in) high, of coarsely toothed, heart-shaped leaves. These are edged in white, more so higher up the plant, with the smallest, uppermost leaves often pure white. Variegation is boldest in spring and early summer, and barely noticeable by winter. The heads of four-petalled, slightly fragrant white or mauve flowers appear in late spring, followed by the seed pods, green at first, when they are lovely in fresh flower displays.

This could never be called a choice treasure, self-seeding as prolifically as it does and thriving in most soils and light shade, even dry shade. Its light-reflective quality is ideal in woodland gardens, on dry banks and at the base of dull shrubs, such as philadelphus or lilac. In mixed borders, it complements bergenias, grape hyacinths (*Muscari*), lungworts (*Pulmonaria*) and dicentras. Though biennial, its large basal leaves perform as weed-smothering ground cover.

Sow outdoors in late spring or early summer; thereafter the plant more than amply renews itself. The variegated form comes true from seed provided there are no green-leaved forms nearby. The seedlings are green to start with and take on variegations later; markings vary in quality, and you may want to weed out the less attractive seedlings.

Lunaria annua 'Variegata Alba'

SILYBUM MARIANUM

Family: Compositae
Height: 1.2m (4ft)
Spread: 60cm (2ft)
Flowering time: Autumn
Aspect: Sun
Soil: Well drained

The leaf veins of blessed thistle, Our Lady's milk thistle or holy thistle, so the legend goes, were stained white by the Virgin Mary's milk as she nursed her child; accordingly, in some old herbals, eating this plant was said to increase the flow of milk.

A hardy evergreen thistle for the back of the border, a wild garden or rough banks, it produces flat rosettes of broad, undulating, lobed, spiny leaves, shiny green marbled with white veining. Branching, 1.2m (4ft) high stems carry small purple thistles in summer.

If sown in spring, blessed thistle behaves like an annual, flowering that summer; if sown in autumn, it behaves like a biennial, flowering the following summer. It thrives in any well-drained soil and sun, self-seeding freely and soon naturalizing, especially on waste ground.

In spite of its extreme spininess, it is much loved by slugs and snails. Its leaves, stems, flower bracts and roots have all been used as vegetables, boiled before eating.

To condition the leaves for cut flower displays, dip the stem ends in boiling water for a few seconds, then let them stand in cold water for several hours.

TROPAEOLUM MAJUS 'ALASKA'

Family: Tropaeolaceae
Height: 25cm (10in)
Spread: 15-25cm (6-10in)
Flowering time: Autumn
Aspect: Sun
Soil: Poor

This compact variety of garden nasturtium, or Indian cress, is unique. Its radially veined, disc-like leaves are light green, conspicuously marbled and striped with creamy white. The single, funnel-shaped flowers, carried well above the foliage, come in a typical nasturtium range of white, yellow, salmon, orange, scarlet, crimson and bicolours.

Sow this hardy annual in spring in ordinary to poor, dry soil and sun. Once established, it makes weedproof, temporary ground cover 25cm (10in) high, clothing the ground with showy flowers and foliage through autumn, and easily pulled up at the end of the season. It is equally good in window boxes, pots and hanging baskets. Its young shoots, however, are especially vulnerable to blackfly.

This plant could equally well appear in the herb section. The seeds were once taken against scurvy and the juice used as an antiseptic. Its leaves and, to a lesser extent, its flowers have a peppery taste like that of watercress (to which it is related) and are traditionally used to flavour summer salads.

Tropaeolum comes from the Greek word for trophy. According to ancient legends, nasturtiums first arose from the blood of a Trojan warrior; the round leaves symbolized his shield and the spurred flower his helmet.

ZEA MAYS

Family: Gramineae
Height: 90cm-1.5m (3-5ft)
Spread: 30cm (12in)
Flowering time: Summer
Aspect: Sun
Soil: Light, rich, well drained

Maize, or sweetcorn, is actually a giant grass, whose stately architectural form is largely unappreciated when the plant is grown commercially. The variegated garden forms are striking in colour and use, traditionally as focal points among lower-growing plants. The Victorians also grew ornamental maize in large pots in greenhouses. Seed selections include 'Gracillima Variegata', 90cm (3ft) high, with slender, green and white striped leaves, and the coarser 'Gigantea Quadricolor' 1.5m (5ft) high, with leaves striped longitudinally in bands of varying widths of creamy white, green, carmine and purple.

Start the seeds under glass in gentle heat in early spring, harden off and plant outdoors after risk of frost is over. In favourable climates, they can be sown outdoors in mid-spring. The seedlings are green, becoming variegated as they mature. Select those with the best variegations for planting out; some seedlings remain dull green. Provide light, rich, well-drained soil, shelter and sun, and a steady supply of water.

This was one of the few variegated plants of which Gertrude Jekyll approved.

Tropaeolum majus 'Alaska' and Furcraea foetida 'Mediopicta'

Right: Zea mays 'Gracillima Variegata'

Silybum marianum

In *A Gardener's Testament*, she advocated cutting back the central stem '....the lower shoots, which are always the best striped, multiply, and make a beautifully compact plant of quite unusual aspect.'

You can grow variegated sweetcorn in pots, grouped with pots of lilies or *Pelargonium fragrans*. For a sub-tropical effect, plant them with *Melianthus major*, cannas, and stooled ailanthus or catalpas.

TENDER PLANTS

IN COOL TEMPERATE climates, late spring marks the start of an annual garden ritual: the putting out of tender and half-hardy plants to enliven the garden through summer until the first frosts. Some, such as agaves, add an exotic, tropical touch; others, such as pelargoniums and fuchsias contribute an old-fashioned, cottage-garden charm. Garden centres are crammed full of seductive, 'summer-only' plants – and it's so easy to be seduced. Many combine attractive flowers and foliage, while others are primarily foliage plants. They can be used as formal bedding, as informal infill, tucked into mixed beds and borders or, perhaps most popular of all, in flower-pots, tubs, urns and window boxes, especially near the house.

Many of the plants listed below can continue to give pleasure after their outdoor season finishes. If grown in manageable-size containers, these can simply be moved to a cool, sunny spot indoors or into a conservatory or greenhouse, having been checked first for any sign of pest or disease and treated as necessary. Others, such as tender fuchsias, need a period of dormancy and have little to offer visually then. And a few, such as coleus, are best used for cuttings and the mother plants discarded.

Where maximum colour is wanted, or shady spots need brightening, variegated plants are ideal. The variegated form of *Helichrysum petiolare*, for example, can weave together disparate plants, creating a unified tapestry of foliage and flowers. It is equally effective used vertically, in pots or hanging baskets, or horizontally, in the open ground, and can make considerable growth in a single season. Variegated forms of busy Lizzy (*Impatiens*) can add floral and foliar colour to a shady bed or, in pots, to either side of a shadowed entrance way. Caladiums are brilliant and exotic in their variegations, but tolerate deep shade, bringing light and colour to the darkest corner of the garden during summer.

In warmer climates, most of these plants can remain part of the permanent garden framework, and may achieve considerable size. Ivy-leaved pelargoniums, for example, can grow 3m (10ft) high and as much across in frost-free climates, and cover an arch or trellis, or spread across the side of a house or over a garden wall.

**Abutilon pictum
'Thompsonii'**

**Abutilon × hybridum
'Savitzii'**

ABUTILON

The spotted flowering maple, *Abutilon pictum* 'Thompsonii', formerly *A. striatum* 'Thompsonii', is a traditional, upright Victorian dot plant. It was grown annually from cuttings, used in large-scale bedding schemes and discarded in autumn. It is also a greenhouse and house plant.

The yellow mottling on its evergreen, maple-like leaves is caused by a harmless virus, but to many, the effect is restless and fidgety. Its orange, red-veined, bell-shaped blooms appear in summer. *A.* × *hybridum* 'Savitzii' has a bushy, dwarf habit with striking, cream maple-shaped leaves blotched green.

The soft, shrubby flowering maple, *A. megapotamicum*, is altogether more graceful; *A. m.* 'Variegatum' has slender, pointed leaves, attractively blotched and tessellated with bright yellow, and small, red and yellow blooms. All need pruning in spring, to encourage well-branched growth. They are of borderline hardiness and can survive outdoors in cool, temperate climates against a sunny, sheltered wall; otherwise lift and overwinter in a cool, frost-free spot.

Family: Malvaceae
Height: 60-180cm (2-6ft)
Spread: 60-180cm (2-6ft)
Flowering time: Summer and autumn
Aspect: Sun or light shade
Soil: Fertile, well drained
Minimum temperature: 5°C (41°F)

AGAVE

A rosette-forming, evergreen perennial succulent on a grand scale, *Agave americana* is Mexican in origin. Although it is potentially permanent planting in mild areas, such as California, south-west England, and the Mediterranean, where it has been naturalized for over 200 years, in colder areas the species and its variegated forms need overwintering under glass. They are especially effective as patio specimens in terracotta pots, which control their size and make them portable.

A. americana is also known as the American aloe, confusing since *Aloe* is a quite distinct South African genus; and as the century plant, referring to its reputation of

Family: Agavaceae
Height: 1.8m (6ft)
Spread: 1.8m (6ft)
Flowering time: Summer
Aspect: Full sun
Soil: Very well drained, sandy
Minimum temperature: 5°C (41°F)

**Agave americana
'Variegata'**

flowering when 100 years or more old. In fact, it can produce its tall, candelabra-like spikes of flowers after 10-15 years in hot climates, 30-40 years in cool ones. Up to thirty side shoots, carried at right angles to the main spike, bear dense masses of pale yellow-green, lily-like flowers, with protruding yellow anthers. The flower spikes grow very quickly, and in the wild reach 10m (33ft) high in a month. They derive sustenance and water from the mother rosette, which dies after flowering, but the young offsets remain intact.

The thick, leathery, grey-green leaves, triangular in section, spring from a short trunk and have fierce brown terminal spines and toothed margins. Their rigidity comes from a flax-like fibre. The finest variegated forms are 'Medio-picta', with a broad, central yellow stripe; 'Stricta', with leaves striped in yellow and white; and 'Variegata', edged in creamy yellow.

A. victoriae-reginae, the Queen Victoria century plant, forms a slow-growing, domed rosette of broadly oval leaves 15-25 cm (6-10in) long. These are dark green, finely edged with white, spineless along the edges but terminating in a short black spine. After 20-30 years, it produces its slender flower stem, up to 4m (15ft) high and bearing pale cream flowers.

Sun and sandy, well-drained soil are essential. If agaves are container-grown, crock the pot well and use soil-based potting mixture, with grit or sharp sand added. In the open ground, they look good in rocky, arid schemes, with palms and other visually strong plants. They can also make an impenetrable hedge. In containers, they look noblest on their own, as a piece of sculpture, rather than demeaned by a ruffle of lobelia or petunias. A containerized agave can, however, look lovely grouped with other sculptural succulents that have equally dramatic form, such as echeverias and sempervivums.

ARACHNIODES SIMPLICIOR

Family: Dryopteridaceae
Height: 30-75cm (12-30in)
Spread: 60cm (2ft)
Flowering time: Non-flowering
Aspect: Light shade
Soil: Neutral to acid, well drained loam
Minimum temperature: 10°C (50°F)

The variegated shield fern, also called *A. aristata* 'Variegata' is an attractive slow-growing, evergreen or semi-evergreen. It carries two to three pinnate, glossy green fronds each displaying a prominent yellowish band on either side of the midrib and down the centre of each pinna. A shaded location or filtered sunlight is ideal; a planting of these ferns under the dappled shade of deciduous trees makes a pleasing effect, but this plant is also an excellent container subject.

It withstands a slight frost, but should not be sited in a cold, exposed location or frost pocket; pot-grown subjects can be over-wintered under cover. Provide loamy, well-drained, neutral to acid soil with high organic content, and make sure plants have a generous supply of water during the period of active growth in spring and early summer. Provide a dressing of balanced fertilizer or manure in spring.

ASPIDISTRA ELATIOR 'VARIEGATA

Family: Liliaceae
Height: 30-60cm (12-24in)
Spread: 60-90cm (2-3ft)
Flowering time: Flowers insignificant
Aspect: Shade
Soil: Deep, well drained
Minimum temperature: 5°C (41°F)

The variegated form of the familiar cast-iron plant, or bar-room plant, is a slow-growing rhizomatous evergreen with long oval, upright, glossy leaves displaying alternating stripes of dark green and creamy white. The plant grows 30-60cm (12-24in) high, 60-90cm (2-3ft) across; insignificant purple flowers are occasionally produced at ground level. It makes a valuable container plant, indoors or out, but in mild climates can be grown outdoors for accent or contrast in full or partial shade; the striking colouring also works well in mass planting. It prefers deep, rich, well-drained soil but is extremely drought tolerant.

CALADIUM

Family: Araceae
Height: 20-90cm (8-36in)
Spread: 25-90cm (10-36in)
Flowering time: Flowers insignificant
Aspect: Shade
Soil: Well drained but moisture-retentive, rich
Minimum temperature: 18°C (64°F)

These beautiful plants are rightly given the common name angels' wings. Their large heart- or arrow-shaped leaves, borne on long stalks, have striking variegations in combinations of green, pink, red and white. They originate from tropical America and require warm conditions, but are partial to deep shade, so ideal for summer colour in a shady garden. They make valuable container plants, for window boxes, pots and tubs, and in cooler climates are sold as house plants.

There are many different selections of *Caladium* × *hortulanum*, also listed as *C. bicolor,* of which the following are recommended: 'Candidum' grows to 90cm (3ft) high and wide, with green-veined and margined white leaves, and there is also a pink form; 'Frieda Hemple', a low-growing form, 45cm (18in) high and 30cm (12in) across, with lush, heavy leaves in rich crimson-red edged with green; 'Little Miss Muffet', a miniature selection 20-30cm (8-12in) high, with lime-green leaves handsomely speckled wine red; 'Red Flash' is veined in crimson and has pink blotches; 'White Christmas', 60cm (2ft) high, with showy, broad, snow white leaves intricately veined and marked with mid-green; and the similar-sized 'White Queen', with leaves shading from white at the centre through soft green towards deep green margins, drawn through with rich red veining.

Caladiums are tuberous perennials mainly grown as annuals, but the tubers can be dug up and stored over winter months, then started into growth indoors before planting out when the soil has warmed up outside. They require well-drained but moisture-retentive soil with good organic content.

**Above: Caladium ×
hortulanum 'Candidum'**

**Left: Caladium ×
hortulanum 'Candidum' pink
form**

**Left: Caladium ×
hortulanum 'Red Flash'**

CANNA

Family: Cannaceae

Height: 1.2-1.8m (4-6ft)

Spread: 60-120cm (2-4in)

Flowering time: Summer to autumn

Aspect: Sun or light shade

Soil: Deep, fertile, moist but well drained

Minimum temperature: 10°C (50°F)

These showy, luxuriant plants can have striking markings that are persistent throughout the summer season. *Canna* × *generalis* 'Bengal Tiger' has large, paddle-shaped leaves displaying numerous longitudinal yellow bands. The leaves are evergreen in frost-free areas; elsewhere this makes a useful ornamental bedding or container plant. Apricot-orange flowers appearing in profusion from summer through autumn form a nice contrast to the foliage; remove flowers as they fade.

Growing up to 1.8m (6ft) high and 1.2m (4ft) wide, it provides an attractive 'tropical' accent when grown as an isolated specimen or focal point. Container planting around a pool or on a patio is effective.

The rare *C. malawiensis* 'Variegata' grows 1.8m (6ft) high, and has broad brown-edged green leaves that are beautifully marked with broad and narrow yellow stripes and have well defined midribs. The plant has showy orange or yellow flowers, according to the form chosen, in summer. It needs bright sunlight, but prolonged exposure to fierce sunlight can scorch the leaf edges.

Cannas are rich feeders, requiring deep, fertile soil that never dries out; but good drainage is essential. They prefer a sunny position, but tolerate light shade. In cool climates, lift rhizomes once the foliage starts to die down, let them dry out, then over-winter in slightly moist peat or soil, in completely frost-free conditions. In spring, start the rhizomes into growth indoors about one month before frosts cease, and plant outside when the soil has warmed up and all danger of frost is past.

Top: Canna malawiensis 'Variegata'

Above: Chlorophytum comosum 'Variegatum'

CHLOROPHYTUM COMOSUM

Family: Liliaceae

Height: 10-45cm (4-18in)

Spread: 10-45cm (4-18in)

Flowering time: Spring and summer

Aspect: Light shade

Soil: Well drained, fertile

Minimum temperature: 5°C (41°F)

The spider plant is one of the most popular house plants, much loved for its tolerance of neglect and its fascinating and graceful method of propagation, by means of plantlets formed at the tips of leafless, arching runners. It is less commonly grown outdoors, but can be equally valuable for summer bedding, for instant infill in beds and borders, as hanging basket plants, in window boxes, and in pots, positioned to cascade over a wall. They can add a lively touch interplanted among ferns in light shade.

Also sold as *Chlorophytum capense*, and commonly called the ribbon plant or walking anthericum in America, *C. comosum* is South African in origin and forms clumps of soft, lance-shaped, evergreen foliage. The species has been replaced in cultivation by its variegated forms. Most popular is 'Vittatum', 30-45cm (12-18in) high and wide, with a broad, central white or pale cream stripe. The similar-sized 'Variegatum' has white-striped green leaves, and 'Picturatum' has green leaves with a yellow central stripe. 'Mandaianum' is tiny, with 10cm (4in) long, dark green leaves centrally striped with yellow. All have insignificant white flowers, which precede the plantlets.

The tiny plantlets form their own thick, rhizomatous roots, and a good mother plant can provide a dozen or more plantlets for planting out in late spring as edging, or to follow sweet-williams (*Dianthus barbatus*), wallflowers (*Cheiranthus*) or forget-me-nots (*Myosotis*). By the end of the season, the plants will have grown considerably, and can be potted up for enjoyment indoors.

The foliage can scorch in hot sun, and drops of water collecting in the leaves can also discolour them when exposed to bright sunlight.

Citrus mitis 'Variegata'

CITRUS

Citrus trees have always held fascination for gardeners in cool temperate climates, and orangeries, forerunners of greenhouses and conservatories, were developed to over-winter them. The compact, bushy, free-flowering and fruiting Calamondin orange, *C. mitis* 'Variegata' (more correctly × *Citrofortunella mitis* 'Variegata') is the variegated form of a popular greenhouse plant. It has leathery, glossy, green and white leaves, fragrant white flowers and small, bright orange, bitter fruit, borne from a young age. The variegated lemon, *Citrus limon* 'Variegata', has green and creamy white variegated foliage and yellow- and green-striped fruit, ripening to yellow.

Keep both cool in winter, moderately watered all year round, mist sprayed when the buds are opening and fed every two weeks with high potash, tomato-type fertilizer when in active growth.

Family: Rutaceae
Height: 90cm-3m (3-10ft)
Spread: 90cm-3m (3-10ft)
Flowering time: Intermittent
Aspect: Sun
Soil: Fertile, well drained, gritty
Minimum temperature: 5°C (41°F)

COLEUS

Flame nettles, or painted nettles, are tender perennials, tropical Asian or African in origin, usually grown as half-hardy annuals. Many people admire their velvety, richly variegated leaves, but others find massed, mixed coleus visually disturbing, and dislike the random variegations of some forms. Nonetheless, if a stunning effect is required, the bright, strong colours of coleus can provide it. First introduced to the West in the mid-eighteenth century, they became a popular subject for Victorian hybridists and were enormously sought after, with plants and seeds changing hands for vast sums of money. *Coleus* is also listed under the genus *Solenostemon*.

The foliage encompasses a brilliant range of colour combinations, including white, cream, yellow, orange, green, red, pink, bronze, deep maroon, and purple. Varie-gations can take the form of edging, veining,

Family: Labiatae
Height: 13-60cm (5-24in)
Spread: 13-60cm (5-24in)
Flowering time: Flowers insignificant
Aspect: Sun or light shade, shelter
Soil: Rich, lime-free, moist but well drained
Minimum temperature: 10°C (50°F)

Coleus 'Display'

Top: Coleus 'Pineapple
Beauty
Right: Coleus 'Nettle'

splashing, mottling or mosaic patterning. Leaf sizes and shapes also vary, from tiny to huge, narrow to broad, fringed, frilled or lace-edged.

There are many seed mixtures, among the finest being 'Fashion Parade', a blend of compact plants 38-45cm (15-18in) high, generously multi-coloured and with leaf shapes ranging through plain oval or lobed leaves, oak-leaf, sabre-leaf, laced and fringed forms; 'Rainbow' selection, 45cm (18in) high, with incredible colour combinations including dazzling multi-colours; and 'Wizard' series, compact, small plants up to 30cm (12in) high, with oval, serrated, medium to large leaves in a wide range of colours.

The 'Carefree' series offers oak-leaved plants up to 30cm (12in) high; 'Dragon' series, 20-30cm (8-12in) high, has large, serrated, gold-edged leaves; the leaves of 'Fiji' are fringed, on plants 45cm (18in) high; 'Mini-Coral' series and 'Milky Way' are only 13-15cm (5-6in) high, with a good range of mixed colours; 'Old Lace' has intricately lacy foliage with colour-contrasting edges; 'Pineapple Beauty', 30-45cm (12-18in) high, has maroon-marked, yellow-green leaves; and the unusual 'Sabre-Leaf Mixed', 20-30cm (8-12in) high, has narrow, graceful leaves on base-branching plants that are particularly tolerant of lower light levels.

Unmixed, or 'separate' seed selections tend to be more expensive. They include 'Molten Lava', 20-30cm (8-12in) high, with carmine-centred, black-edged foliage; 'Salmon Lace', 45cm (18in) high, with salmon-centred leaves edged in green and gold; and the white-edged, scarlet-centred 'Scarlet Poncho', a trailing plant 30cm (12in) high, ideal for hanging baskets. Two more unusual selections are 'Dazzler', variegated fiery red, yellow, green and maroon, roughly following the veins and midribs; and 'Nettle' with lime green leaves, unusually variegated yellow and pink with random maroon veining.

The leaves colour best in full sun, although under glass some summer shade is necessary, to prevent leaf scorch. A steady water supply is essential and a humid atmosphere ideal, since lower leaves drop at a hint of drought. The tiny blue-and-white flowers that appear in summer are best pinched out; this helps keep the plants compact and the foliage looking good, as does frequent pinching out of non-flowering shoots.

Coleus are raised easily from seed, sown indoors in early to mid-spring and planted out after all frosts have passed. The best colour forms can be propagated by cuttings taken in autumn; coleus grown as house plants or brought inside for the winter become lanky and poorly coloured due to lower light levels, and are best replaced.

For bedding, coleus can be edged with the silvery-leaved *Cineraria maritima*, lemon-scented pelargonium, purple iresines, and non-flowering bedding geraniums, such as 'Madame Salleron'.

Coleus are very useful for cut-flower displays, the most exotic and colourful forms appearing as floral rather than foliage material. To condition, dip the stems in boiling water for a few seconds, then let them stand for a while in cold water.

COPROSMA REPENS

This tender, evergreen shrub from New Zealand, also sold as *Coprosma haueri* and commonly called the Tasmanian currant or mirror plant, has a lax habit and glossy, oval leaves. The flowers are insignificant, but female plants, if fertilized by a male, produce attractive berries.

'Beatson's Gold' is a sprawling, almost hardy plant with green and cream leaves. 'Kiwi Gold' is similar, but more prostrate and ground-hugging. 'Marginata' has dark green leaves edged in yellow. 'Picturata', also sold as 'Variegata' has yellow-centred leaves edged in dark green.

'Marble King' is slow-growing, dwarf and especially tender, with creamy white leaves lightly spotted with green. 'Marble Queen' is similar but more robust; leaves are

Family: Rubiaceae

Height: 20-90cm (8-36in)

Spread: 90cm (36in)

Flowering time: Late spring

Aspect: Sun

Soil: Rich, peaty, acid, well drained

Minimum temperature: 2°C (36°F)

Coronilla glauca 'Variegata'

CORONILLA GLAUCA 'VARIEGATA'

Also sold as *Coronilla valentina glauca*, this dense, bushy shrub is not quite hardy, but is worth cosseting, or growing in a greenhouse. Its pale, glaucous, pinnate, evergreen foliage is heavily splashed, edged or striped with creamy white, creating a lacy effect. Clusters of up to ten yellow pea-flowers are carried in the leaf axils, well above the foliage. The blooms, which appear mainly in spring but continue intermittently throughout the year, are sweetly scented by day, scentless at night. They are followed by slender, long-tailed pods. For those who find the combination of flowers and variegated foliage restless, the flowers can be nipped off.

The plant needs a gritty, perfectly drained soil, ideally at the base of a warm wall, or in a corner between two walls. It responds well to trellis-training.

Family: Leguninosae
Height: 3m (10ft)
Spread: 2.5m (8ft)
Flowering time: Late winter or spring
Aspect: Sun
Soil: Rich, loamy, well drained
Minimum temperature: 2°C (36°F)

blotched green at the centres and are more heavily spotted. 'Pink Splendour' is basically creamy white with a green centre, the whole overlaid with pink and purple. One of the stronger cultivars, it can reach 1.2m (4ft) high.

All root quickly from cuttings, given bottom heat, and a single mother plant can provide numerous offspring. Once established, they are drought-tolerant and do well in coastal locations. Otherwise, grow them in a greenhouse, or as summer bedding in cool temperate climates. The cool, glossy foliage contrasts well with high-key summer flowers, such as verbena.

FELICIA AMELLOIDES

Also known as *Agathaea coelestis* and *Aster capensis*, the blue daisy, or blue marguerite, is a tender South African perennial, grown as a half-hardy annual in cool climates. The yellow-centred, mauve, marguerite-like flowers are carried above the foliage, and offer a valuable alternative to ageratum, for edging, bedding or container growing. Compared to many other members of the genus, which close their flowers at a hint of cloud, it keeps its flowers open for most of the day.

There are two variegated forms: the older and smaller 'Variegata', with round to oval, mid-green, evergreen leaves edged in creamy white, some mottled white in the centre and a few all-white; and the similar but newer, 'improved' and larger 'Santa Anita Variegata'.

Felicia is intolerant of cold soils, especially wet ones. Trim any straggling growth, and deadhead regularly, to encourage further

Family: Compositae
Height: 30-45cm (12-18in)
Spread: 25-45cm (10-18in)
Flowering time: Midsummer
Aspect: Full sun
Soil: Well drained
Minimum temperature: 5°C (41°F)

Felicia amelloides 'Variegata' growing with verbena

flowering. In mild winters, it may survive intact, but it is safer to take cuttings in autumn and overwinter them under glass.

FICUS

Although normally grown as house plants, tender ornamental figs can be used as dot plants in summer bedding schemes, as temporary, containerized patio plants or as permanent planting in frost-free zones. The most elegant tree species is weeping fig, *Ficus benjamina*, potentially huge as a permanent outdoor plant; *F. b.* 'Variegata' has glossy, rich green, pointed leaves, heavily and randomly splashed with white. The variegated rusty fig, *F. rubiginosa* 'Variegata', makes a lower, spreading tree with similar shaped leaves, heavily edged in white, and rusty brown felted beneath.

The rubber plant, *Ficus elastica*, has little grace, at least in its house plant size. Variegated forms include 'Variegata', with yellow-edged and patched, drooping leaves; 'Schrijvereana', with light green and cream patched leaves; 'Doescheri', with large, broadly oval leaves, grey green, dark green and creamy yellow, with a pink midrib; and the smaller, narrower leaved 'Tricolor', with green, pink and creamy white patched leaves.

For ground cover in humid, frost-free zones or summer display in pots or hanging baskets, the variegated trailing fig, *F. radicans* 'Variegata' (syn. *F. sagittata* 'Variegata') has wiry stems and pointed, leathery leaves, greyish-green splashed with creamy white; the creeping fig, *F. pumila* 'Variegata', has tiny, thin, heart-shaped leaves, edged and spotted with creamy white. Both have nodal roots and can also be trained as self-clinging climbers, when they can reach 3m (10ft) or more high.

Family: Moraceae
Height: 5cm-9m (2in-30ft)
Spread: 20cm-6m (8in-20ft)
Flowering time: Flowers insignificant
Aspect: Sun or light shade
Soil: Fertile, well drained
Minimum temperature: 15°C (59°F)

FUCHSIA

Family: Onagraceae
Height: 20-90cm (8-36in)
Spread: 20-90cm (8-36in)
Flowering time: Summer
Aspect: Sun or light shade
Soil: Rich, moist but well drained
Minimum temperature: 5°C (41°F)

Tender fuchsias form a continuum with hardy ones (see page 152), with similar flowering, range of growth habits and cultivation needs, except the requirement for overwintering in frost-free conditions. In 'borderline' areas, mulching the roots is often all the protection needed; above-ground growth dies back but sprouts again in spring.

They are particularly suitable for container growing, since the containers can be easily moved under cover when frost threatens. Cut back the growth by a quarter to one-third, either in autumn, which saves overwintering space, or in spring.

Variegated tender fuchsias include the Victorian 'Avalanche', with double, scarlet and purple blooms and yellowish, green-veined foliage; the robust, upright 'Avon Celebration', with semi-double, white, mauve and green-tipped blooms and heavily variegated, yellow-green foliage; 'Avon Gold', with profuse, medium-sized pale pink and lavender blooms, and creamy gold and green foliage; and 'Gilt Edge', with small, reddish-orange single blooms and silver-edged leaves.

'Gartenmeister Bonstedt', upright, bushy and ideal for bedding, has olive green leaves veined in red, and brick red blooms; 'Golden Marinka', with a cascading habit ideal for hanging baskets, has cream and golden variegated foliage and a profusion of single, red flowers; 'Golden Lena', has pink and purple, semi-double flowers and modest, creamy yellow leaf edges; the old Victorian 'Sunray' has small, salmon pink and rosy purple flowers, and leaves variegated pale green, creamy white and cerise, with a silvery white cast.

Gazania rigens 'Variegata'

GAZANIA RIGENS

This tender, evergreen, clump-forming perennial of South African origin was called *Gazania splendens*, and is commonly known as treasure flower. It is grown as a half-hardy annual for summer bedding, pots and tubs. Its orange-yellow, dark-centred daisies are temperamental, opening only in sun and shutting in mid-afternoon. The form 'Variegata' has long, dark green leaves edged with gold and cream; 'Aureovariegata' has yellow-splashed leaves.

Well-drained soil, ideally sandy, is essential. In mild areas you can risk leaving plants outdoors through winter, perhaps cloching them to help keep moisture off while maintaining good air circulation; otherwise take cuttings in late summer, or lift plants and overwinter them under glass. They tolerate wind and salt spray, making them useful for seaside planting.

Family: Compositae
Height: 15-20cm (6-8in)
Spread: 30-45cm (12-18in)
Flowering time: Summer
Aspect: Full sun
Soil: Well drained, sandy
Minimum temperature: 2°C (36°F)

HELICHRYSUM PETIOLARE

Formerly *Helichrysum petiolatum*, and commonly called the liquorice plant, this half-hardy or moderately hardy sub-shrub is valuable for its graceful wands of grey-felted, heart-shaped, evergreen leaves, which offer cool contrast to hot, vibrant summer flower colours. It is usually partnered with the pinks, reds and oranges of fuchsias, pelargoniums, busy Lizzies (*Impatiens*) and petunias, but also makes a good foil for shrubs such as roses, ceanothus and purple-leaved forms of *Cotinus coggygria*, and climbers such as *Vitis vinifera* 'Purpurea'.

Growth habit depends on locale, but the plant is normally lax and quick-growing. In window boxes, hanging baskets or tubs, the stems gracefully arch and trail, often turning up at the tips and creating an attractive, layered effect. Against a warm wall, they weave their way up and through adjacent plants, visually knitting them together, and

Family: Compositae
Height: 2.4m (8ft) grown vertically; 15cm (6in) grown as ground cover
Spread: 60cm-2.4m (2-8ft)
Flowering time: Flowers insignificant
Aspect: Sun
Soil: Well drained, poor
Minimum temperature: −1°C (30°F)

can reach 2.4m (8ft) in height and spread. In borders, they spread horizontally, and are excellent for last-minute cover of bare soil, or as short-term ground cover on a hot, sunny bank. The root system is very small compared to the top growth, doubling their value as container plants, or as bedding plants where root space is limited.

'Variegatum' has creamy white leaf edges, with occasional leaves splashed with white; 'Roundabout' is similar, but slower growing and diminutive, with a rather speckled effect.

In spite of their grey, furry appearance, the leaves wilt and scorch if deprived of water in hot weather – plants in containers need frequent watering. They rarely flower in cool temperate climates outdoors, but the small, papery flowers are, in any case, insignificant. Given dry soil and atmosphere, the plants may overwinter successfully outdoors, but it is safer to take cuttings in late summer or early autumn, and overwinter them under glass or on a sunny windowsill.

The stems can be tricky in cut flower arranging. They do not last in florist's foam, and soft-tipped stems need their cut ends briefly dipped in boiling water. With mature, woody stems, just scrape the lowest 2.5cm (1in) of stem.

IMPATIENS

Family: Balsaminaceae
Height: 30-90cm (12-36in)
Spread: 30-90cm (12-36in)
Flowering time: Summer
Aspect: Sun or light shade
Soil: Rich, moist but well drained
Minimum temperature: 10°C (50°F)

There are several variegated forms of the much-loved, old-fashioned busy Lizzie, or patient Lucy, *Impatiens walleriana*. This is a fast-growing, tender, bushy evergreen perennial from Zanzibar. 'Variegata' has pointed, oval, pale green leaves, irregularly margined with white. The single, bright pink flowers are typically spurred. *I.w. petersiana* has rosy pink flowers and long, narrow, leaves, bronzy green with red veining. Both, however, are rare and largely superseded by the brilliant, multi-coloured variegations of the F1 New Guinea hybrids, derived largely from *I. linearifolia* and *I. hawkeri*.

Named hybrids include 'Aflame', with pale pink flowers and leaves marbled yellow and green and tinged with red; 'Arabesque', with yellow-centred and red-veined, green leaves up to 15cm (6in) long, and bright pink flowers; 'Cheers', with crinkled yellow leaves narrowly striped with green, and small coral flowers; and 'Flare' with green leaves centrally splashed yellow, and scarlet flowers. Mixed flower colour seed strains are also available, such as 'Firelake Hybrid Mixed', which has variable foliage colour: some leaves are all green, others have creamy white central splashes, and are sometimes veined in deep red.

Impatiens New Guinea hybrid 'Flare'

Nerium oleander 'Variegata'

With their robust, compact growth and huge flowers, up to 8cm (3in) across, the New Guinea hybrids are ideal for bedding, especially in light shade, although full sun is tolerated in cool, northerly climates. They are also stalwart subjects for window boxes, tubs and hanging baskets, and make useful, instant infill in shady beds.

Busy Lizzies are grown as half-hardy annuals, sown in spring and planted out after all danger of frost is over. They also root easily from cuttings, inserted in seed compost or a jar of water.

Regular pinching out of growing tips encourages branching. A continual supply of moisture is essential, and high humidity helpful. The succulent stems are vulnerable to wind, so shelter is also important. Given rich soil, regular feeding and copious water in the growing season, plants can reach 1.2m (4ft) or more high. Red spider mite and aphids can be troublesome.

NERIUM OLEANDER 'VARIEGATA'

Family: Apocynaceae
Height: 60cm-6m (2-20ft)
Spread: 30cm-4.5m (12in-15ft)
Flowering time: Summer to autumn
Aspect: Sun
Soil: Well drained, rich
Minimum temperature: 10°C (50°F)

In its native Mediterranean habitat, oleander, or rose bay, forms thickets along damp ravines and water courses. It is an erect, branching, suckering shrub or small tree grown for its terminal clusters of luxuriant, periwinkle-like flowers. These are single rose pink in the species, and single or double, white, yellow, orange, pink, red or purple, sometimes fragrant, in cultivars. A popular greenhouse plant, it benefits from summering outdoors, which ripens the wood and promotes future flowering. In very mild locations, train it against a wall in full sun or receiving most sun in the afternoon; in frost-free zones, it makes an attractive hedge.

The double pink-flowered 'Variegata' has conspicuous, wide yellow stripes on its leathery, lance-shaped, dark green leaves. Like the species, it is excellent for container growing, where its size can be curbed. Use a fairly rich, loam-based growing medium.

Place in full sun, water and feed copiously in the growing season, cease feeding and water barely at all when dormant; the drier the roots, the lower the temperature it can tolerate.

Oleander tolerates hard pruning. Prune flowering shoots by half after flowering; cuttings will root in a jar of water, placed in a warm spot. It is also tolerant of pollution, and of salt, making it an excellent maritime plant.

Scale insects and mealybug can be problems if plants are grown under glass. All parts of oleander are extremely poisonous; it is known as the 'horse killer' in India, where it is used as a funeral flower.

OSTEOSPERMUM 'SILVER SPARKLER'

Family: Compositae
Height: 30-45cm (12-18in)
Spread: 30-45cm (12-18in)
Flowering time: Summer
Aspect: Full sun, shelter
Soil: Light, sandy
Minimum temperature: 2°C (36°F)

This is one of many hybrids of the South African sub-shrub formerly known as *Dimorphotheca*. 'Silver Sparkler' makes low, spreading, tufty mats of narrow evergreen leaves variegated light green and creamy white. Its pure white daisies are produced singly over several months, but open only in sun, when pollinating insects are most likely to be about.

Heat, light, shelter and excellent drainage are essential. In mild winters, it may survive outdoors, but taking cuttings of non-flowering shoots in late summer and overwintering them under glass is safer. Its growth habit makes it perfect for edging or sprawling over paving stones, tucked in cracks between paving slabs or in the front of borders. It is also good for coastal planting.

Osteospermum 'Silver Sparkler'

PELARGONIUM

Family: Geraniaceae

Height: 20cm-3m (8in-10ft)

Spread: 20cm-3m (8in-10ft)

Flowering time: Summer, but potentially year-round

Aspect: Sun or light shade

Soil: Free-draining

Minimum temperature: 1°C (34°F)

As with hostas, the number of variegated pelargoniums is overwhelming; dividing them into zonal, ivy-leaved and scented-leaved forms is the best approach. (Regals, or Martha Washington pelargoniums, the fourth main group, are rarely variegated.)

All need free-draining soil and, ideally, full sun, although scented-leaved forms tolerate light shade and golden-leaved zonals can scorch in hot, bright sun. Avoid over-feeding and overwatering, and, if pot grown, overpotting, since these conditions result in lush foliar growth but reduced variegation, especially yellow variegations fading to dull green in zonals. There will also be few, if any, flowers and, in the case of scented-leaved types, reduced scent. Frequent pinching back, especially of young plants and ivy-leaved types, encourages branching and generous flowering.

SCENTED-LEAVED PELARGONIUMS

Of the three types, the scented-leaved are the most subtle and variable in growth habit, and in leaf size and shape. Their scents, originally for the purpose of deterring foraging animals, range from strident to delicate – those listed below are acceptably pleasant. The flowers are generally small, but have a delicacy, and often intricate beauty, that is lacking in the more showy zonal and regal pelargoniums. The most robust types can provide cut foliage material for flower arranging virtually all year round. Mature shoots last best, stripped of their lowest leaves, dipped briefly in boiling water if woody, and given a long, cool drink.

Scented-leaved plants are good in pots, urns and raised beds, especially near paths or patios, where they can release their fragrance when touched or brushed against in passing. They are also suitable for herb gardens, since many are traditional ingredients in cookery, cosmetics and herbal medicine. They are ideal for

Pelargonium 'L'Elégante'

window boxes, where their beauty and fragrance can be appreciated from indoors and out.

Pelargonium crispum 'Variegatum', the variegated lemon geranium, is a short-jointed, bushy plant, making 30-60cm (1-2ft) high, erect spires of small, fan- or wedge-shaped, crinkled, cream-edged, lemon-scented leaves. Its medium-sized flowers are mauve. It needs a little extra cosseting, since it is vulnerable to disease in wet, cold conditions. (See photograph overleaf.) 'Old Spice' is similar in appearance, but has a sweeter, spicier scent.

P. × *fragrans* 'Variegata', or 'Snowy Nutmeg', has small, greyish-green, white-edged, three-lobed, indented leaves with a scent variously reminiscent of pine, lemon

Right: Pelargonium crispum 'Variegatum'

Above: Pelargonium 'Bird Dancer'

and nutmeg. The small, white flowers are veined and spotted red. Compact, bushy and naturally branching, it rarely exceeds 45cm (18in) high and wide.

'Lady Plymouth', or 'Grey Lady Plymouth', a sport of *P. graveolens*, has deeply lobed grey leaves, edged in white and scented with a mixture of rose, pepper and citrus. Its small, pale pink flowers are marked in purple. A branching, spreading species, it can reach 90cm (3ft) high and wide.

P. quercifolium, the oak-leaved geranium, has deeply lobed, mid-green leaves with dark central blotches, and a pungent scent. Its relatively large mauve flowers are spotted and veined purple. There are several forms, with growth ranging from erect to compact or trailing.

P. 'Chocolate Peppermint', a hybrid of *P. quercifolium*, has three-lobed leaves, with dark brown, central butterfly markings. The foliage is strongly mint-scented, with a hint of chocolate.

P. 'Variegated Clorinda', another hybrid of *P. quercifolium*, has gold and green, tri-lobed foliage scented like cedar and camphor, and large pink flowers. It makes a large plant, up to 90cm (3ft) high and wide.

IVY-LEAVED PELARGONIUMS

These hybrids of *P. peltatum* are excellent stand-bys for hanging baskets, window boxes and tubs. The stems of ivy-leaved types are brittle and must be handled with care, otherwise cultivation is straightforward. Many have contrasting leaf veining or zoning to a certain degree, but the following are the most striking.

'Crocodile', an Australian cultivar, has prominent yellow, cobweb-like veining over its dark green leaves, caused by a harmless virus, and single, purple-red blooms. It is sometimes listed as 'Fishnet', 'Sussex Lace' or 'Alligator'.

'Elsi', with double, scarlet blooms, is a naturally upright, unbranched plant, needing

Above: Pelargonium 'Miss Burdett-Coutts'

Above: Pelargonium 'Mrs Quilter'

frequent pinching out to encourage branching. Its green leaves are narrowly edged in creamy white.

'Flakey' is a miniature ivy-leaved form with greyish-green, white-edged leaves, tinged pink if grown in dry, light conditions. The sparse flowers are white, with lilac markings. It resembles a scaled-down version of 'L'Elégante', an old Victorian form with greyish-green leaves marbled and edged in creamy white, with pink overtones if grown in dry, light conditions. Its profuse single, white flowers have lilac markings. (See photograph on p. 41.)

'Magaluf' has silvery green leaves, edged in creamy white, and single neon-pink flowers, with darker spots on the upper two petals.

'White Mesh', sometimes confused with 'Crocodile', has semi-double, rich pink flowers and creamy white veining.

'Wood's Surprise' has soft mauve, double blooms, and white and green marbled leaves.

ZONAL PELARGONIUMS

The variegated, fancy-leaved or ornamental-leaved zonal pelargoniums make by far the largest category. Some have flowers equal in beauty to their leaves, others have modest flowers, often pinched out in bedding schemes. The variegation ranges from subtle, with elegant slivers of white, gold or bronzy black on green, to strident, especially with tricolour forms. These can be slow-growing or difficult to propagate, and consequently more expensive.

Though traditionally used in bedding, variegated zonals are good mixers, in smaller quantities, for tubs and window boxes. Generally, the more strident the variegation, the more subdued its neighbours should be.

'Bewerly Park' has a black-zoned leaf, and double, pale pink flowers.

'Bird Dancer', an American miniature zonal raised by M. Bird, has dark-edged, deeply pointed leaves and spidery, elegant, single, pale salmon blooms (See photograph on p. 42.)

'Butterfly Lorelei' has green leaves, with a central yellow butterfly-shaped zone, and double, pale salmon flowers.

'Caroline Schmidt' an old cultivar, has crinkled, silvery green leaves edged in creamy white, and large, bright red, double flowers. It is excellent for bedding, with vigorous, upright growth.

'Chelsea Gem' has cream-edged, silver-green leaves, and double, pale pink flowers. Compact and bushy, it is also good for bedding.

'Contrast' has yellow-centred leaves, surrounded by rings of russet and maroon, rimmed in yellow and splashed with green. Its single, red flowers are small, and best removed.

'Distinction', wide-spreading and bushy, has dark green, serrated foliage with a narrow black zone, and single, scarlet flowers.

'Dolly Varden' has grey-green leaves, edged in pale yellow, with a brownish-red zone, and single, red flowers.

'Falklands Hero', a relatively modern tricolour, has green, yellow and red leaves, and single red flowers. It is similar to the popular form 'Mr Henry Cox' (see below), but bushier and more muted.

'Frank Headley' is a dwarf form with profuse, single, salmon pink flowers and small, silvery green, white-edged leaves.

'Freak of Nature', an unusual, compact Victorian form, has white-centred, green-rimmed leaves carried on white main stems and stalks, and single, red flowers.

'Friary Wood' has pale gold leaves with a chestnut brown zone, and large, double, white-eyed, pinky mauve blooms. It is compact and bushy.

'Golden Harry Hieover', a Victorian bicolour, has pale to golden green leaves, with a chestnut brown zone, and profuse, single scarlet blooms.

'Happy Thought' has a pale yellow butterfly marking in the leaf centre, surrounded by an orange bronze ring and a bright green outer edge. The flowers are single, bright rose. 'Pink Happy Thought' is similar, with single pink blooms.

'Lass O'Gowrie', a slow-growing tricolour, has grey-green, cream-edged leaves with a cerise zone, and small red flowers.

'Marechal MacMahon', an old compact, bushy cultivar, has golden foliage zoned with rich brown and edged in pale yellow, and small red flowers, best removed.

'Miss Burdett-Coutts' is a slow-growing tricolour, with green-centred leaves, red zone, and wide creamy white edges. The single, red flowers are best removed. (See photograph on p. 43.)

"Mr Henry Cox', also sold as 'Henry Cox' or 'Mrs Henry Cox', is a Victorian favourite, with green leaves irregularly margined in gold, a deep red and black zone, and pale pink, single flowers. It is slow-growing and not free-branching, so needs regular pinching out.

'Mrs Pollock', another Victorian tricolour, has green-centred leaves, with a chocolate brown and scarlet zone and yellow leaf margins, and small, orange-red, single blooms.

'Mrs Quilter' is naturally branching and wide-spreading, with lime green leaves zoned in a chestnut brown, and sparse, small, salmon flowers, best removed. (See photograph on p. 43.)

'Orbit Series' is a group of early-flowering zonals with seventeen distinct flower colours in the white, pink, salmon and red range, and vivid bronze or red-brown leaf markings. They make compact, sturdy, well-branched plants.

'Ringo Series' have very clear and distinctive, dark brown, almost black leaf zones, and a good range of typical flower colours.

'Spitfire', a tall, upright, cactus-flowered zonal, has rolled, quill-shaped, bright red petals and green leaves edged and splashed in creamy white.

'Turkish Delight' has gold-centred leaves with a red and bronze zone and green edges, and single, orange-red blooms.

'Vina', a bushy, floriferous dwarf zonal, has golden leaves with a chestnut zone, and double, apricot pink blooms.

Plectranthus coleoides
'Variegatus'

PLECTRANTHUS COLEOIDES 'VARIEGATUS'

An evergreen sub-shrub, white-edged Swedish ivy is related to coleus, though less often seen outdoors. Its common name refers to its popularity in Sweden for use in hanging baskets and window boxes; it actually originates from tropical Africa. Initially upright but soon trailing, its succulent, square stems carry oval, scalloped, hairy leaves, grey-green with white margins, that give off a distinct odour when crushed. Its insignificant tubular, mauve flowers appear sporadically, and are best removed.

Provide a steady supply of moisture in

Family: Labiatae
Height: 60cm (2ft)
Spread: 60cm (2ft)
Flowering time: Intermittent, pinch out flowers
Aspect: Bright but indirect light
Soil: Rich
Minimum temperature: 10°C (50°F)

Right: Zantedeschia
elliottiana

Top: Tradescantia
blossfeldiana 'Variegata'

Above: Tradescantia zebrina

the growing season, or the lower leaves dry up and fall off; high humidity is required in hot weather. Pinch out the growing tips regularly, to keep compact, and replace old plants annually from cuttings, which root easily. Colouring is best in bright light, providing moisture is adequate, but protect from intense direct sunlight.

tinged centre; and 'Quadricolor', with uneven, metallic green, pink, white and cream stripes.

Pinch out the growing tips regularly to induce bushiness, and remove all-green shoots, as soon as they appear. Water generously in the growing season and mist regularly in hot, dry weather.

TRADESCANTIA

Family: Commellinaceae
Height: 15cm (6in)
Spread: 45-60cm (18-24in)
Flowering time: Spring and summer
Aspect: Bright but indirect light
Soil: Rich
Minimum temperature: 10°C (50°F)

Familiar trailing, evergreen house plants with outdoor potential for window boxes and hanging baskets, wandering Jews, or inch plants, have oval leaves clasping trailing stems, slightly angled at each joint.

Tradescantias are quick-growing and rapidly become leggy, but are easily propagated from tip cuttings rooted in potting medium or water. Shearing old plants and rooting the trimmings in a 10cm (4in) pot can provide several dense, new plants each growing season.

Tradescantia albiflora is represented by the variegated forms 'Albovittata', with large, white-striped, dark green leaves; and 'Tricolor', with white and purple striped, green leaves.

T. blossfeldiana 'Variegata', also listed under *T. cerinthoides* 'Variegata', has leaves randomly and unevenly striped in cream, or sometimes all cream, and becomes tinged pink if grown in full sun.

T. fluminensis is similar to *T. albiflora* and some references list them as synonymous, but the former has more pointed leaves. *T.f.* 'Variegata' has creamy white-striped, yellow-green leaves with purple undersides; 'Quick-silver' is more robust, without any hint of purple to its leaves.

T. zebrina, also confusingly called the inch plant or wandering Jew, is a trailing tradescantia with silvery white and green striped leaves with striking purple under-sides, and pink, three-petalled blooms. The forms commonly grown are 'Discolor', with slender silvery stripes bordering a copper-

ZANTEDESCHIA ELLIOTTIANA

Family: Araceae
Height: 75cm (30in)
Spread: 45cm (18in)
Flowering time: Early summer
Aspect: Sun or light shade
Soil: Rich, moisture-retentive
Minimum temperature: 10°C (50°F)

The golden arum lily, also listed as *Richardia elliottiana*, is a tuberous-rooted perennial with large arrow-shaped, deciduous, dark green leaves, spotted with silver. The attraction of the flower spike, in early summer, is its clear, golden yellow spathe. Smaller and less hardy than the better known *Zantedeschia aethiopica*, this plant needs a protective winter mulch in mild areas. Elsewhere, it is best grown in pots of rich, loam-based potting medium, and moved under glass for the winter. Feed and water generously during the growing season, then gradually reduce both after flowering, and keep plants nearly bone dry in winter to encourage a period of dormancy.

HERBS

Herbs as a category, whether for culinary, medicinal, cosmetic or even magical use, have existed for thousands of years, and knowing plants' utilitarian virtues, whether of historical or present-day interest, enhances the pleasure of growing them. They are planted in mixed or herbaceous borders as often as in herb gardens. This chapter concentrates on culinary herbs only – herbs with other uses are included in Perennials and Trees and Shrubs.

Wherever they are grown, herbs tend to contribute generously to the garden scene. Their usually modest flowers, especially those of the *Labiatae* and *Umbelliferae* families, attract bees and butterflies which further enliven a garden. Herb foliage, whether plain or, as here, strikingly variegated, acts as a foil to nearby flowers, whose beauty can pale when seen in unrelieved mass.

Not all herbs, in the widest definition, are aromatic, but those that are have become firm favourites. Touching aromatic herbs helps to release their scent, so site them near a path or patio, or at the front of a border, where they can be brushed or touched in passing.

ARMORACIA RUSTICANA 'VARIEGATA'

Family: Cruciferae
Height: 90cm (3ft)
Spread: 45-60cm (18-24in)
Flowering time: Summer
Aspect: Sun or light shade
Soil: Deep, well drained
Minimum temperature: −23°C (−10°F)

Also sold as *Cochlearia officinalis*, horse-radish is an indestructible, tenacious perennial herb with inedible, dock-like leaves and edible roots, traditionally served freshly grated, as a sauce with roast beef. It is extremely tough, and in Britain is naturalized along roadsides and wasteground.

The tiny white flowers and shabby leaves of the species are dull, but 'Variegata', with leaves generously splashed with creamy white, is more interesting and equally tasty.

Plant the roots in spring, and dig up as needed in the following year. In autumn, store roots in sand-filled boxes for winter use. Inevitably, a few thin side roots remain in the ground, and these will sprout the following spring. Invasiveness can be a problem.

Armoracia rusticana 'Variegata'

Family: Labiatae
Height: 25-30cm (10-12in)
Spread: 25-30cm (10-12in)
Flowering time: Summer
Aspect: Sun or light shade
Soil: No special requirements
Minimum temperature: −23°C (−10°F)

MELISSA OFFICINALIS 'VARIEGATA'

Lemon balm's deliciously sharp, self-descriptive scent, which even a glancing touch releases, is among the strongest of all herbs. The dull green species, however, is more a menace than an asset in all but wild gardens, with its prolific self-seeding, tenacious, thick roots and tendency to look worn out and suffer from rust by late summer.

'Variegata', also listed as 'Aurea' or 'Aureovariegata', has the fragrance of the species but is altogether more attractive and tidier. Its serrated, heart-shaped leaves are dark green irregularly splashed with yellow, retained all year round. Massed plants make a beautiful, informal pattern, and the colouring is lovely with dark-leaved perennials, such as liriope, and shrubs, such as *Viburnum davidii*.

An evergreen perennial, it starts spring as a tight basal rosette, eventually 25-30cm (10-12in) high and wide, with sparse, taller stems of minute white flowers in summer.

It thrives in almost any soil, in sun or light shade, and is easily increased by division: any tiny rooted bits planted in the growing season quickly establish. Space plants 30cm (12in) apart. Unfortunately, its self-sown seedlings tend to be all green; pinching out the flower heads prevents seeding, and also keeps the plant compact.

Immensely attractive to bees, balm is traditionally rubbed onto beehives. It was formerly used in surgical dressings and as furniture polish. Balm tea is said to be soporific, calming the heart and the nervous system and relieving melancholy, and dried balm leaves are an essential ingredient in herb pillows.

The foliage is short-lived when cut, but submerging the whole stem overnight in water helps extend its life.

MENTHA

Two variegated mints are worth growing, the better known being the strongly scented variegated pineapple or apple mint, *Mentha suaveolens* 'Variegata', formerly *M. rotundifolia* 'Variegata'. Its small, rounded, woolly and wrinkled, grey-green leaves are liberally splashed with brilliant creamy white. Some shoots are all white; others, unfortunately, all grey-green. It grows 25-30cm (10-12in) high, more compact and less invasive than some mints. The more robust *M. × gentilis* 'Variegata', sometimes sold as *M. × g.* 'Aurea', has oval leaves, splashed, veined and striped in bright yellow and green, on purplish stems 45cm (18in) high.

Both have modest, lipped mauve flowers, typical of the *Labiatae* family, although variegated apple mint is shy to flower. Both make good ground cover in sun or shade, provided the soil is rich and moist; colouring is best in sun. Space plants 60cm (2ft) apart. They eventually become overcrowded and suffer accordingly, unless regularly lifted, divided and replanted in freshly enriched soil.

Family: Labiatae
Height: 25-45cm (10-18in)
Spread: 60cm (2ft)
Flowering time: Summer
Aspect: Sun or shade
Soil: Rich, moist
Minimum temperature: −23°C (−10°F)

Above: Melissa officinalis
'Variegata'

Left: Mentha suaveolens
'Variegata'

Above: Origanum vulgare
'Gold Tip'

Right: Mentha × gentilis
'Variegata'

Far right: Salvia officinalis
'Tricolor'

To keep mint roots confined, grow them in buckets sunk in the ground.

Though highly ornamental, both plants are also flavourful and useful. Mint was an Elizabethan 'sweet' herb, strewn on floors, and was also used as a salve. Today, mint tea is taken for headaches, indigestion and insomnia; mint flavours confectionery, chewing gum and toothpaste; and mint sauce or jelly with lamb is a traditional partnership. As with most herbs, its aroma is most fully developed just before flowering.

For flower arranging, dip the stem ends in boiling water and follow with a long drink; apple mint is the longer lasting of the two.

ORIGANUM VULGARE 'GOLD TIP'

A form of perennial marjoram, or dittany, this relatively new cultivar forms dense, weed-smothering clumps 45cm (18in) high and wide. Its small, oval, bright gold-tipped green leaves grow in tidy rosettes up the stiff, wiry stems. In midsummer, it carries profuse heads of tiny mauve flowers. Its neat, tufty habit is suitable for formal edging, but it is equally suitable for growing in cracks between paving slabs, in container gardens and rockeries. Provide sun and well-drained soil. Clipping back lightly after flowering keeps the plant compact. It is an ideal foil for grey-leaved plants, such as *Festuca ovina* 'Glauca' and *Helichrysum petiolare*.

A bee plant, marjoram was also traditionally given to cows as nourishment after calving. It was an Elizabethan strewing herb, and predated hops as a flavouring for ale and beer. It was given to comfort the bereaved, and planted on graves, and was a herbal remedy for indigestion, toothache, headache and insomnia. Today, it is an essential ingredient in Italian cooking.

Family: Labiatae
Height: 45cm (18in)
Spread: 45cm (18in)
Flowering time: Midsummer
Aspect: Sun
Soil: Well drained
Minimum temperature: −34°C (−30°F)

SALVIA OFFICINALIS

Culinary sage is represented by two variegated forms. S.o. 'Tricolor' has pale-edged, grey leaves, irregularly splashed with cream, pink, red and purple – altogether providing two more colours than its varietal name suggests. S.o. 'Icterina', or golden sage, is splashed greeny grey and yellow. Variously listed as shrubs, sub-shrubs and perennials, both make rounded, semi-evergreen bushes, 'Icterina' up to 45cm (18in) high and wide, 'Tricolor' slightly less. They grow straggly with age, but are easily increased by cuttings taken in mid-spring. Young plants produce the most vivid foliage, another reason for regular renewal.

Neither form is very hardy and the plants can suffer in cold winters. Both need sun, and light, well-drained soil; spring planting and a warm spot against a wall in full sun are ideal. Lightly clip over in mid to late spring, to encourage basal growth.

The flavour is that of ordinary, grey-leaved sage, a well-known complement to the richness of pork and an ingredient in Derby sage cheese. As a medicinal herb, sage was used to treat fevers, headaches, cold, coughs, greying hair and even memory loss. According to folklore, where sage grows strongly in a garden, the wife rules the house.

Variegated sages provide only a modest amount of foliage for flower arranging; dip the cut ends in boiling water and follow with a long drink.

Family: Labiatae
Height: Up to 45cm (18in)
Spread: Up to 45cm (18in)
Flowering time: Summer
Aspect: Sun
Soil: Well drained
Minimum temperature: −18°F (0°C)

Salvia officinalis 'Icterina' with Lamium galeobdolon 'Variegatum'

**Above: Symphytum ×
uplandicum 'Variegatum'**

**Right: Salvia officinalis
'Icterina' and
'Purpurascens' in a mixed
planting**

SYMPHYTUM ×
UPLANDICUM
'VARIEGATUM'

Family: Boraginaceae
Height: 30cm (12in)
Spread: 60cm (2ft)
Flowering time: Late spring to early summer
Aspect: Sun or shade
Soil: Cool, moist
Minimum temperature: −29°C (−20°F)

This dramatic hybrid of the native perennial comfrey (*S. officinale*) is shade-tolerant and ideal ground cover in cool, moist, rich soil in woodland or waterside gardens or among shrubs. It is sometimes listed as *S. peregrinum* or *S. asperrimum* 'Variegatum', and known in common parlance as Russian comfrey.

Its rather coarse, evergreen foliage forms clumps 30cm (12in) high. The leaves are spear-shaped, hairy and grey-green, with generously broad, creamy white margins. The variegations remain all year round, but plants are liable to revert. Heads of milky, lilac-pink buds open into nodding, tubular, mauve or blue flowers, carried on leafy stems 90cm (3ft) high, in late spring and early summer.

The leaves are most handsome just before flowering, but they soon become shabby; cutting back hard after flowering encourages fresh basal growth, which is fully recovered by the end of summer. Space plants 60cm (2ft) apart and propagate by division or from root cuttings.

Comfrey is excellent for compost-making, and said to heal bruises, wounds and broken bones, hence its old name, bone-set. In Bavaria, the leaves are dipped in batter and fried. Comfrey tea is said to aid digestive and respiratory problems. Although the flowers and young leaves wilt quickly when picked, the mature leaves are long-lasting, and good for flower arrangments. To condition them, dip the ends in 2.5cm (1in) of boiling water, then let them stand in deep, cool water for several hours.

THYMUS

Family: Labiatae
Height: 8-30cm (3-12in)
Spread: 30-38cm (12-15in)
Flowering time: Summer
Aspect: Full sun
Soil: Light, well drained
Minimum temperature: −23°C (−10°F)

Thyme leaves are tiny, so variegations inevitably read as *petit point*. Nonetheless, these evergreen shrubs or woody-based perennials are valuable garden assets, their delicacy serving as contrast to bolder plants. Lemon-scented thyme, *Thymus × citriodorus* has several variegated forms including 'Silver Queen', with grey-green leaves edged in silver; 'Variegatus', or 'Silver Posie', with pale green leaves edged with creamy white; and 'Golden King', with golden-edged leaves, two-thirds gold to one-third green. All are bushy, dome-shaped plants, 23-30cm (9-12in) in height and slightly more across, with clusters of tiny, two-lipped mauve flowers in summer.

The hybrid 'Doone Valley' forms dense mats, 8cm (3in) high and 30cm (12in) across, of dark green foliage heavily marked and mottled with gold. Large heads of lilac flowers appear in late summer.

All prefer full sun, shelter and light, well-drained soil. They are wonderful plants for cracks in pavings, where 'careless' footsteps release their pungent aroma, and in container gardens, rock gardens and dry stone walls; tiny rooted sprigs inserted in any of these soon thrive and spread. As with most woody herbs, thymes benefit from a light clipping after flowering, and harder pruning in mid-spring.

Thyme is another butterfly and bee plant, traditionally grown near hives; honey from areas where thyme grows wild has a distinctive flavour. Roman soldiers bathed in thyme-scented water before battle, to increase their courage. It was a strewing plant, and used to treat chest and throat complaints, including whooping cough. Thyme tea is taken to aid indigestion. In cooking, it is a welcome addition to most savoury dishes.

Thymus × citriodorus 'Silver Posie'

PERENNIALS

PERENNIALS – NON-WOODY plants that live for several years, theoretically capable of flowering repeatedly – form the bulk of many gardens. Some perennials qualify as ground cover, needing little attention once the individual plants knit together to create weed-suppressing clumps, carpets or mounds. Others are prima donnas, needing ongoing cosseting, rigorous watering or feeding regimes, or protection from winter wet or cold, summer sun, predators or diseases. Some perennials are herbaceous, dying back to a long-lived rootstock in autumn, and sprouting again in spring; others are semi-evergreen or evergreen, providing year-round cover. Perennials range in size from diminutive to mammoth, and in rate of growth from slow to fast, in some cases, perhaps too fast!

Traditional herbaceous perennial borders have largely given way to mixed plantings, in which shrubs, small trees, perennials, biennials, annuals and bulbs are juxtaposed for ongoing seasonal interest. Perennials are especially valuable in newly planted mixed borders, while shrubs are still small and, if correctly spaced, leave large gaps to fill. Many perennials, only a year after planting, can be divided into two or three, each rooted portion replanted to grow and be further subdivided, if need be.

Although some variegated perennials listed below are common garden favourites, available from most large garden centres, others are unusual, available only by catalogue or by visiting specialist nurseries. Such plants may be more expensive, but the fact that a single plant has the potential to produce as many as you need should more than balance the extra expense and effort.

ACORUS

Family: Araceae
Height: 45-90cm (18-36in)
Spread: 15-60cm (6-24in)
Flowering time: Summer
Aspect: Sun
Soil: Moist, rich, loamy
Minimum temperature: −29°C (−20°F)

Sweet flag, *Acorus calamus*, is a European and British waterside plant, with strap-shaped leaves 60-90cm (2-3ft) high, each pleated along one side. Its superficial similarity to iris gives sweet flag its common name, though it actually belongs to the Arum family. 'Sweet' refers to the warm, cinnamon-like fragrance emitted when the leaves or rhizomatous roots are bruised or crushed. The form in garden use is 'Variegatus', with green leaves neatly, strikingly and vertically striped in creamy white, tinged rosy pink or burnt sienna at the base in spring. Its greenish-yellow flowers, looking like tiny cattle horns, appear in summer, but are of little value compared to the foliage with its long-lasting variegation.

Sweet flag is a plant for boggy ground, stream or pond sides, or shallow shelves in artificial pools, in up to 25cm (10in) of water, where its reflections are an added bonus. It is also lovely in a setting of sea-washed stones; or for bold contrast in colour and form, planted with the purple-leaved *Rheum palmatum* 'Atrosanguineum' or bronze-tinted rodgersias.

A. gramineus 'Variegatus', the Japanese sweet flag, or grassy-leaved sweet flag, is a diminutive, dainty plant. It has fan-like sprays of dark green, grassy, evergreen foliage, striped with cream, coming from slender, creeping rhizomes. It grows up to 45cm (18in), usually less, and needs shallower water. Its green flower spathe is hardly noticeable among the leaves and is of no decorative value. Although sometimes sold as a house plant for a cool, sunny spot, Japanese sweet flag is actually quite hardy. The rare *A. g.* 'Pusillus', or 'Albovariegatus', is small enough to be used effectively in dish and terrarium gardens.

All prefer sunlight, and are best planted in mid-spring, in a situation with moist, rich, loamy soil. They are easily propagated by division.

Acorus calamus 'Variegatus'

AEGOPODIUM PODAGRARIA 'VARIEGATUM'

Family: Umbelliferae
Height: Up to 25cm (10in)
Spread: 60cm (2ft)
Flowering time: Summer
Aspect: Sun or shade
Soil: No special requirements
Minimum temperature: −34°C (−30°F)

Ground elder, *Aegopodium podagraria*, strikes terror into the heart of most gardeners since it spreads rapidly by rampant, running roots. The tiniest piece of root left in the soil is capable of generating a whole new plant. (Ironically, in the United States it is sometimes sold to the unwary as ground cover.) The garden form 'Variegatum' is vigorous and tolerant but non-invasive, with attractive leaf edges and splashes of creamy white, on a fresh green ground.

Variegated ground elder grows in almost any soil and in sun or shade, although its variegations are especially valuable for enlivening a dim spot, such as at the base of a shady wall or under trees or hedges that let some light through their foliage. It grows up to 25cm (10in) high, often less. Its white summer flowers are insignificant and can be nipped off, to keep the foliage fresh-looking. On the other hand, the typical umbellifer seed heads, if picked and air-dried while still green, are marvellous in dried flower displays.

The species was probably introduced into medieval England as a herbal remedy against gout, hence one of its common names, gout weed. From its compound, elder-like leaves came its most common name, ground elder. The origin of its third common name, bishop's weed, is uncertain, but one explanation is that its weedy persistence is enough to make even a bishop swear! The leaves were once boiled and eaten like spinach.

Aegopodium podagraria 'Variegatum'

AJUGA REPTANS

Family: Labiatae

Height: 15cm (6in)

Spread: 30cm (12in)

Flowering time: Early summer

Aspect: Sun or light shade

Soil: No special requirements

Minimum temperature:
−34°C (−30°F)

The carpet or common bugle is a native British plant of damp meadows and woodlands, its rosettes of dark green, shiny, deeply veined leaves, 5cm (2in) high, and blue flower spikes in spring up to 15cm (6in) high, are modestly attractive. The plants were once grown in herb and cottage gardens as a wound herb. In today's gardens, the species has largely been replaced by coloured-leaf and variegated forms, which make weed-suppressing evergreen ground cover in sun or light shade, in any ordinary soil that doesn't dry out.

Carpet bugles are stoloniferous, spreading quickly by long runners that form after flowering in spring and root as they go. In the right conditions, carpet bugles can become rampant and smother less robust subjects nearby, and are often excluded from alpine and rock gardens for that reason. On the other hand, in bone-dry or starved soils, results can be disappointing.

Ajuga reptans 'Burgundy Glow' has basically wine-red leaves, mottled with mauve and pink and finely edged in cream; colouring is best in sun. It is good with silver and blue foliage, such as rue (*Ruta*), *Artemisia* 'Lambrook Silver', *Centaurea gymnocarpa*, *Hosta sieboldiana* or *Melianthus major*.

A. r. 'Multicolor', also sold as *A. r.* 'Rainbow' and *A.r.* 'Tricolor', is beetroot red with a coppery, metallic sheen and paler edges in winter; in spring it becomes vividly splashed and mottled with many colours, variously described as red, orange, green, bronze, pink, apricot and cream. Its sparse, deep blue flower spikes appear in early summer. As with 'Burgundy Glow', it colours best in the sun but is shade-tolerant. This is perhaps the most visually arresting variegated bugle, since the markings bear no relationship to the leaf form. Some may find the irregular patterning discordant, but it is undoubtedly eye-catching, especially planted with silver-leaved senecios or purple-leaved

cotinus or Japanese maples.

A. r. 'Variegata', sometimes sold as *A. r.* 'Argentea', is the least robust and visually strident of the three. Its grey-green leaves are marked with splashes of creamy white overlaid with pink, and form relatively tight, neat cover. Its pale blue flower spikes are sparse. Unlike the red-leaved forms, it prefers light shade, where it would complement ferns, trilliums, erythroniums, Solomon's seal (*Polygonatum*) and other woodland plants.

You can interplant variegated ajugas with dwarf spring bulbs or use them to underplant roses and other deciduous shrubs and trees. Their leaf form and carpeting habit contrast well with more upright, bold-leaved plants, such as hostas, bergenias, iris and phormiums. Plant ajugas whenever the ground isn't frozen or waterlogged, spaced 30cm (12in) apart; water until the plants become established and weed until they knit together. They are vulnerable to mildew, so treat with fungicide if necessary.

Top: Ajuga reptans 'Multicolor'

Above: Ajuga reptans 'Variegata'

AQUILEGIA VULGARIS

Family: Ranunculaceae

Height: 30-75cm (12-40in)

Spread: 30-45cm (12-18in)

Flowering time: Late spring, early summer

Aspect: Sun

Soil: Moist, but well drained, rich loam

Minimum temperature: −25°C (−13°F)

Columbines, or granny's bonnets, with their delicate, maidenhair fern-like foliage and spurred flowers, are enchanting but not particularly long lived, and flowering can be disappointing on dry soils. The variegated forms are part of the Vervaeneana group, sometimes listed as *Aquilegia vulgaris* 'Variegata' or *A. v.* 'Woodside'. They have golden marbled and mottled foliage and various coloured flowers, including pure white, said to have the cleanest, clearest and most striking variegations; mid-pink, the most common; and deep red. Heights vary as well, so check with supplier. Variegation usually, but not always, comes true from seed, and columbines also cross-breed freely, so variegated forms should be grown well away from others, since seed is the primary source of propagation.

ARABIS

Family: Cruciferae

Height: Up to 15cm (6in)

Spread: 20-45cm (8-18in)

Flowering time: Spring and summer

Aspect: Sun

Soil: Well drained

Minimum temperature: −29°C (−20°F)

These low-growing sun lovers form evergreen, spreading mats of greyish-green rosettes, overlaid with sheets of tiny, white, scented flowers in spring and summer. Rock gardens are the traditional home, but they make good front-of-border plants, and can be naturalized in bare or rocky spots, or allowed to tumble over dry banks or raised walls. Arabis thrives in any well-drained soil, ideally limy, and is easily propagated by cuttings or division.

Arabis caucasica 'Variegata', formerly *A. albida* or *A. alpina* 'Variegata', the white rock cress, forms mounds 15cm (6in) high, 30cm (12in) or more across, of creamy yellow-edged leaves in loose rosettes. It is robust, and can be invasive; clipping after flowering keeps it tidy. A traditional component of formal spring bedding, with wallflowers (*Cheiranthus*), polyanthus and bellis, it is also a traditional companion of alyssums and aubrietas.

A. ferdinandi-coburgii 'Variegata' has

Artemisia vulgaris 'Variegata' and Lamium maculatum 'White Nancy'

compact rosettes of narrow, tiny, shiny, white-edged and generously splashed leaves, tinged purple in winter. *A. f-c.* 'Old Gold' is similar, but with gold and green leaves. Both grow 8cm (3in) high and up to 30cm (12in) across.

ARISAEMA SPECIOSUM

Family: Araceae
Height: 60-90cm (2-3ft)
Spread: 45cm (18in)
Flowering time: Spring
Aspect: Sun or light shade
Soil: Rich, well drained, but moisture-retentive
Minimum temperature: −12°C (10°F)

Barely qualifying as variegated but worth including for its fascination value, the Himalayan cobra lily has three-lobed, brown-edged, rich green leaves on mottled brown and green stalks (perhaps the variegated stalks tip the scale in its favour!). A member of the Arum family, in spring it carries typical arum flower spathes that are maroon striped with green on the outside, although these are somewhat hidden by 60-90cm (2-3ft) high leaves. Most intriguing, if not strictly relevant, is its creamy white spadix, with a dangling purple tail at the tip, 60cm (2ft) long.

Plant the tubers 10cm (4in) deep in a sheltered spot in sun or light shade, in rich, well-drained but moisture-retentive soil. A wild or woodland garden, with leaf-enriched soil and dappled light, is ideal.

The cobra lily is a relative of the common American Jack-in-the-pulpit (*A. triphyllum*), whose leaves are plain green but whose hooded spathes are striped and flushed purple, green and white. Increase by division or seed.

ARTEMISIA VULGARIS 'VARIEGATA'

Family: Compositae
Height: 60-75cm (24-30in)
Spread: 60cm (24in)
Aspect: Full sun
Soil: Well drained, ordinary or poor
Minimum temperature: −23°C (−10°F)

This hardy aromatic perennial, a variegated version of the native British mugwort or St John's plant, makes a handsome show until midsummer, after which it is likely to deteriorate. It grows 60-75cm (24-30in) high, slightly less across. Its creamy white speckled, lacy leaves have pale cottony

Arabis caucasica 'Variegata'

undersides. Preferred growing conditions are full sun and well-drained, ordinary or poor soil.

The species was a traditional herb, which in both Eastern and Western folklore was believed to have magical, protective properties against evil spirits, fatigue and disease. On a more practical level, the leaves were used as insect repellent, and to flavour alcoholic drinks, such as absinthe.

Family: Araceae

Height: 20-45cm (8-18in)

Spread: 30cm (12in)

Flowering time: Spring

Aspect: Sun or light shade

Soil: Well drained but moisture-retentive

Minimum temperature: −23°C (−10°F)

ARUM

Glossy, spear-shaped arum foliage has a schedule all its own, emerging from the soil in mid-autumn and continuing to grow through winter until it reaches its full size in mid-spring. It dies back after flower spathes appear in spring, eliminating it as ground cover but making it an especially valuable source of winter and early spring foliage for the gardener and flower arranger. Its sturdy, drumstick-like stalks of bright orange-red berries appear before the leaves in autumn.

Arum italicum 'Pictum' has clearly defined variegation, with intricate white veining that ends neatly parallel to and just short of the leaf margin. Its typical arum spathes are pale green, tinged purple at the base. If happy and left undisturbed, it slowly forms a colony, with seedlings popping up, often some distance away. Seedlings take two years for variegations to show. Although there is some confusion between the two, *A. i.* 'Marmoratum' is generally larger and broader leaved, with less distinct, softly marbled veining.

A. maculatum, commonly called lords and ladies, cuckoo pint or soldiers and sailors, grows wild in English woodlands and hedgerows. The specific name *maculatum* refers to spots; some forms have heavily spotted leaves, but others are plain green.

Arum 'Itma', a hybrid (*italicum* × *maculatum*), recently discovered by British grower Bill Baker, has the most splendidly dramatic markings of all – nearly black blotches demarcate very pale leaf veins. It grows 20-30 cm (8-12 in) tall and produces spathes very similar to *A. maculatum*.

Grow arums in sun or shade and, ideally, in moisture-retentive, well-drained, leafy, cool soil. They are vulnerable to slugs.

Gardening writer Gertrude Jekyll loved using arum leaves with cut daffodils. To condition the cut foliage, stand the leaves for several hours in deep water. To prevent the longer stems from curving while being conditioned, pack them into a narrow tube, such as a cigar tube or toothbrush holder.

Above: Arum italicum 'Pictum'

Right: Arum 'Itma' (maculatum × italicum)

ASTRANTIA MAJOR 'SUNNINGDALE VARIEGATED'

Family: Umbelliferae

Height: Up to 30cm (12in)

Spread: 45cm (18in)

Flowering time: Summer

Aspect: Light shade

Soil: Rich, moist

Minimum temperature: −29°C (−20°F)

Masterwort is an alpine meadow plant originally introduced into physic gardens and now naturalized in grassy places. The species is modest, forming clumps of broadly lobed, deciduous, serrated leaves, each on its own stem, up to 30cm (12in) high. In summer, wiry, branching stems up to 60cm (2ft) high carry pincushion-like, dusky pink, green and white flowers, each with a starry ruff of bracts. (The generic name, *Astrantia*, is Greek for star-like.)

'Sunningdale Variegated' is as handsome as the species is modest, especially in spring, when its bold splashes of cream and yellow are sharpest. Unfortunately, the contrast gradually fades; trimming back the foliage after flowering encourages a second flush of bright new growth for autumn.

Although tolerant of a wide range of conditions, astrantia prefers soil that is rich and moist but well drained, and light shade, where it forms dense clumps. Some authorities state that full sun creates the strongest variegation; others insist on light shade. Possibly, given sufficiently moist soil, a sunny aspect is ideal; but in soil that tends to be dry, shade is preferable. Astrantia spreads by underground runners and is easily increased by division in spring.

Variegated astrantia can enliven the ground under light-foliaged trees, such as birch, in woodland or wild gardens, or create a focal point in a mixed border. It combines well with purple and white martagon lilies, the purple-leaved *Viola labradorica* 'Purpurea', and euphorbias, or with creamy-edged hostas and pale yellow flowers such as the primulas shown in the photograph. Plant 45cm (18in) apart.

Both the leaves and flowers are much loved by flower arrangers; the flowers are especially long-lasting when cut.

Above: Astrantia major 'Sunningdale Variegated'

Left: Astrantia major 'Sunningdale Variegated' in flower with Hosta crispula

Above: Aubrieta deltoidea 'Variegata'

Right: Athyrium nipponicum 'Pictum'

Right: A close-up of Athyrium nipponicum 'Pictum'

ATHYRIUM NIPPONICUM 'PICTUM'

Also listed as *Athyrium nipponicum* 'Metallicum' and *A. goeringianum* 'Pictum', the Japanese painted fern is an elegant relative of the lady fern, *A. felix-femina*. It is unique among hardy ferns, in its silvery-green variegated, maroon-stemmed fronds. These are deciduous, lacy and doubly pinnate, up to 45cm (18in) high.

Grow in sheltered light shade, in free-draining but moisture-retentive, humus-rich soil. It can also be grown as a cool greenhouse plant, in free-draining potting mixture, with leaf mould and coarse sand added. Propagate established crowns by division in spring.

Only the mature fronds are suitable for cutting, and are delightful arranged with garden pinks (*Dianthus*).

Family: Polypodiaceae
Height: 45cm (18in)
Spread: 45cm (18in)
Flowering time: Non-flowering
Aspect: Light shade
Soil: Free-draining, humus-rich
Minimum temperature: −34°C (−30°F)

AUBRIETA

There are several variegated forms of this popular spring-flowering rock-garden plant. *Aubrieta deltoidea* 'Variegata' has wedge-shaped, silver-edged evergreen foliage, with occasional all-white leaves, and clear purple flowers. 'Nana Variegata' is a miniaturized version excellent for container gardens. 'Argenteovariegata', also called *A. albomarginata*, has silver-splashed leaves and blue flowers. 'Aureovariegata', also called 'Aurea', has gold-edged leaves. Most grow 5-15cm (2-6in) high and 45-60cm (18-24in) across.

Plant in full sun, in well-drained, ideally limy soil, on a dry bank, in a wall, in crevices in a rock garden, or as edging to beds and borders. Cut back after flowering to keep growth compact.

Family: Cruciferae
Height: 5-15cm (2-6in)
Spread: 45-60cm (18-24in)
Flowering time: Spring
Aspect: Full sun
Soil: Well drained
Minimum temperature: −29°C (−20°F)

BALLOTA NIGRA 'VARIEGATA'

Family: Labiatae
Height: 20-30cm (8-12in)
Spread: 20-30cm (8-12in)
Flowering time: Summer
Aspect: Light shade
Soil: Well drained
Minimum temperature: −23°C (−10°F)

Also called 'Archer's Variety', this is a creamy white-splashed variety of the wild black horehound, also called 'stinking roger' because of its unpleasant-smelling, hairy, nettle-like leaves. The variegated form has only a slight, pungent aroma, mildly reminiscent of curry. It grows 20-30cm (8-12in) high and wide. Insignificant mauve flowers are carried in whorls in the leaf axils in summer. The variegated form is not stable, often reverting to green, and does not come true from seed. Well-drained soil and light shade are the best conditions.

BARBAREA VULGARIS 'VARIEGATA'

Family: Cruciferae
Height: 15cm (6in)
Spread: 23cm (9in)
Flowering time: Late spring to late summer
Aspect: Sun or light shade
Soil: Rich, moist
Minimum temperature: −29°C (−20°F)

Land cress, winter cress or common yellow rocket, as the species is called, grows wild in English hedgerows, stream sides, damp banks and waste grounds. The peppery, acrid taste of its evergreen, glossy, toothed leaves is reminiscent of cress, and the plant is cultivated, less so nowadays than previously, for use in winter salads. (It can also be lightly boiled and eaten, like cabbage.)

In 'Variegata', the 15cm (6in) high basal rosettes are liberally splashed with creamy yellow. The branching heads of small yellow flowers are carried on long, leafy stems, up to 45cm (18in) high, from late spring to late summer, but detract from the impact of the foliage. They are best pinched out, which also encourages more leaves and discourages biennial behaviour (dying after flowering).

The cultivar enjoys the same conditions as the species, sun or light shade and rich, moist soil. It comes true from seed, but established clumps can also be lifted and divided in spring. It is an ideal subject for inclusion in an ornamental vegetable garden, but is also suitable for front-of-the-border positions.

If you want to add a few leaves to salads, especially those containing radicchio or lollo rosso, pick older, larger, outer leaves, leaving the central rosette intact.

BRUNNERA MACROPHYLLA

Family: Boraginaceae
Height: 45cm (18in)
Spread: 45cm (18in)
Flowering time: Late spring to early summer
Aspect: Light shade
Soil: Rich, well drained
Minimum temperature: −29°C (−20°F)

Siberian bugloss, formerly *Anchusa myosotidiflora*, with its delicate sprays of rich blue flowers in late spring and early summer, is an obvious relative of forget-me-not (*Myosotis*). Its heart-shaped, deciduous leaves continue to grow through summer, eventually becoming rather coarse and straggly, but it is useful ground cover, especially in wild or semi-wild gardens or corners.

There are three, quite distinct variegated forms, all with leaf clumps 45cm (18in) high and wide. 'Variegata', or 'Dawson's White', has grey-green leaves broadly edged with creamy white, some nearly all white. 'Hadspen Cream' has light-green leaves margined with creamy yellow. 'Langtrees' has rough, dark-green leaves bordered with silver spots.

All, but especially 'Variegata', need light shade, shelter and moist but well-drained, rich soil; the variegated leaf areas easily bruise, dry out and turn brown in hot sun, wind or drought.

If reversion starts to occur, remove plain green leaves; some authorities suggest that regular lifting, dividing and replanting helps prevent reversion.

**Above: Brunnera
macrophylla 'Variegata'**

**Left: Barbarea vulgaris
'Variegata'**

**Left: Ballota nigra
'Variegata'**

Above: Convallaria majalis 'Variegata'

Right: Cyclamen coum

Above: Cyclamen hederifolium

Left: Calamintha grandiflora 'Variegatus'

CALAMINTHA GRANDIFLORA 'VARIEGATUS'

Family: Labiatae
Height: 45cm (18in)
Spread: 45cm (18in)
Flowering time: Early summer
Aspect: Sun
Soil: Well drained, but not dry
Minimum temperature: −23°C (−10°F)

Occasionally listed as *Satureja grandiflora* 'Variegata', this is a pleasantly modest, old-fashioned, aromatic herbaceous perennial. Its numerous upright stems create a dense bush, up to 45cm (18in) high and wide, ideal for a rock garden or herb garden, at the front of a border, or in gaps between paving stones on a patio or wide path. Provide sun and well-drained but not bone-dry soil.

The mint-like, mint-scented leaves are heavily marked with cream. In early summer, the plant is covered in a haze of profuse, pink, sage-like flowers. Like many plants of the *Labiatae* family, this is attractive to bees.

CONVALLARIA MAJALIS 'VARIEGATA'

Family: Liliaceae
Height: 20cm (8in)
Spread: 30cm (12in)
Flowering time: Spring
Aspect: Sun
Soil: Moist but well drained
Minimum temperature: −29°C (−20°F)

Lily-of-the-valley needs no description, but this treasure, occasionally sold as 'Albostriata' or 'Striata', has green and gold, vertically striped leaves, up to 20cm (8in) high, with the gold stripes meticulously following the leaf veins. Although its striking, almost sculptural appearance has contemporary appeal, it was grown as long ago as 1835. The creamy white flowers are slightly smaller than in the species, but the fragrance is equally rich and penetrating; flowers are sometimes followed by bright red berries.

A hardy deciduous woodland plant, 'Variegata' likes moist but well drained, humus-rich, sandy soil. Like the species, it can take time to settle down and often confounds, refusing to grow in seemingly ideal conditions, but thriving in poor, dry, heavy or otherwise unsuitable soil. Unlike the species, it is tolerant of and colours best in sun, becoming dull or reverting in shade. Remove any leaves that revert, but expect slight fading, even in sun, as the season progresses.

Plant the thongy rhizomes firmly, horizontally at 2.5cm (1in) deep and 30cm (12in) apart, in late autumn. If numbers allow, plant in two or three likely sites in your garden and observe which locale they prefer. You can also lift an entire clump from an established colony and replant it in a new site.

Lily-of-the-valley, in all its forms, looks best in informal swathes, whether through light woodland or rough grass, or through lower-growing plants in a mixed border. It can also, technically, be incorporated into a herb garden, since the dried, powdered flowers and roots were once used as a heart tonic, diuretic and love potion.

CYCLAMEN

Family: Primulaceae
Height: 10-15cm (4-6in)
Spread: 30cm (12in)
Flowering time: Early autumn through winter
Aspect: Light or deep shade
Soil: Moist but well drained
Minimum temperature: −23°C (−10°F)

Unlike many rarities featured in this book, the best cyclamen for variegation is also the easiest, most adaptable and widely available hardy species. Formerly *Cyclamen neapolitanum*, the current specific name *hederifolium* refers to the ivy-like, lobed leaves, though wide variation occurs in leaf shape as well as in variegation, a showy silver and grey marbling on a dark green ground. The leaf undersides are a rich, dull crimson.

The leaves usually follow the lightly fragrant, elegant flowers, pink with darker mouths, which appear mainly in early autumn and may continue, on and off, into winter. The leaves, prostrate at first, form a dense ground cover 10cm (4in) high, with the patterns created by the leaf overlap additionally striking. The leaves are fully mature in winter, and die back in early summer.

There are several named forms, including the white-flowered 'Album' and 'Bowles' Apollo', which has heavily marked leaves and pink flowers.

Leafy, moist but well-drained, cool soil in light or deep shade is ideal, but these plants are exceptionally tolerant. Among the few variegated plants that thrive in dry shade, *C. hederifolium* is ideal for naturalizing under hedges or trees, even pine and cedar, or along

woodland walks. Their display season from autumn to spring makes them good partners for woodland ferns, such as *Athyrium* or *Blechnum*, which are at their best from spring to autumn. On a smaller scale, plant them in shady rock gardens.

The tubers are long-lived, and can eventually grow 30cm (12in) or more across, producing 150 leaves annually. Pot-grown plants are less risky than dried tubers, but more expensive. Plant 5cm (2in) deep and 30cm (12in) apart, with the domed, smooth side down, in late summer or early autumn. The roots, flowers and foliage emerge from the rim of the upper surface. They self-seed where happy, but seedlings may need a cover of wire netting or light twigs, as temporary protection against birds. Mulch occasionally with peat or leafmould with a little bonemeal added.

Winter-flowering *C. coum*, 10-15cm (4-6in) high, is variable. Some plants have plain green leaves, others are heavily marbled with white, and there are several selected forms. All are ideal for growing under trees, where dry, shady conditions and root-riddled soil would deter less vigorous subjects.

Disporum sessile 'Variegatum'

Family: Liliaceae
Height: 45cm (18in)
Spread: 30cm (12in)
Flowering time: Spring
Aspect: Semi-shade
Soil: Humus-rich
Minimum temperature: −29°C (−20°F)

DISPORUM SESSILE 'VARIEGATUM'

Fairy bells, also listed as *Oakesiella variegata*, is a rhizomatous Japanese woodland plant resembling Solomon's seal, to which it is related. Its stalkless, lance-shaped leaves, irregularly striped green and white, are carried on erect stems from which hang creamy white, bell-shaped flowers in spring. Blue-black berries are sometimes produced after the plant flowers, which is usually in April or May. Plant the rhizomes 8cm (3in) deep, 30cm (12in) apart, in cool, humus-rich soil in semi-shade.

Dracunculus vulgaris

DRACUNCULUS VULGARIS

The sinister-looking dragon plant, also listed as *Arum dracunculus*, just merits inclusion for its purple-blotched, snake-like fleshy stems and fan-shaped, deeply divided, white-striated leaves. It is, however, grown for its intriguing spathe, greenish outside and velvety, rich crimson-purple inside. The deep maroon, nearly black spadix contained within smells of fresh faeces, to attract pollinating dung beetles and bluebottles. Once pollinated, the odour disappears and scarlet berries eventually follow.

Mediterranean in origin and deciduous, it thrives in sun, especially in cool areas, or light shade and well-drained soil, especially sandy loam. In cool climates, the base of a wall in full sun is ideal. Plant the tuberous roots with 8cm (3in) covering of soil in autumn. Lift and divide every few years, to prevent overcrowding and degeneration.

Family: Araceae
Height: 90cm (3ft)
Spread: 45cm (18in)
Flowering time: Early summer
Aspect: Sun or light shade
Soil: Moist, well drained, humus-rich
Minimum temperature: −6°C (20°F)

EPIMEDIUM

Family: Berberidaceae
Height: 23-45cm (9-18in)
Spread: 30-45cm (12-18in)
Flowering time: Spring
Aspect: Light shade
Soil: Leafy, humus-rich
Minimum temperature: −23°C (−10°F)

The forms of barrenwort, or bishop's hat, listed below are most markedly variegated in spring. Although the variegations fade to dull green, they are so dramatic that their inclusion is justified. The new spring foliage, comprised of several oval or heart-shaped leaflets carried on a wiry stem, has copper or crimson variegations, roughly following the veins. In autumn, the leaves are again tinged russet or bronze, remaining so through winter. Clip off the old, untidy foliage in late winter, to reveal the new leaves and tiny nodding, spurred flowers.

Woodland dwellers by nature, epimediums make excellent evergreen or semi-evergreen, dense ground cover in light, cool shade, such as under trees and shrubs. Partner with ferns, alliums, hellebores or *Tiarella cordifolia*. Though fairly tolerant, they dislike drought, and prefer leafy, humus-rich soil. Epimedium clumps spread slowly by underground rootstock and can remain undisturbed for years. Propagate by division.

Epimedium diphyllum forms a mounded shape up to 30cm (12in) high and wide. It has narrow, heart-shaped, evergreen leaves, that are bright green, crinkled, slightly mottled and irregularly edged with maroon, and bears white flowers.

E. × perralchicum 'Fröhnleiten', an evergreen hybrid 45cm (18in) high and 30cm (12in) across, has foliage marbled with reds and bronze in spring, and again in autumn. Bright yellow, starry flowers are borne in spring.

E. × versicolor 'Sulphureum' is one of the most robust and easy-going. Its 30cm (12in) high, semi-evergreen foliage is marbled reddish-purple in spring and bronze in autumn; its pale yellow, pink-tinted flowers appear in early spring.

E. × warleyense, another semi-evergreen hybrid, has bright green leaves tinged with red-purple, and unusual orange-red and yellow flowers. More compact, it grows 23cm (9in) high.

Epimedium diphyllum

Above: Eryngium bourgatii
Left: Eryngium variifolium

Left: Eryngium 'Calypso'

ERYNGIUM

Sea hollies have an exotic appearance, intriguing and sometimes stately, or even sinister, rather than pretty. Inhabitants of alpine slopes as well as seashores, their spininess protects them from grazing animals, and the waxy leaf coating helps reduce transpiration. The branching stems of thistle-like flowers, with attractive, prominent bracts, last for weeks in the garden and are easily air dried for winter displays.

From the Spanish Alps comes *Eryngium bourgatii*, with intricate and fiercely spiny, flat rosettes of deeply cut, greenish-grey foliage, veined and spotted in white. Its appearance has been likened to crumpled wire mesh. In summer, it carries 30-45cm (12-18in) high, wiry stems of blue-purple thistles. Thrifts (*Armeria*) or silver-foliaged, low-growing artemisias or pinks (*Dianthus*) would complement its form and enjoy similar growing conditions.

E. variifolium, a hardy evergreen North African species from the Atlas mountains, forms basal rosettes of less heavily spiny, dark-green, toothed leaves, with sharp white veining and marbling. In late summer, leafy stems up to 60cm (2ft) high, carry small, metallic-blue thistles. Again, partner it with sun-lovers – seakale, phlomis, cistus or gypsophila.

E. 'Calypso' originated in Holland and has atypical rounded and fleshy green leaves with broad cream edging tinged pink in late summer; the amethyst-blue flowers last for several weeks from midsummer. It grows up to 90cm (3ft) and 30cm (1ft) across. Though strikingly handsome, the plant is slow-growing and difficult to propagate; it needs a sunny position and good drainage and may require staking.

Eryngiums need full sun and perfect drainage, whether sandy, gravelly or limy soil. Where happy, they self-seed, but can also be propagated by division and root cuttings.

Family: Umbelliferae
Height: 30-90cm (12-36in)
Spread: 30-60cm (12-24in)
Flowering time: Summer
Aspect: Full sun
Soil: Well drained
Minimum temperature: −23°C (−10°F)

ERYSIMUM

Family: Cruciferae
Height: 30-45cm (12-18in)
Spread: 30-45cm (12-18in)
Flowering time: Summer
Aspect: Full sun
Soil: Well drained, poor
Minimum temperature: −12°C (10°F)

These variegated alpine wallflowers are short-lived, semi-evergreen sub-shrubs, closely allied to the immensely popular biennial bedding wallflowers (themselves actually short-lived perennials but grown as biennials replaced annually), and sometimes listed in catalogues under *Cheiranthus*. The dome-shaped *Erysimum linifolium* 'Variegatum' grows 30-45cm (12-18in) high and wide, with mauve summer flowers and cream variegated leaves; *E. mutabile* 'Variegatum' is similar, but its specific name refers to its flowers that open scarlet and gradually change to reddish-mauve. Ideal for sunny borders, banks and rock gardens, they need full sun, well drained, even dry and poor soil, and shelter. Propagate from cuttings.

ERYTHRONIUM

Family: Liliaceae
Height: 20-30cm (8-12in)
Spread: 20-30cm (8-12in)
Flowering time: Spring
Aspect: Light shade
Soil: Moist but well drained, humus-rich
Minimum temperature: −23°C (−10°F)

These hardy, tuberous, spring-flowering perennials thrive in rough, leaf-strewn grass, under light-foliaged trees or along woodland paths.

Erythronium dens-canis, the European dog-tooth violet, has jade green leaves, up to 25cm (10in) high, mottled with bronze and overlaid with a slight metallic sheen – hence the American common name, trout lily. Its English common name comes from the fang-like appearance of its tubers, best planted from pots rather than while dormant and dried. Its gracefully pendant, cyclamen-like spring flowers have reflexed petals and range from pink, rose and lilac to white.

The American species *E. revolutum* has green leaves mottled with brown and flowers ranging from white to pink, carried in late spring. Cultivars include 'Rose Beauty', with deep pink blooms, 'Citronella', with yellow blooms, and 'White Beauty', white flowers with yellow centres. These grow 20-30cm (8-12in) high and wide. The tubers tend to dry out quickly and fresh tubers should be planted as soon as bought.

They prefer cool, moist but well-drained, humus-rich soil. For an old-fashioned meadow garden, plant with snowdrops, winter aconites, primroses, small crocus, doronicums, muscari, and species narcissi. They self-seed and form large clumps from offsets where happy; lift and divide the clumps occasionally in late summer, to prevent overcrowding.

EUPHORBIA

Family: Euphorbiaceae
Height: 30-120cm (1-4ft)
Spread: 30-90cm (12-36in)
Flowering time: Early spring to early summer
Aspect: Sun or light shade
Soil: Well drained
Minimum temperature: −23°C (−10°F)

Spurges are supreme foliage plants, with their orderly, often architectural, leaf arrangement, accentuated by variegations in the forms described below. Their flowers are insignificant but surrounded by dish- or saucer-shaped bracts, that are fascinating and often plain green, reinforcing the foliar impact. The evergreen forms are especially valuable in winter.

The milky sap the plant exudes when cut gives it its second common name, milkweed. This is a skin irritant and care should be taken when handling spurges, especially against inadvertently getting sap in the eyes.

Most well-drained soils in sun or light shade suit euphorbias, although glaucous-leaved and red-variegated forms colour best in full sun.

Euphorbia amygdaloides is the British native wood spurge, found along roadsides, in hedges and light woodlands. Its evergreen leaves and stems are tinged purple. The rather rare but beautiful *E. a.* 'Variegata' (minimum temperature −18°C/0°F) has creamy white leaf margins, and a creamy white ruff around the sharp lime green flowers, which appear in early summer. It grows 45-60cm (18-24in) high, and its roots are wide spreading, making considerable, bushy clumps in time.

Drawbacks are its vulnerability to mildew, and its tendency to revert to plain green, counteracted by propagating and replanting regularly from cuttings. Grow alongside

Above: Erythronium revolutum 'Rose Beauty'

Above: Erysimum linifolium 'Variegatum'

Right: Erysimum mutabile 'Variegatum'

Above: Erythronium dens-canis

pulmonarias or hardy geraniums, or as ground cover around old-fashioned rose bushes.

E. *sikkimensis* needs richer, moister conditions than most spurges. It is spectacular in spring, when its brilliant purple and red new shoots, described as resembling ruby glass, appear. The young leaves are tinged and veined red. Although they fade as the season progresses, the pink, bronze and red veining and edging to the soft green leaves remain attractive. The loose, flat, greenish-yellow flower heads are enhanced by red bracts. This is a large plant, 90-120cm (3-4ft) high, more in good conditions. Grow it as a back-of-the-border subject, where it may need staking, or as a wild garden plant, left to flop at will.

E. *wallichii*, 60-75cm (24-30in) tall and 45cm (18in) wide, has dark green leaves with purplish edges and distinct white midribs. Large, yellow-green bracts surround the small flowers which appear in early summer. It is tolerant of full sun, but best in partial shade.

E. *characias* 'Variegata' is a handsome plant, its green-grey leaves margined and streaked with creamy white. Smaller and less hardy than the species, it grows 45-60cm (18-24in) high and wide, and needs overwintering in cool, frost-free conditions.

E. *c. wulfenii* 'Burrow Silver', a new introduction, is a variegated form of the king of euphorbias. It makes statuesque, shrubby clumps, up to 90cm (3ft) high, of soft creamy yellow and green foliage that changes in emphasis as the season progresses. The narrow, evergreen leaves droop in very cold weather but return to their ruff-like form as temperatures increase. To reach their fullest potential, they need shelter.

The tips of young stems curl in autumn, turn reddish-purple over winter and produce domed, lime green flower bracts the following spring and early summer. They should then be cut down to ground level, to allow the next year's stems room to grow. Plant with silvery helichrysums or artemisias, acanthus, figs, eucalyptus or purple sage. 'Burrow Silver' is superb overhanging paving or in large, terracotta pots as focal points, and is

**Euphorbia characias
'Variegata'**

especially welcome in dry gardens.

Spurge is much loved by flower arrangers, but the cut ends must be seared with a flame, or dipped in boiling water for a few seconds, to stem the flow of sap. Propagate cultivars by division or cuttings, species plants by seed.

FILIPENDULA ULMARIA 'VARIEGATA'

Meadowsweet, or queen of the meadows, is a native British plant found in wet meadows, riversides and ditches. In spring it forms large basal clumps of attractively divided leaves. In summer it sends up branching stems, up to 1.2m (4ft) high, of creamy white plumes, with an overpoweringly sweet smell. It was a sacred herb of the Druids, often associated with death. In medieval times, it was used as a strewing herb, to counteract unpleasant household smells, and its flowers were used as a substitute for honey and to flavour mead.

The variegated form is more compact, its dark green leaves up to 30cm (12in) high and centrally splashed with yellow – a rather restless effect, attractive to some but not to others. To keep its foliage in top condition, the young flower stems are normally removed.

Like the species, the variegated form needs deep, moist soil, and shade in hot areas. It associates well with waterside plants such as hostas, loosestrife (*Lythrum salicaria*), and willow gentian (*Gentiana asclepiadea*). It is easily increased by division.

Family: Rosaceae
Height: 30cm (12in)
Spread: 30cm (12in)
Flowering time: Summer
Aspect: Sun or shade
Soil: Deep, moist
Minimum temperature:
−34°C (−30°F)

Above: Fragraria × ananassa 'Variegata' with Lysimachia nummularia 'Aurea'

Far left: Filipendula ulmaria 'Variegata'

Left: Fragraria × ananassa 'Variegata' in flower

FRAGARIA × ANANASSA 'VARIEGATA'

Family: Rosaceae

Height: 15cm (6in)

Spread: Spreads indefinitely

Flowering time: Spring and summer

Aspect: Sun or light shade

Soil: Well drained

Minimum temperature: −29°C (−20°F)

The species is the European wild strawberry, an evergreen carpeting plant with white flowers in spring and summer, wide-questing runners, and small but delicious, fragrant, tiny berries. 'Variegata' makes robust ground cover, 15cm (6in) high and spreading indefinitely. It enjoys a cool spot in sun or light shade and any well-drained soil, particularly akaline ones. Its rich green, divided leaves are irregularly, heavily and randomly splashed with white, especially effective in winter and most marked on mature plants. At its best when it can weave its way through and over plain-leaved perennials, it is an ideal unifier but suffers from reversion; annual replanting helps.

Interestingly, the species qualifies as a herb since its leaves were once brewed and taken as a spring tonic, after a winter diet deficient in vitamins and minerals. It was also the symbolic fruit of the Virgin Mary and, before her, Venus.

Above: Geranium phaeum 'Variegatum'

Right: Geranium macrorrhizum 'Variegatum'

Right: Fritillaria imperialis 'Argenteomarginata'

FRITILLARIA IMPERIALIS 'ARGENTEOMARGINATA'

Family: Liliaceae
Height: Up to 1.5m (5ft)
Spread: 23-30cm (9-12in)
Flowering time: Spring
Aspect: Full sun
Soil: Well drained
Minimum temperature: −23°C (−10°F)

The variegated crown imperial fritillary is a stately show-stopper, with its clusters of deep orange, pendant bellflowers, containing drops of sweet nectar in their stamens, topped by tufts of white-edged, green, leaf-like bracts. The flowers are carried on bare, reddish-purple stems, covered with a tidy ruff of variegated leaves on the lower half.

In the mixed border, groups of fritillaries, even of three bulbs, are more comfortable-looking than single plants. A dark setting and foreground of forget-me-nots (*Myosotis*) would be ideal. Lift and thin old clumps as soon as the leaves turn yellow, and plant fresh bulbs then – they send out roots early, and shrivelled bulbs may well fail. Grow in well drained, rich soil and full sun; on poorly drained or suspect soil, make a little bed of sand in each planting hole. Their strong, foxy odour makes the flowers unsuitable for cutting.

GERANIUM

Family: Geraniaceae
Height: 20-50cm (8-20in)
Spread: 25-60cm (10-24in)
Flowering time: Late spring and early summer
Aspect: Sun or shade
Soil: Well drained
Minimum temperature: −29°C (−20°F)

This genus is often confused with the related *Pelargonium* genus, tender evergreen sub-shrubs with showy, large flowers. Botanical geraniums are undemanding hardy herbaceous ground cover plants, some especially valuable for dry shade, under trees and as underplanting for shrub roses. The common name, cranesbill, refers to the beak-like seed case seen as the flower fades.

Geranium macrorrhizum 'Variegatum' is among the most effective weed-smothering ground covers. Forming carpets 20cm (8in) high and twice that across, its rounded, lobed, semi-evergreen leaves are fresh green with creamy white swirls. They are tinted scarlet in autumn and have an attractive winter presence. Magenta-pink flowers rise just proud of the leaves, in a single, brief flush in early summer. Its woody, surface-running roots are easily divided in spring, and its wide-spreading but non-invasive nature makes it ideal for weaving between clumps of contrasting foliaged plants, such as *Alchemilla mollis*, day lilies and large-leaved hostas. The leaves are scented, most noticeably when touched or bruised, a reason for planting along a path or patio's edge.

G. × monacense 'Muldoon', also sold as *G. × m.* 'Variegatum' and formerly as *G. punctatum* 'Variegatum', is a shade-loving, deciduous hybrid. Its dense, woody root system makes weed-proof ground cover 45cm (18in) high and 60cm (2ft) across. Each of the five lobes on the angular leaves has a maroon spot. The young leaves may be pale yellow, contrasting dramatically with the spots. They gradually turn green, with irregular cream and crimson splashes. Dull purple flowers appear in late spring and early summer.

G. phaeum 'Variegatum' is the variegated form of mourning widow, or dusky cranesbill, so-called from its nodding, reflexed, five-petalled, dark maroon (almost black) flowers, appearing on lax stems in late spring and early summer. A relatively tall geranium, it forms clumps 50cm (20in) high and half that across, of soft green, hairy leaves heavily splashed with creamy white and strikingly blotched with wine red. Tolerant of deep, dry shade, it is ideal for enlivening a wild or woodland garden, interplanted with honesty and bluebells. In borders, interplant with dark purple tulips, such as 'Queen of the Night'. It is propagated by division and also self-seeds, but seedlings are variable.

Geranium × monacense 'Muldoon'

GLECHOMA HEDERACEA 'VARIEGATA'

Family: Labiatae

Height: 10-15cm (4-6in)

Spread: 30-90cm (1-3ft)

Flowering time: Spring and summer

Aspect: Sun or shade

Soil: Ordinary, moist but well drained

Minimum temperature: −12°C (10°F)

Also known as *Nepeta hederacea* and *N. glechoma* or, commonly, as ground ivy, the rampageous species is represented in cultivation by the slightly less robust variegated form 'Variegata'. Though still a potential menace in open beds and borders, it is useful, large-scale ground cover under trees, and enchanting grown as a trailing plant in hanging baskets, pots and window boxes.

A fully hardy, evergreen carpeter, rooting from the nodes, it has pretty round, scalloped, fresh green leaves that are irregularly edged and splashed with white and occasionally tinged with purple. Its whorls of insignificant lilac-blue flowers appear in spring and summer.

It is happy in sun or shade and any moist but well-drained soil; but unfortunately is much loved by slugs. As newly planted ground cover, it needs regular weeding until plants knit together.

Above: Glechoma hederacea 'Variegata'

Right: Hemerocallis fulva 'Kwanzo Variegata'

HELLEBORUS LIVIDUS

Family: Ranunculaceae

Height: 45cm (18in)

Spread: 30cm (12in)

Flowering time: Spring

Aspect: Light shade

Soil: Rich, moist but well drained

Minimum temperature: −12°C (10°F)

Although William Robinson, in his Victorian classic *The English Flower Garden*, exiled green-flowered hellebores to the wild garden, they are more valued as garden plants today. *Helleborus lividus* suffers from confused nomenclature, being variously called *H. argutifolius* and *H. lividus corsicus*. Deep purple stems bear three-part, glaucous green, prickly-edged leaves that are waxy, polished and laced with paler veining.

The foliage forms bushy clumps from which emerge sturdy flower stems 45cm (18in) high, in winter topped by clusters of fat, round buds that open to pink-tinged, apple green, cup-shaped flowers in spring. After flowering, the stems die and are followed by new foliage.

It is less hardy than many hellebores and, like most, resents disturbance. It needs moist but well-drained, rich soil, light shade and shelter, and may require staking. Good plant partners include species narcissi, euphorbias, squills and ferns. It can also be grown in pots in a cold greenhouse, where its delicate scent is more noticeable. The leaves take glycerine well, for dried flower displays.

Helleborus lividus

HEMEROCALLIS FULVA 'KWANZO VARIEGATA'

Family: Liliaceae
Height: 1.2m (4ft)
Spread: 90cm (3ft)
Flowering time: Summer
Aspect: Sun or light shade
Soil: Fertile, not too dry
Minimum temperature: −34°C (−30°F)

This is the variegated form of the old-fashioned tawny, copper-coloured or fulvous day lily. Orange, fragrant double flowers with red centres are carried in clusters and last only a day, hence the name, but are produced over a long period in summer. The flower buds, fresh or dried, are considered a delicacy in the Orient, where they have been cultivated as crops for centuries.

It is a tough plant, happy in sun or light shade, and any fertile, but not bone-dry, soil.

Its light green, variably white-striped foliage emerges in early spring and forms large, grassy, arching clumps, 1.2m (4ft) high and 90cm (3ft) across. It has rapidly colonizing, rhizomatous roots and is easily increased by division. Partner with contrasting foliage, such as those of hostas, ferns, campanulas, geraniums, polygonums or delphiniums, or repeat the grassy theme with subtle variations, juxtaposing 'Kwanzo Variegata' with *Curtonus paniculatus*, *Iris sibirica*, *Crocosmia* and ornamental grasses. Slugs can be a problem.

HEUCHERA

Family: Saxifragaceae

Height: 15cm (6in)

Spread: 30cm (12in)

Flowering time: Spring and summer

Aspect: Sun or light shade

Soil: Rich, well drained

Minimum temperature: −29°C (−20°F)

Coral bells are so called from their dainty sprays of small, bell-shaped flowers carried on wiry, 30cm (12in) high stems in spring and summer. The rounded, hairy, slightly crinkled evergreen leaves form low, weed-smothering mounds 15cm (6in) high and twice that across.

Heuchera 'Snowstorm', an American introduction, has extensive creamy white marbling to the leaves, flushed pink in winter. It grows in sun or light shade and rich, well-drained soil. The crowns become woody in time, producing fewer flowers. Top dress with leafy compost to encourage fibrous roots to form, or lift and divide in late summer, discarding the old, central woody portion and replanting the remaining roots deeply. A good front-of-the-border plant, it combines well with plain green-leaved subjects, or garden pinks (*Dianthus*).

× *Heucherella* 'Bridget Bloom' is a bi-generic hybrid between *Heuchera* and the related *Tiarella*. It looks like a compact heuchera, forming clumps of attractively marbled evergreen leaves. The charming pink and white flowers, on 45cm (18in) spikes, appear earlier than heuchera flowers and sometimes continue, on and off, until autumn. Provide light shade and rich, moist but well-drained soil; otherwise growth and flowering are poor, especially in dry soil.

Heuchera 'Snowstorm'

HEXASTYLIS SHUTTLEWORTHII 'CALLAWAY'

Family: Aristolochiaceae

Height: 8-12cm (3-5in)

Spread: 30-45cm (12-18in)

Flowering time: Early summer

Aspect: Shade

Soil: Slightly acid, moist but well drained

Minimum temperature: −23°C (−10°F)

This selected American cultivar is both more vigorous and more strongly marked than the species. Also known as *Asarum shuttleworthii* 'Callaway' and commonly called the southern mottled wild ginger, it has heart-shaped leaves, 8cm (3in) across, beautifully mottled in silvery grey and dark green. These form a low-growing, broad mass of evergreen foliage, 8-12cm (3-5in) high and up to 45cm (18in) across. The vase-shaped violet flowers, spotted with dark brown, appear in early summer, but are typically hidden by the foliage.

It is an ideal plant for woodland conditions, requiring a slightly acid soil that drains easily but receives a constant supply of moisture. Being very shade-tolerant, it actually thrives in the shadier locations where other plants may not do so well, making excellent ground cover. Propagate by division in spring.

HOSTA

Family: Liliaceae

Height: 8cm-1.2m (3in-4ft)

Spread: 25-75cm (10-30in)

Flowering times: Early summer to early autumn

Aspect: Sun or shade

Soil: Tolerant of most conditions

Minimum temperature: −34°C (−30°F)

This is perhaps the most outstanding genus of herbaceous foliage plants, with a daunting and ever-increasing number of variegated forms. Variegation ranges from narrow margins to central splashes. In the vast majority, it follows the leaf form and emphasizes the orderly, sculptural quality of the leaf clumps, especially in those with layered, overlapping leaves radiating from a central crown, such as *Hosta sieboldiana* 'Frances Williams'.

The palette is largely cool, relatively limited and therefore relatively subtle, another asset in terms of general garden use. It ranges from white through cream, beige, pale yellow, deep yellow, pale, medium and dark green, blue-green, grey-green and grey. Some leaves are matt, others are glossy; all are visibly veined but some are dramatically so, with corrugated or puckered textures.

Most variegated forms are bicoloured, and those that have several shades or tints of green or yellow and white are still restrained compared to, say, coleus or the more strident ajugas. Some forms are at their best in spring, gradually fading to plain green as the season progresses; a few begin life dull-looking in spring and gradually take on their variegations as the leaves mature; and others retain their strong colour contrast from the time the leaves unfurl until the first autumn frost – an important factor in selection. A few turn bright yellow briefly in autumn, before dying back.

Formerly called funkias or plantain lilies, hosta species are mostly Japanese in origin, the rest coming from China or Korea. They range in size from miniature, such as the 8cm (3in) high *H. lancifolia* 'Inaho', to huge, such as the 1.2m (4ft) *H. sieboldiana* 'Frances Williams'. The leaves range from narrowly lance-shaped to spoon-shaped or broadly round and pointed. Some are almost stalk-less, others are carried on tall, sturdy stalks, occasionally themselves variegated. All are deciduous, but their thick, fleshy, dense and deep roots, once established, prevent weeds establishing themselves, even when the plants are dormant.

The trumpet-shaped flowers are secondary, but modestly charming; a few forms are scented. The flowers appear from early summer to early autumn, according to type. They range from white through washed-out mauve to rich, deep violet, and are carried on slender, leafless stalks.

CULTIVATION AND CARE

Hostas are tolerant, surviving in sun or shade and most soils, including sand, clay and chalk, the last only if heavily and regularly manured. Cool, light shade produces the most

Hosta sieboldiana 'Frances Williams'

Above: Hosta fortunei 'Albopicta'

Right: A mixed planting of hostas, polygonatum and origanum

Above: Hosta undulata undulata

Above: Hosta 'Thomas Hogg'

luxurious foliage; although hostas grown in sun produce more flowers, their leaves (and flowers) are smaller and variegations may bleach out. Shade from house or garden walls is preferable to shade from trees, especially in urban areas, where sooty deposits on the tree leaves drip onto and mar the hosta leaves below. Smooth or shiny-leaved hosta forms, such as 'Thomas Hogg' and *H. ventricosa*, tend to shed the soot better than forms with deeply corrugated leaves. Although hostas are hardy, the new shoots appear early in spring and can be damaged by frost, so frost pockets are best avoided.

Hostas will grow in dry or wet, but not waterlogged, soil. Generally, the sunnier the spot, the damper the soil should be, and the higher the humidity. Whatever the aspect, the richer and deeper the soil, the better, especially if hostas are competing with tree roots. Under trees, digging good-sized planting holes and filling them with enriched soil is worth the extra effort, and an annual mulch of well-rotted compost or leafmould, whatever the conditions, promotes healthy growth and a good show.

Established clumps can remain untouched for years, but division is the normal method of propagation. Younger plants can be lifted and divided any time of year, but ideally in spring or fall. With old clumps, it is easier to take pie-shaped wedges from the clump, using a sharp spade, leaving the mother plant *in situ* and filling the hole with rich soil.

Slugs and snails are the main enemies, and it is sensible to scatter slug pellets around hostas in early spring.

A word of warning: some variegated hostas only assume their true colours when mature, young plants remaining plain green, so don't condemn the supplier prematurely. On the other hand, saving the label and receipt is sensible.

USING HOSTAS IN THE GARDEN

Height, form and colour, as usual, are the determining factors, but because of the sheer visual solidity of a hosta, siting is particularly

Hosta fortunei 'Aurea
Marginata' and Hedera
colchica 'Sulphur Heart'

Hosta fortunei 'Marginata
Alba'

important. This is especially true for the larger forms which, when well established, are automatic focal points. As well as mixed border stalwarts, they are excellent by the waterside, in light woodland, edging hard surfaces such as paths or patios, or in tubs or large terracotta pots. Hostas adjacent to stone, brick, gravel or weathered wood make an extremely effective textural contrast. When hostas are planted at the base of a garden statue or fountain, or near a garden bench, these features are enhanced.

It is easy to be enticed into collecting hostas. Specialist nurseries offer over 100 forms and their catalogues often state that, as well as the numerous forms listed, others – rare, difficult to propagate, or not yet named – are available upon application. Displaying a collection, especially of variegated forms, is a challenge. In large gardens, clumps of a single, variegated form can be surrounded by plain-leaved plants. An alternative, especially in small gardens, is to group variations on a limited theme. Several forms of green-leaved, white-margined hostas could be grown together, creating subtle variation within an

overall unified effect. A more sophisticated visual pun would combine green-edged, white-centred hostas with their reverse – white-edged, green-centred forms. Random mixtures of variegated hostas, however, display neither their restful nor their statuesque qualities which would be shown in a more careful grouping.

Hostas are supreme mixers and it might be easier to list unsuitable plant partners than suitable ones; there are so many facets of the hosta character that suggest planting schemes. Their oriental origins, for example, make them ideal for partnering with Japanese maples, magnolias, primulas, tree peonies, bamboos, nandinas and *Fatsia japonica*. Hostas at the base of an out-of-season camellia are a less obvious connection, but both are oriental in origin, with complementary foliage and flowering times, and both can thrive against a wall that does not get direct sun.

Hostas' waterside connotations suggest huge-leaved gunneras, rodgersias and rheums, together with grassy-leaved water and waterside iris, sweet flag and sedges. The architectural forms suggest architectural plant partners: acanthus, aralia, stag's horn sumach (*Rhus typhina*) and New Zealand flax (*Phormium tenax*), for example.

The scale and solid leaf forms are complemented by delicate, lacy contrast: the tiny-leaved mind-your-own business, *Soleirolia soleirolii*; delicate ferns, such as the royal fern, *Osmunda regalis* or the sensitive fern, *Onoclea sensibilis*; bronze-leaved fennel or dicentras.

Hosta colours, according to type, are another source of inspiration, whether used as contrast, such as grey-leaved variegated hostas with red or purple forms of *Cotinus coggygria*, or in the harmony of yellow-edged hostas partnered with yellow-leaved feverfew or the golden form of creeping Jenny, *Lysimachia nummularia* 'Aurea'.

The flowers suggest other members of the lily family as potential company: lilies themselves, day lilies, Solomon's seal (*Poly-*

gonatum), *Ophiopogon* species, or mondo grass, grape hyacinths and lily-of-the-valley.

Lastly, hostas' main role as ground cover brings to mind many reliable ground covers with forms offering pleasant contrast – alchemillas, astrantias, ajugas, numerous hardy geraniums and euphorbias, bergenias, heucheras, polygonums, and even the modest but effective lesser periwinkles (*Vinca minor*).

HOSTAS AS CUT FOLIAGE

Young leaves can be tricky, but immersing them completely in tepid or cold water for several hours or overnight before arranging helps keep them turgid. As you submerge the leaf, re-cut the tip of the stem under water. This treatment also suits mature leaves of temperamental types, such as *H. fortunei* 'Albopicta'.

Older, mature foliage needs no special preparation, but re-cut the tips of the stems under water before arranging.

CLASSIFYING HOSTAS

The presentation and description of variegated hostas is challenging, to say the least. Division into white- and yellow-variegated forms seems the obvious solution, but 'creamy white' and 'creamy yellow' are often used by different catalogues to describe the same plant, which, indeed, may be creamy yellow in sun, creamy white in shade, or begin the season one colour and fade to the other.

Further confusion is added by the enormous number of new cultivars constantly appearing in the United States, Britain and Japan, some virtually identical; by the simultaneous use of Japanese and English species and varietal names; and by the renaming of old cultivars, combined with the stubborn refusal by some growers to adopt the new names. Not infrequently is a particular cultivar given markedly differing descriptions in different catalogues, and deemed not to exist in others. Except for the most widely available, undisputed forms, it is best to see a variegated hosta at the nursery or garden centre before making a decision.

The list below includes variegated species and cultivars, followed by a list of hybrids, by far the largest category, and still growing. Hostas are relatively expensive, being propagated commercially by division, a slow and limited process. New introductions are always more expensive still, partly from novelty as well as limited stocks, but micro-propagation is proving successful with some forms, and may ultimately bring numbers up and costs down.

SPECIES AND CULTIVARS

Hosta crispula is a striking species, sometimes confused with *H. fortunei* 'Marginata Alba'. Its large, long, broad and pointed, dark green leaves, 60cm (2ft) high, have wavy margins and are generously edged in white, though young plants produce all-green leaves. Shelter is best, since wind can turn the leaf margins brown. Its lilac flowers appear in early summer.

H. decorata decorata, also known as *H. decorata marginata*, is a Japanese subspecies with rounded, dark green, matt leaves, 60cm (2ft) high, with tidy white margins that continue down the stalks. Its deep lilac flowers appear in early summer.

H. elata 'Aureomarginata', also known as *H. montana* 'Variegata', has enormous pointed leaves, up to 75cm (30in) high, grey-green, broadly margined in yellow. The margins are attractively uneven, as if applied quickly by brush. It starts into growth early, and may need some frost protection. Its flowers are white.

H. fortunei 'Albopicta', one of the most ubiquitous variegated hostas, has large, deeply veined, heart-shaped leaves but the stalks are quite short. Its young, unfurling leaves are pale butter yellow, edged in lime and dark green. The centre slowly becomes darker and duller, fading to pale green and, by midsummer, the whole leaf becomes two tones of soft green. The dense clumps are 45-60cm (18-24in) high, 60cm (2ft) across, and produce pale lilac flowers. Best in light shade and shelter. (See photograph on p. 84.)

The similar-sized cultivar 'Gold Standard' behaves in the reverse way, its deeply veined, medium-sized, green leaves become golden yellow, thinly edged in green, as the season progresses.

'Aurea Marginata', or 'Yellow Edge', is also widely available. Its deep green leaves carry broad, uneven, creamy yellow borders that remain colourful well into autumn. The clumps are 75cm (30in) high, 60cm (2ft) across. (See photograph on p. 86.)

'Marginata Alba' is a magnificent, vigorous form, with broad, whitish edged, sage green leaves, grey underneath. It needs shade to produce the best colour contrast, but is relatively tolerant of exposure to wind. It grows to 75cm (30in) high and 60cm (2ft) across. (See photograph on p. 86.)

Rarer variegated cultivars of this species include the distinctive 'Gloriosa', with 45cm (18in) high, cupped, dark green leaves, edged in white; 'Hyacinthina Variegata', with grey-green leaves broadly margined in white, 60cm (2ft) high; 'Phyllis Campbell', with blue-green leaves marbled yellow in spring, but later fading, 60cm (2ft) high; 'Spinners', with large, sage green leaves edged in creamy white and remaining colourful until the first frost; and 'Sundance', with dark green leaves thickly edged in creamy white, 45cm (18in) high.

H. gracillima 'Variegata' is a charmingly diminutive form, with 15cm (6in) high, narrow green leaves edged in cream. It spreads quickly from stoloniferous roots, making good ground cover.

H. helenioides 'Albopicta' has broad yellow margins to its narrow, 30cm (12in) high leaves, with the colouring continuing down the stalks. It forms clumps 45cm (18in) across.

H. lancifolia, a late-flowering species with dark green, shiny, arrow-shaped leaves, has produced two variegated cultivars of note: 'Chinese Sunrise', 30cm (12in) high, with green-edged, gold leaves, fading to green; and the miniature 'Inaho', only 8cm (3in) high, with gold-streaked green leaves.

H. sieboldiana 'Frances Williams' is a variegated form of the distinct, huge, quilted, grey-leaved species. Its waxy, broad, pointed, blue-grey leaves have irregular, wide, creamy beige margins that deepen in colour as the summer progresses. It forms splendid clumps 75cm (30in) high and 45cm (18in) wide, but takes time getting established and is best in light shade. It turns bright yellow in autumn; the starry seedcases that follow the white flowers last all winter, and are good in dried flower displays. The new 'Frances Williams Improved' has wider leaf margins. The slightly smaller *H.* 'Northern Halo' has white-margined, heavily textured blue leaves, but is slow-growing.

H. sieboldii, formerly *H. albomarginata*, has small, overlapping, elliptical green leaves, 30cm (12in) high and narrowly edged with white, and violet flowers in midsummer. Its wide-spreading rootstock makes it a good colonizer. Cultivars include 'Kabitan', with green-edged, yellow leaves; the more compact 'Louisa', of American origin, with bright green, white-edged leaves and white flowers; and the temperamental and difficult 'Shirokabitan', with green-edged, white leaves 10cm (4in) high.

H. tokudama is like a small-scale *H. sieboldiana*, with puckered, heart-shaped, slightly cupped, blue-green leaves, 35cm (14in) high. Variegated forms include the unusual 'Aureo-nebulosa', with cloudy, mottled, yellow-centred, blue-green leaves; and 'Variegata', with yellow-green broken stripes.

H. undulata undulata, also called *H. u.* 'Mediovariegata' or, for simplicity, *H. undulata*, has low, rich green, wavy-edged leaves, 20cm (8in) high, each with a large central creamy white splash. *H. u. univittata* is more vigorous and taller but otherwise similar, forming densely packed mounds of wavy-edged, shiny green leaves, 30cm (12in) high, boldly striped with creamy white in the centre. New leaves are produced all summer. It carries violet flowers. (See photograph on p. 85.)

Above: Hosta 'Francee' with Lamium maculatum 'Beacon Silver'

Right: Hostas 'Shade Fanfare' (foreground) and 'Yellow Splash' (behind)

H. ventricosa 'Aureomaculata' has large, heart-shaped leaves 75cm (30in) high, splashed with creamy white in spring, but fading in summer. Young leaves are produced through the season. The flowers, like those of the following cultivar, are an attractive deep violet. (See photograph on p. 89.)

The equally large 'Aureomarginata', also sold as 'Variegata', has irregular borders of pale and deep yellow on its rich green leaves, and retains its bright variegation all summer.

HYBRIDS

This selection is necessarily incomplete, but the following gives an idea of the range available.

'Antioch' has magnificent arching leaves, mid to dark green at the centre, surrounded by mottled lighter green, with uniform, wide, creamy white margins, and lavender flowers.

'Celebration', 15cm (6in) high, has green-edged, creamy white leaves, much loved by slugs and in need of shade.

'Francee' has 60cm (2ft) high, rich green leaves edged in white, and pale lilac flowers.

'Fringe Benefit' is aptly named for its puckered, greeny-blue leaves, 60cm (2ft) high, edged in white when mature.

'Ginko Craig' has 30cm (12in) high, lance-shaped, white-margined green leaves and mauve blooms.

'Goldbrook Grace' is a new introduction, with 30cm (12in) high, green-margined gold leaves, retaining their colour well in shade.

'Golden Tiara' has 30cm (12in) high, heart-shaped green leaves edged in gold.

'Ground Master', named for its ground-covering qualities, has wavy-edged green leaves margined in creamy white, 25cm (10in) high, and purple flowers.

'Lunar Eclipse' has white-edged, heavily corrugated gold leaves, 45cm (18in) high, that grow more impressive as the season progresses. The flowers, carried in mid-summer, are near-white.

'Resonance' is similar to 'Ground Master', with cream-edged, undulating, 20cm (8in) high leaves.

'Reversed' has blue-grey margins to its creamy white, 40cm (16in) high leaves. It is temperamental, needing shade and shelter.

'Sea Sprite' is a tiny form only 10cm (4in) high, with wavy-edged green margins to its creamy yellow leaves. Its stoloniferous roots spread rapidly, and it carries lilac flowers.

'Shade Fanfare' has 45cm (18in) high, light green leaves, yellow in sun, with broad, creamy white margins. It is a strong, quick grower, ideal for ground cover, and its lavender flowers are carried freely.

'So Sweet', a recent introduction from America, forms an impressive mound of glossy, pale to mid green leaves margined broadly in yellow, and strongly fragrant, pure white flowers.

'Sugar and Cream' is also quick-growing and from America, with large, undulating, cream-edged leaves, up to 60cm (24in) high. It carries fragrant, lilac-tinged white flowers in late summer.

'Thomas Hogg', sometimes sold as *H. undulata* 'Albomarginata', is one of the easiest, most vigorous white-edged cultivars. Its large, pointed, rich green, waxy-smooth leaves are broadly margined in white, forming clumps 60cm (2ft) high and as much across. The smooth leaf surfaces make them less liable to collect sediment from dripping trees. Its tall, lilac flowers are carried in early summer.

'Wide Brim' is a new, fast-growing hybrid with rounded, ribbed, blue-green leaves, broadly and irregularly edged in pale gold. It grows 45cm (18in) high, and its densely packed spikes of pale lilac flowers are carried in midsummer.

'Yellow Splash' is a narrow-leaved hybrid, broadly edged in cream. Contrast remains strong all summer and autumn. It is a compact form, 30cm (1ft) high.

HOUTTUYNIA CORDATA 'CHAMAELEON'

Family: Saururaceae
Height: 15-25cm (6-10in)
Spread: 45cm (18in)
Flowering time: Summer
Aspect: Sun or semi-shade
Soil: Cool, moist
Minimum temperature: −29°C (−20°F)

This highly fashionable creeping plant has bright red branching stems and heart-shaped, orange-scented, deciduous leaves, strikingly and irregularly patterned with yellow, green, pink, red and bronze. The curious, single white flowers with conical green centres appear in summer.

The species, which has slightly metallic, blue-grey leaves, grows wild in the ditches of Japan, and 'Chamaeleon' makes good ground cover, 15-25cm (6-10in) high, in cool, moist soil or shallow water. Plant in semi-shade if the soil is liable to be at all dry; given a steady supply of moisture, full sun produces the best leaf colour. It can be invasive, so partner it with equally strong-growing plants: bamboo, montbretias (*Crocosmia*), rushes or polygonums, for example. Plant the rhizomes 8cm (3in) deep, 45cm (18in) apart; propagate by division in spring.

Some reputable authorities list 'Variegata' as synonymous with 'Chamaeleon'; others, equally reputable, list it as a separate but similar cultivar.

IRIS

Family: Iridaceae
Height: 30-60cm (12-24in)
Spread: 45cm (18in)
Flowering times: Late spring to midsummer
Aspect: Requirements vary, from full sun to cool shade
Soil: Requirements vary, from dry soil to shallow water
Minimum temperature: −29°C (−20°F)

There are half a dozen good variegated forms of this huge, and hugely popular, genus. Fortunately, they vary widely in their cultivation needs, from shallow water to dry soil and from cool shade to hot sun, so it is possible, whatever your garden, to grow at least one. All share the same marked verticality in leaf form, in each case reinforced by vertical stripes.

Iris ensata 'Variegata', formerly *I. kaempferi* 'Variegata', the Japanese flag, is a cultivar of a species particularly favoured by the Japanese, and the subject of much hybridization both in Japan and in the West. 'Variegata' has bright green and white foliage, especially striking in spring. The deciduous

Left: Houttuynia cordata
'Chamaeleon'

leaves, up to 60cm (2ft) high, have a prominent midrib, which distinguishes them from the closely related I. *laevigata*. Its huge, violet, velvety blooms are beardless, but have a yellow streak on the falls in place of the beard. They are carried, up to four per stem, in midsummer.

Provide cool, moist but not waterlogged, rich, acid soil, ideally with plenty of well-rotted organic matter incorporated, and full sun or light shade. Plant in early autumn or spring, or lift, divide and replant in late summer after flowering, spacing the rhizomes 45cm (18in) apart. It rarely flowers the first season after planting.

I. *foetidissima* 'Variegata', the only reliably evergreen variegated iris, is a form of the native English gladwin, stinking gladdon or roast-beef plant, found in thickets and woods on dry, chalky soil. (The roast-beef aroma of its leaves is only released if the leaves are crushed, so *foetidissima* is a bit overdramatic.) 'Variegata' forms clumps of dark grey-green leaves, 45cm (18in) high, broadly margined with white down one side; they are whitest in heavy shade, and remain variegated all year round. The leaves form typical, flat fans, the outermost leaves in each fan sometimes being slightly curved. It seldom flowers, so the brown pods of brilliant orange seeds for which the species is grown are also absent.

'Variegata' is especially valuable for enlivening dry shade, such as under trees or at the foot of a wall that does not receive direct sun. It makes a nice group with other chalk- and shade-loving plants, such as hart's tongue fern (*Asplenium scolopendrium*), *Helleborus foetidus* and *Daphne laureola*. Incorporate leaf mould into the soil when planting; set rhizomes 45cm (18in) apart. The species was formerly grown in herb gardens, the decoction of the root being used as a purgative, often mixed with ale.

I. *japonica* 'Variegata' also has creamy white-striped leaves but is semi-evergreen, and to thrive needs a hot, sunny spot, such as the base of a wall that receives full sun

(minimum temperature −12°C/10°F). Its 30cm (12in) high leaves form slightly angled fans, and it carries branching sprays of orange-crested, purple-veined, white orchid- or butterfly-like blooms in late spring. The shrubby germander, *Teucrium fruticans*, with its silvery grey leaves and penchant for similar growing conditions, would form an attractive backdrop.

Given well-drained soil, the rhizomes are quick to spread. Ensure vigorous growth by lifting, dividing and replanting 45cm (18in) apart every couple of years immediately after flowering. Slugs can be a problem.

I. laevigata 'Variegata', a form of the Japanese water iris, has dramatic, soft green and white, grassy foliage, which remains fresh-looking throughout the growing season, although it is deciduous. This, together with its purple-blue flowers, marked with gold on the falls, makes it one of the best water-side plants, for shallow water or permanently moist soil. It grows 60cm (2ft) high and forms clumps 45cm (18in) wide. Increase by lifting, dividing and replanting after flowering.

I. pallida, the old-fashioned, bearded Dalmatian iris or great purple flag, has two variegated forms. 'Argentea Variegata' has stiff fans of strongly striped, glaucous green and white leaves, 38cm (15in) high. Its flowers, carried in late spring or early summer, are relatively modest but the foliage increases in attractiveness as the season progresses. The more robust, taller and rarer 'Variegata', also sold as 'Aurea' and 'Aurea Variegata', has glaucous green and yellow foliage, 60cm (2ft) high and inclined to bend over at the tips. The upper extremities of the leaves may turn brown by late summer, but can be cut off. Its tall, branching spikes of lilac-blue blooms appear in early summer, and are variously described as elder- or vanilla-scented.

Both form large clumps in well-drained soil and sun: ideal in mixed borders filled with sun-loving plants, such as pinks (*Dianthus*), catmint (*Nepeta*) or gypsophila.

I. pseudacorus 'Variegata' is a yellow-

striped form of the British native golden flag, found in marshes, watersides and wet fields. At its best in spring, its fan-like sprays of foliage eventually reach 90cm (3ft) high but gradually fade, the buttercup yellow becoming green by the end of summer. Its yellow flowers, with their distinct brown markings, appear in early summer. 'Variegata' prefers sun or light shade and rich, moisture-retentive soil, bog or shallow water.

In folklore, the golden flag was thought to avert evil, and in herbal medicine, it was used as an astringent. The variegated form is long lasting when cut, much loved by flower arrangers, especially for spring displays or in oriental-style arrangements.

Above: Iris pseudacorus 'Variegata' and Iris laevigata 'Variegata'

Far left: Iris pallida 'Variegata'

Left: Iris laevigata 'Variegata' and mixed candelabra primulas

**Above: Lamium maculatum
'Chequers'**

**Right: Lamium maculatum
'Beacon Silver'**

**Right: Lamium maculatum
'White Nancy'**

LAMIUM

Family: Labiatae
Height: 10-30cm (4-12in)
Spread: 45-90cm (18-36in)
Flowering time: Early summer
Aspect: Sun or light shade
Soil: Well drained, humus-rich
Minimum temperature: −29°C (−20°F)

Deadnettles are useful, robust, shade-tolerant ground cover, often consigned to 'second string' positions in the garden and taken for granted rather than nurtured. The wild species grow in open woods and hedges in Europe. Cultivars thrive in any well-drained, even dry soil as long as there is plenty of humus, but they resent winter wet. Many forms are tolerant of sun but will grow most luxuriantly in cool shade.

Lamium galeobdolon 'Variegatum', also known as *Lamiastrum galeobdolon* 'Variegatum', *Galeobdolon luteum* 'Variegatum' and *G. argentatum*, is the rampageous variegated form of the British native yellow archangel. Its floppy, looping runners carry pairs of semi-evergreen, silver-splashed and marbled leaves, flushed purple in winter. In early summer, whorls of hooded yellow flowers are carried all along the stems.

It spreads quickly, up to 90cm (3ft) a season, the runners forming a weed-suppressing tangle 30cm (12in) high with stems rooting at the nodes. Though excellent for colonizing wild gardens, rough banks, hedge bottoms and large areas under trees or shrubs, even the dense, dry shade of beech, it is unsuitable for confined spaces or growing near choicer plants. It is lovely with its long strands hanging, waterfall fashion, over retaining walls.

Propagation is, if anything, too easy, any rooted section potentially an independent plant. It is naturally variegated and comes true from seed. To encourage new, tidy growth, trim back annually in late winter or early spring. 'Silver Carpet', also sold as 'Silberteppich', is less invasive, growing 20cm (8in) high and 45cm (18in) across, with silver leaves netted and veined in green, and yellow flowers.

L. maculatum is also naturally variegated and self-rooting, but much more compact and less invasive. Its dark green foliage is centrally striped with white and makes a ground-hugging mat, 20cm (8in) high and 60cm (24in) across. Its hooded, washed-out magenta flowers can be awkward to accommodate, but 'Album', with white flowers, and 'Roseum', with clear pink flowers, are alternatives. For a startlingly bright effect in cool shade, choose the compact, 10cm (4in) high 'Beacon Silver', that has silvery leaves, narrowly edged in green and slightly mottled in maroon, with pink flowers; the similar, but heavily mottled, 'Chequers' or the more subtle white-flowered 'White Nancy'; or the slightly weak, shade-loving 'Aureum', 15cm (6in) high, with white-striped, golden leaves and mauve-pink flowers. All make good small-scale ground cover, front-of-border plants, or even edging.

LIGULARIA TUSSILAGINEA 'AUREO MACULATA'

Family: Compositae
Height: 60cm (2ft)
Spread: Up to 1.2m (4ft)
Flowering time: Late summer
Aspect: Light shade
Soil: Rich, moist
Minimum temperature: −23°C (−10°F)

The leopard plant has remarkably bold foliage, even for a variegated plant. The Victorians grew it as a greenhouse pot plant as well as in borders, and its beauty has only recently been rediscovered. A vigorous, rhizomatous herbaceous perennial, Japanese in origin, it is also known as *Farfugium grande*, *Farfugium tussilagineum* 'Aureomaculatum', *Ligularia kaempferi* 'Aureo Maculata' and *Senecio kaempferi* 'Aureo Maculata'. Its large, round leaves, up to 30cm (12in) across, are spotted yellow; a very rare form spotted with pink and white exists. The leaves are carried on 30cm (12in) stems and form loose clumps, excellent for filling large areas, especially in waterside schemes. Its sturdy, branching, woolly stems carry bright yellow daisies in late summer.

Rich, moist, even boggy soil in light shade is vital, and shelter from strong winds, since the leaves burn. Frequent watering may be necessary in dry summers. It is only moderately hardy, so protect with a winter mulch or, in cold districts, overwinter in a cool greenhouse. Propagate by division in spring. Slugs and snails can be troublesome.

Ligularia tussilaginea 'Aureo Maculata'

LIRIOPE MUSCARI

Family: Liliaceae

Height: 30cm (12in)

Spread: 45cm (18in)

Flowering time: Autumn

Aspect: Sun or light shade

Soil: Well drained, lime-free

Minimum temperature: −23°C (−10°F)

Attractive rather than arresting, *Liriope muscari* 'Variegata', the variegated lily turf, will never be a bestseller but is worthy of wider use. Also known as *L. platyphylla, L. graminifolia densiflora* and *Ophiopogon graminifolius*, it forms dense clumps of foliage that spread slowly but steadily. The dark, shiny, arching evergreen leaves are striped with creamy white but gradually fade to green. Unusually, new foliage appears in midwinter, in reasonable weather. In autumn, the plant carries tightly packed spikes of tiny bauble-like violet flowers, neither profuse nor showy but valuable for their timing. In hot climates, shiny black berries follow, but early frosts prevent berry formation.

Although hardy, it prefers shelter; wind can brown foliage and destroy flowers. Plant in well-drained, even dry, lime-free soil. It is salt-tolerant and does well in coastal gardens; suited by sun or light shade, but flowering is best in sun. Once planted it needs virtually no attention. Propagate by division in spring.

Its tidy, predictable habit makes it good as formal edging to paving, shrub plantings or mixed borders, and it is excellent informal ground cover, especially in the dry shade of trees. Good plant associations include the autumn-flowering *Nerine bowdenii, Colchicum autumnale* and *Schizostylis coccinea*, or *Euphorbia robbiae* and the purple-leaved berberis, *B. thunbergii* 'Atropurpurea'.

Where available, the following American cultivars increase the colour choice in variegated forms. 'John Burch', 30cm (12in) high and wide, has distinct yellow marginal variegation. 'Gold Banded' has arching leaves narrowly banded with gold down the centres. 'Silver Sunproof' displays foliage that is almost white in full sun, more green or yellow-green when grown in partial shade. All carry lavender flowers in late summer.

Right: Liriope muscari 'Variegata'

NYMPHAEA

Family: Nymphaceae

Height: 15cm (6in)

Spread: 30-150cm (1-5ft)

Flowering time: Summer

Aspect: Sun

Soil: Rich, heavy

Minimum temperature: −23°C (−10°F) (except tropical forms)

Water lilies are quintessential plants grown for the beauty of their flowers, but some also have variegated leaves. These range from miniature to mammoth and from hardy to tender, suitable for planting in water depths from 15cm (6in) to 90cm (3ft). The maroon, wine red or purple variegations to the green leaves are attractive without competing with the flowers, and make a sympathetic background for frogs and toads.

Hardy hybrids with variegated foliage include 'Marliacea Chromatella' ('Golden Cup'), with yellow flowers and bronze-mottled leaves, and 'Paul Hariot', with maroon-spotted leaves and prolific apricot flowers that fade to coppery red. The hardy dwarf form *N. pygmaea* 'Helvola' has tiny, yellow, semi-double flowers and maroon-blotched leaves. For fragrance, choose *N. odorata* 'Sulphurea Grandiflora', with heavily mottled maroon leaves and scented, star-shaped yellow flowers.

Tropical hybrids are difficult in cold climates, requiring overwintering in pools under glass, but many are exquisite and fragrant. They include blue-flowered types absent from the range of hardy water lilies. Their large flowers are carried on long, erect stems, and are excellent for cutting. Tropical forms with variegated foliage include 'Evelyn Randig', with magenta flowers and mottled purple leaves; and the deep blue 'King of the Blues', with maroon-spotted leaves.

Plant the rhizomatous roots in spring, in perforated aquatic plant pots in heavy loam. Cover newly planted roots with gravel, to weight them and prevent muddy water. Thin out crowded leaves and remove faded leaves in summer, to prevent the water fouling. Propagate by dividing established roots in spring, discarding the old central section and replanting the outer, young sections in fresh loam. Blackfly can be a problem, but a strong jet from a hose knocks them into the water, where they are eaten by fish.

PHLOX

Family: Polemoniaceae

Height: 10-90cm (4-36in)

Spread: 45-60cm (18-24in)

Flowering time: Late spring to late summer

Aspect: Light shade

Soil: Well drained but moist, humus-rich

Minimum temperature: −29°C (−20°F)

There are two variegated cultivars of this old-fashioned cottage garden herbaceous perennial, and one variegated dwarf form. The 90cm (3ft) high, rather temperamental *Phlox paniculata* 'Norah Leigh' has striking leaf variegations of mid and light green and ivory, and soft lavender flowers. The newer 'Harlequin' has less prominent variegations, but a stronger constitution, and violet flowers.

Provide plenty of moisture and good, rich soil; chalk and heavy clays are unsuitable. 'Norah Leigh', in particular, is weak unless given optimum conditions. Dark backdrops are ideal, and adjacent plants with blue or purple flowers, such as *Echinops ritro*, *Caryopteris* or *Ceratostigma*. Phlox also form an attractive partnership with the variegated fuchsia, *F. magellanica* 'Versicolor'.

Thin crowded stems of esablished plants in early spring, to promote healthy growth. Top-dress annually with well-rotted organic matter, and stake on exposed sites. Border phlox suffer from eelworm, and are best propagated from root cuttings. You can 'tamper' with the flowers in two ways: pinching out the growing tips when stems are 25cm (10in) high encourages side shoots to form flowers; and if the flower colour is wrong for the scheme, you can nip out the buds and use the plants as foliage features only.

The variegated rock phlox, *P. × procumbens* 'Variegata' (*P. amoena* 'Variegata') is robust, quickly forming low cushions, 10cm (4in) high and 45cm (18in) wide, of leathery, evergreen, creamy white and green leaves. Occasionally leaves are all creamy white, and young foliage is tinged with pink. The rosy purple flowers appear in late spring and early summer.

Grow in light shade and rich, sandy soil. Divide or take heel cuttings after flowering. Phlox are excellent for rockeries, crevices in paving or tumbling over drystone walls.

Phlox paniculata 'Norah Leigh'

PHORMIUM

Family: Liliaceae
Height: 50cm-3m (20in-10ft)
Spread: 30-90cm (1-3ft)
Flowering time: Summer
Aspect: Sun
Soil: Fertile, well drained
Minimum temperature:
−6°C (20°F)

These architectural, majestic plants, with clumps of evergreen foliage like giant iris, are sometimes listed as perennials, sometimes as shrubs. They manage to embody tropical, aquatic and arid imagery at the same time, and enhance schemes based on any of these themes, as well as mixed beds and borders. Contrasting them with perennials, such as bergenia or *Gunnera manicata*, or shrubs of rounded habit, such as sage, is especially effective. They are brilliant in containers, and in practical terms, container growing allows you to move them indoors in severe winter weather.

The amount of variegation varies from leaf to leaf, and from plant to plant, so ideally you should select the individual plants yourself.

P. cookianum, at 60-90cm (2-3ft) high and 30cm (12in) across, is more compact and has greener leaves than the more familiar *P. tenax*, or New Zealand flax. Variegated cultivars of *P. cookianum* include 'Variegata', with white-margined leaves; 'Tricolor', with green- and white-striped leaves thinly margined in purple-red; and 'Cream Delight', 60-90cm (2-3ft) high, which has creamy yellow leaves edged and finely striped with green. The flowers are greeny brown bells, carried on stiff spikes.

Variegated forms of New Zealand flax all have red-brown flowers. 'Variegatum' is tall-growing, up to 3m (10ft) high. The leaves are finely striped with light and medium green, interspersed and edged with wide creamy yellow bands. Some leaves are barely variegated, others are almost entirely cream. 'Veitchii' is an old dwarf form, with narrow leaves banded and striped with creamy yellow.

Hybrids between the two species include 'Yellow Queen', or 'Yellow Wave', with arching yellow leaves narrowly margined in green, 90cm (3ft) high; 'Aurora', with leaves vertically striped with bronze, red, salmon pink and yellow; 'Dazzler', 50cm (20in) high,

with purple, bronze, pink and scarlet striped leaves; and 'Sundowner', with grey, purple, cream and pink leaves.

Grow in sun, shelter and well-drained soil. They are excellent for coastal planting. Though reasonably hardy, the leaves can be damaged by the weight of heavy snow and battered by winter storms. In autumn, you can bunch the leaf clumps together, and tie in several places to a stake. They can be cut to ground level by hard frost but roots usually send up new growth; mulching at the onset of winter helps. Propagate by division.

They are long-lasting when cut and good for large-scale cut flower displays. The broad leaf bases can be cut to tapered points, to take up less space in a vase.

Phormium 'Dazzler'

PHYSOSTEGIA VIRGINIANA 'VARIEGATA'

Family: Labiatae
Height: 90cm (3ft)
Spread: 45cm (18in)
Flowering time: Late summer
Aspect: Full sun or slight shade
Soil: Rich, moist, well drained
Minimum temperature:
−29°C (−20°F)

This is a finely variegated form of the native North American obedient plant, also called false dragonhead. It is 'obedient' because the flower stems are curiously 'hinged', so that when a flower is pushed into a different position, it stays in place. The foliage, however, is more outstanding than the flowers – lance-shaped, toothed, mid green leaves distinctly edged in white. Plants grow to 90cm (3ft) high and 45cm (18in) across; the rose-purple flower spikes are borne in late summer.

Plant in full sun or light shade, in rich soil that is moist but well drained. Physostegia makes a good border plant, the erect clumps of brightly edged foliage forming a striking display; it is also useful material for flower arranging. It spreads by a running rootstock; propagate by division in autumn or early spring, selecting the sturdiest outer roots.

Physostegia virginiana 'Variegata'

Phormium cookianum 'Cream Delight'

PODOPHYLLUM HEXANDRUM

Family: Berberidaceae

Height: 30-45cm (12-18in)

Spread: 30cm (12in)

Flowering time: Spring

Aspect: Partial shade

Soil: Moisture-retentive with high organic content

Minimum temperature: −23°C (−10°F)

The Himalayan mayapple, also known as *Podophyllum emodi*, provides seasonal interest in its delicate flowers and striking fruits, as well as the variegated foliage. The leaves emerge in folded, umbrella-like form at the tops of the stems in spring. When open they are deeply three-lobed and the unusual coloration is cool lime green covered in chocolate brown mottling, which lasts well into summer. Plants grow 30-45cm (12-18in) high with a spread of about 30cm (12in). The white to rose-pink, cup-shaped flowers appear in spring, held upright above the foliage. These give way in summer to shining red, fleshy, plum-shaped fruits about 5cm (2in) long.

This is an ideal subject for growing in a situation with semi-shade or dappled woodland light, and the plant forms excellent ground cover. The soil should be moisture-retentive, and also containing a high level of organic matter. Cut back the stems in late autumn as necessary; propagate by division in spring.

POLYGONATUM

Family: Liliaceae

Height: 60-90cm (2-3ft)

Spread: 30-60cm (1-2ft)

Flowering time: Late spring or early summer

Aspect: Light shade

Soil: Cool, humus-rich, moist

Minimum temperature: −29°C (−20°F)

There are several variegated forms of Solomon's seal, a deciduous, shade-loving woodland and cottage-garden plant of great charm. All have gracefully arching stems with alternate, shiny green leaves and pendant, green-tipped white bell flowers along the stem undersides in late spring or early summer. The leaves turn an attractive golden yellow before dying back in autumn.

Although true of most plants, it is particularly true of Solomon's seal that the larger the clump, the more effective visually: an ample drift of Solomon's seal in light woodland, a wild garden or under deciduous trees is perfect. It can be included in a herb garden, since its fleshy, slow-spreading rhizomatous roots were once taken in ale or applied as a poultice, to heal bruises and broken bones – plants suitable for a shady herb garden being particularly valuable! Hostas and lilies-of-the-valley, with which it shares a dainty elegance and close botanical relationship, associate well with Solomon's seal, as do ferns. The stems can be preserved for winter flower arrangements by being placed in a solution of half glycerine, half water, for four days, then hung upside down to dry.

Polygonatum × *hybridum*, often sold, incorrectly, as either of its parents, *P. multiflorum* or *P. odoratum*, is the most common Solomon's seal. The flowers are carried in clusters on 90cm (3ft) high stems, and are often followed by greeny black berries. The form 'Variegatum' has leaves striped and edged with creamy white. *P. falcatum* 'Variegatum', 60cm (2ft) high, has strongly marked white-edged leaves and vigorous growth.

P. odoratum 'Variegatum' has green leaves edged with off-white, and scented white bells carried singly or in pairs on angled stems 60cm (2ft) high. 'Grace Barker' (also listed as *P.* × *hybridum* 'Striatum'), 60cm (2ft) high, has white-striped foliage and flowers late in the season.

Grow Solomon's seal in sandy, humus-rich soil and light shade, never in hot, dry conditions. Propagate by lifting and dividing in spring. Solomon's seal sawfly larva can strip the leaves down to midribs. Spray with an appropriate insecticide in late spring, when the eggs are laid, and use pellets against slugs.

POLYGONUM CUSPIDATUM 'AUREA-MACULATA'

Correctly called *Fallopia japonica*, but traditionally known as *Polygonum cuspidatum*, the terrifyingly robust great Japan knotweed is much easier to plant than to control or eradicate. Recommended in old gardening books, it is beautiful but too invasive for all but the largest gardens. It makes vast colonies of graceful, russet-red stems carrying heart-shaped leaves, which are striped or completely yellow or creamy white in the form 'Variegatum', with young shoots pink-tinged. Frothy white flower panicles appear in late summer. The stems remain intact, and attractive, after the leaves fall.

Grow in any soil and in light shade; waterside or copse planting is ideal. It can also be grown as a clump in a lawn, the size of the clump controlled by regular mowing up to the edges. Established bamboo or rhododenron thickets are suitably strong partners.

The leaves become dull as they age; cutting the stems down in early summer encourages a second, fresh spurt of growth; remove any all-green shoots as soon as seen. Their scale and abundance make them useful for adding mass to flower arrangements. Dip the cut stems in boiling water for a few seconds, then allow them to stand for several hours in cold water.

Family: Polygonaceae

Height: 1.8m (6ft)

Spread: 3m (10ft)

Flowering time: Late summer

Aspect: Light shade

Soil: No special requirements

Minimum temperature: −34°C (−30°F)

Polygonatum odoratum 'Variegatum'

PULMONARIA

Family: Boraginaceae

Height: 30cm (12in)

Spread: 30-45cm (12-18in)

Flowering time: Early spring to summer

Soil: Rich, moisture-retentive

Aspect: Light shade

Minimum temperature: −29°C (−20°F)

One of the first plants to flower in spring, and virtually weatherproof, lungwort is so called because, in the eyes of old herbalists, the spotted leaves resembled lungs, and were once used to treat chest complaints. In folklore, the spots were said to be caused by drops of the Virgin's milk or tears falling on the leaves. These are more or less evergreen, and spotted and bristly in some, but not all, species and cultivars. New foliage follows flowering, and grows coarser as the season progresses.

Lungwort is excellent ground cover in moisture-retentive, rich soil and light shade, under deciduous shrubs and trees, against a sunless wall, and so on; but the leaves are liable to burn and wilt in direct sunlight. Its flowering overlaps tulips, daffodils, doronicums, wallflowers, primroses, grape hyacinths, aubrieta and alyssums, and it can be used as formal edging. In informal shady borders, combine variegated and green-leaved forms with hostas and the quick-spreading sensitive fern, *Onoclea sensibilis*. To propagate, lift and divide in spring. Occasional self-seeding occurs, but not invasively so.

Pulmonaria longifolia has flat, basal rosettes, 30cm (1ft) high and 45cm (18in) across, of long, narrow, pointed, dark green, white-spotted leaves. Dense terminal clusters of rich blue flowers continue late into summer. The form 'Mournful Purple' has dark green leaves blotched with light green, and drooping clusters of rose and purple flowers set in dark calyces. 'Roy Davidson' has wider leaves than the species, giving a bolder effect. The foliage is dark green spotted with silver-grey, and the early spring flowers are an attractive soft blue. It is tolerant of heat and humidity but needs partial shade, and makes excellent ground cover.

P. officinalis grows wild in European woods, especially on chalky soil. Also called spotted dog, from its leaves, or soldiers and sailors, from its mixed pink and blue flowers,

Pulmonaria longifolia

Pulmonaria saccharata

this species is usually represented by the improved form 'Cambridge Blue', with light blue flowers opening from pink buds in early spring.

P. saccharata has rough-textured leaves, marbled silver and grey-green, and more dramatic than *P. officinalis*. Its blue flowers appear in early spring. There are several cultivars. 'Reginald Kaye' has large silver spots in the leaf centres, and smaller spots along borders. 'Alba' has large, pure white flowers in mid to late spring. 'Argentea', also

called 'White Windows', has frosted, heavily spotted silver leaves, and flowers in early spring. 'Leopard' has spotted leaves and pinkish-red flowers; 'Mrs Moon' is similar, with lilac-red flowers. 'Tim's Silver' has a satiny, silvery leaf surface with a fine green rim, and blue flowers in mid to late spring. *P. angustifolia* 'Beth's Pink' has broad, heavily spotted leaves and coral red flowers.

SAXIFRAGA

Family: Saxifragaceae
Height: 2.5-45cm (1-18in)
Spread: 15-30cm (6-12in)
Flowering time: Late spring and early summer
Soil: Cool, rich, well drained
Aspect: Light shade
Minimum temperature: −18°C (0°F)

This huge genus, forming the backbone of many rock gardens, is well represented with variegated species and cultivars. Those listed here are the most widely available; for connoisseurs, specialist nurseries stock rarer plants. There are many different types of saxifrages, requiring different growing conditions, but the following need or prefer light shade and moist but well-drained soil.

Saxifraga cuneifolia 'Variegata' has tidy rosettes of creamy yellow blotched, evergreen leaves and sprays of dainty white flowers in late spring and early summer. It grows 15-20cm (6-8in) high and 30cm (12in) across.

S. stolonifera, also sold as *S. sarmentosa*, is better known as the house plant mother-of-thousands, or strawberry geranium. It is the traditional ground cover under greenhouse staging, but is actually moderately hardy, making quick-spreading ground cover outdoors, where it thrives in the shade of evergreen shrubs, or at the foot of a wall out of direct sun.

Its loose rosettes, 15cm (6in) high and 30cm (12in) across, are composed of red-stemmed, round, evergreen leaves, marbled pale green and veined red, with red undersides and tinged red in winter. It spreads rapidly by runners, or stolons, and its airy sprays of pale pink and white flowers appear in early summer. The less hardy form 'Tricolor' has green leaves irregularly edged in pink and white.

S. × *urbium* 'Aureapunctata', also sold

as *S. umbrosa* 'Aureapunctata' or 'Variegata' is the variegated form of the long-suffering and tolerant London pride, usually grown in dry, airless shade and poor soil where little else will survive. Its gold-speckled, leathery, evergreen rosettes are eye-catching, if not restful, and it carries dainty, starry pink flowers in late spring. It makes a good edging plant.

For rock or container gardens, the dwarf hybrid 'Bob Hawkins' is only 2.5-5cm (1-2in) high and 15cm (6in) across. Its oval, evergreen leaves are splashed with white and it carries tiny, creamy white flowers in summer on 5cm (2in) high stems. 'Hi Ace' is another low-growing rock subject, with crimson flowers in spring, and cream and green variegated foliage.

Saxifraga × urbium
'Aureapunctata'

Scrophularia auriculata 'Variegata'

SCROPHULARIA AURICULATA 'VARIEGATA'

Family: Scrophulaceae
Height: 60-120cm (2-4ft)
Spread: 30cm (12in)
Flowering time: Summer
Soil: Rich, moist
Aspect: Sun or light shade
Minimum temperature: −23°C (−10°F)

Also sold as *S. aquatica* 'Variegata', the variegated figwort forms spectacular basal clumps of wavy-edged, broad green leaves irregularly splashed and striped in cream. The square-sectioned, tall, rigid, branching stems carry smaller variegated leaves and in summer, tiny red-brown, beady flowers. Likened by one gardening writer to rodents' eyes, the flowers add nothing and are best nipped out, which also keeps the basal foliage fresh looking. The basal leaves are evergreen, and are valuable for winter interest. Ideal for the bog or wild garden, this plant combines well with ligularias.

Grow in rich, moist soil in sun or light shade. Lift and divide in spring, or take cuttings. Slugs can be troublesome.

For flower arranging, put the cut stems in boiling water for few seconds, then completely submerge in warm water for several hours. Short lengths of stem, 23-30cm (9-12in) long, last longest.

SEDUM

Family: Crassulaceae
Height: 10-45cm (4-18in)
Spread: 40-60cm (16-24in)
Flowering time: Late summer to autumn
Soil: Well drained
Aspect: Sun or light shade
Minimum temperature: −23°C (−10°F)

Stonecrops are 'toughies', thriving wherever their roots can gain a foothold; some alpine species are invasive, but the following are not. Valuable for being one of the few succulent hardy genera, stonecrops are easily propagated by division.

Sedum albo-roseum 'Mediovariegatum', more popularly known as *S. spectabile* 'Variegatum', and commonly as the Japanese stonecrop or ice plant, grows 30-40cm (12-16in) high and twice as wide. Its upright shoots of fleshy, glaucous, blue-grey leaves, each with a creamy yellow centre, carry large, flat heads of starry pink flowers, extremely attractive to butterflies and bees. The flowers remain fresh looking for weeks in the garden and attractive well into winter providing some welcome colour.

Its cool appearance is especially arresting seen against red or purple foliage of Michaelmas daisies (*Aster novi-belgii*), and its sculptural quality is enhanced by a setting of gravel. It is a good container plant and tolerates most soils; remove any green shoots as soon as seen.

The tuberous-rooted, slightly tender *S. sieboldii* 'Variegatum' is more popular as a windowsill house plant and will not survive the winter outdoors in cold climates, but makes good summer infill in rock gardens and hanging baskets. Its long, trailing stems carry whorls of three or four creamy, yellow-centred leaves, occasionally edged in red, and in late summer, pink flowers. In autumn, the leaves take on a rosy tinge. Grown at ground level, it forms low mounds 10cm (4in) high and 40cm (16in) across. It likes heavy, limy, well-drained soil, and is much loved by slugs.

The hardy *S. spurium* 'Tricolor' also forms mats 40cm (16in) across, of trailing, hairy red stems, 10cm (4in) high. These carry whorls of round, succulent, creamy white, pink and green, toothed, semi-evergreen leaves topped by branching heads of small, starry, purply pink flowers. It is good on banks, and in rock gardens.

Sedum sieboldii 'Variegatum'

SEMPERVIVUM

Family: Crassulaceae
Height: 2.5-8cm (1-3in)
Spread: 20-30cm (8-12in)
Flowering time: Midsummer
Aspect: Full sun
Soil: Very well drained, gritty
Minimum temperature:
−23°C (−10°F)

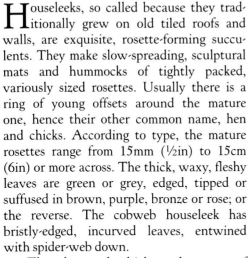

Houseleeks, so called because they traditionally grew on old tiled roofs and walls, are exquisite, rosette-forming succulents. They make slow-spreading, sculptural mats and hummocks of tightly packed, variously sized rosettes. Usually there is a ring of young offsets around the mature one, hence their other common name, hen and chicks. According to type, the mature rosettes range from 15mm (½in) to 15cm (6in) or more across. The thick, waxy, fleshy leaves are green or grey, edged, tipped or suffused in brown, purple, bronze or rose; or the reverse. The cobweb houseleek has bristly-edged, incurved leaves, entwined with spider-web down.

The elongated, thick, scaly stems of starry, red or yellow flowers in midsummer are crude by comparison to the foliage. After flowering, the rosette producing the flower stem dies, but leaves young offsets to carry on.

The generic name, *Sempervivum*, comes from the Latin for immortality, and refers to the plants' ability to cling to life in the most inhospitable, hot, dry conditions; they originate in rocky terrains in southern Europe and western Asia. Houseleeks are ideal for container growing in trough gardens or alpine pans, or for planting in rock gardens or crevices in walls. Exposure to full sun intensifies their waxy or hairy coverings. They can also be grown in the cracks between paving stones, and are sometimes used as formal edging, perhaps an unsympathetic role.

Because there are over 50 species, and numerous varieties and hybrids, all basically similar but with minor variations in form, naming is very confused. Some have been classified under the separate genus, *Jovibarba*.

S. arachnoideum, the cobweb or spider houseleek, has tiny, 15mm (½in) wide rosettes of red-edged, green leaves covered with thick white down. They thrive in chinks in sunny walls, where little else will grow. The form 'Laggeri' ('Tomentosum') is the hardiest.

S. calcareum, the glaucous houseleek, is closely allied to *S. tectorum*, and is sometimes listed as *S. t. calcareum*. It has huge rosettes tipped with chocolate brown, up to 12.5cm (5in) across.

S. heuffelii, more correctly *Jovibarba heuffelii*, is unusual in that it forms no offsets, but the mature rosettes, 5-8cm (2-3in) across, divide naturally. It is grey green, with yellow flowers and purple-tipped or flushed foliage, especially in autumn.

S. tectorum, the common or roof houseleek, with 5-15cm (2-6in) rosettes of maroon-tipped leaves, has spawned numerous hybrids and varieties, including 'Commander Haye', purply red with green tips; 'Jubilee', crimson and green; and the similar but larger 'Othello'.

Perfect drainage is essential. Humus-rich soil, with plenty of chippings, suits large types, while smaller, cobwebby types thrive in a minimum of humus; sandy soil mixed with brick rubble is traditional. A layer of chippings over the soil surface helps prevent the leaves coming in contact with wet soil and rotting. Cold wet winters are especially lethal and plants grown in pans may benefit from overwintering in an unheated greenhouse, with maximum ventilation.

Houseleeks are easily propagated from offsets but leaf cuttings, division and seed are other options.

**Sisyrinchium striatum
'Variegatum'**

the petal undersides. When the flower dies, the leaf shoot that produced it also dies. It is particularly attractive when partnered with blue flowers, such as veronica, or blue foliage, such as rue or certain euphorbias.

Grow in any well-drained soil, in a sunny, sheltered location. It appreciates generous feeding. Give protection in harsh winters, when it is safest to bring one or two plants under glass, in case of loss. Lift and divide regularly in late summer, to encourage fresh growth and prolong its life.

SOLEIROLIA SOLEIROLII 'ARGENTEA'

Formerly known as *Helxine soleirolii*, and commonly as mind-your-own-business or baby's tears, the species was described in William Robinson's classic *The English Flower Garden* as a 'rampant little fiend'. It is also known as 'the Corsican curse', from its country of origin and its tenacious, invasive nature.

The variegated form 'Argentea', or 'Variegata', is a silver-edged plant, creating a dense, mossy carpet of minute round leaves and microscopic flowers. Traditionally grown as ground cover under staging in greenhouses or around pot plants, it is ideal for wandering along cracks between paving stones, especially in urban gardens, in cool, damp shade. It grows well at the edges of ponds; or where it can work its way up damp, shady walls. It can grow in sun, but moist soil is essential. On no account should it be introduced into borders or rock gardens, where it is virtually impossible to control or eradicate.

In mild climates, it is evergreen; otherwise, it dies back, but usually shoots fresh from the roots in spring. If it starts to revert, remove the all-green shoots at once. Propagation is by division; the stems root as they touch the ground, and the tiniest pieces are capable of making independent plants.

Family: Urticaceae
Height: 2.5cm (1in)
Spread: Spreads indefinitely
Flowering time: Flowers insignificant
Aspect: Sun or shade
Soil: Cool, moist
Minimum temperature: −6°C (20°F)

SISYRINCHIUM STRIATUM 'VARIEGATUM'

Family: Iridaceae
Height: 45-60cm (18-24in)
Spread: 23-30cm (9-12in)
Flowering time: Summer
Aspect: Sun
Soil: Ordinary, well drained
Minimum temperature: −29°C (−20°F)

Fondly and inexplicably known as 'Aunt May', this is one of those plants whose variegation and flower colour are in perfect harmony. South American in origin and closely related to iris, it produces fans of semi-evergreen, iris-like leaves, grey-green striped vertically with creamy yellow. In summer it bears slender, densely packed spikes of small, satiny, pale yellow flowers, striped purple on

SYMPHYTUM 'GOLDSMITH'

Family: Boraginaceae
Height: 15-25cm (6-10in)
Spread: 60cm (2ft)
Flowering time: Spring
Aspect: Light shade
Soil: No special requirements
Minimum temperature: −29°C (−20°F)

The variegated form of 'proper' comfrey is covered on page 55; this low-growing, evergreen hybrid has broad, creamy yellow edges to its heart-shaped, dark green, hairy leaves. In spring, it carries drooping clusters of blue and white, tubular flowers on 15cm (6in) stems.

It forms easy, useful, weed-proof ground cover, perhaps more suited to rough banks, wild gardens and planting under trees and shrubs than in the border, and tolerates dry shade, but prefers a moist soil. The plant increases by means of long stems which root at their tips, but they are shallow-rooted and easily pulled out, if need be.

TELLIMA GRANDIFLORA 'PURPUREA'

Family: Saxifragaceae
Height: 20cm (8in)
Spread: 30cm (12in)
Flowering time: Early summer
Aspect: Sun or light shade
Soil: Well drained, rich, neutral to acid
Minimum temperature: −29°C (−20°F)

This genus contains only one species, a heuchera-like plant popularly known as fringecup or false alum root. A valuable, if modest, semi-evergreen ground cover, it forms dense, spreading clumps of intricately veined, faintly bristly, scalloped, round leaves. In late spring, it bears wand-like stems of tiny, pink-fringed green bellflowers, becoming ruddy as they age.

'Purpurea', sometimes sold as 'Rubra', has bronzy leaves with dark green veins and beetroot purple undersides. In winter, its tones deepen.

Grow in any well-drained soil in cool semi-shade; it is excellent for town gardens. The centres of the clumps tend to lift out of the ground with age. Top dress or mulch regularly, and divide every few years. Slugs can be troublesome.

For flower arranging, re-cut the stem cleanly under water, then submerge the whole leaf in water for several hours, to make it turgid.

TOLMIEA MENZIESII 'TAFF'S GOLD'

Family: Saxifragaceae
Height: 20cm (8in)
Spread: 30cm (12in)
Flowering time: Early summer
Aspect: Sun or light shade
Soil: Well drained, rich, neutral to acid
Minimum temperature: −18°C (0°F)

This golden-variegated cultivar of the North American species has maple-like leaves that are irregularly speckled with green and primrose yellow in shade, more yellow and white in sun. Its common name, piggy-back, or pick-a-back, plant, comes from the enchanting little plantlets that form on the upper sides of the leaves, where they join the stalk. In early summer, it produces spikes of insignificant, coppery flowers.

Another moderately hardy plant grown as a pot plant, it is excellent in hanging baskets and window boxes, where the weight of the plantlets creates a cascading effect. It is also a good front-of-border and edging plant, and weed-suppressing ground cover for cool woodland. In hot sun, browning is liable to occur.

The plantlets root if they touch the soil, gradually increasing the size and spread of the mound. Pegging or weighting down leaves encourages rooting; a rooted plantlet can be detached and grown on independently.

Tolmiea menziesii 'Taff's Gold'

TOVARA

Family: Polygonaceae
Height: 45-60cm (18-24in)
Spread: 45-60cm (18-24in)
Flowering time: Late summer
Aspect: Shade, shelter
Soil: Fertile, moist
Minimum temperature: −18°C (0°F)

This genus, sometimes listed as *Persicaria*, other times as *Polygonum*, includes the familiar knotweeds of gardens, hedgerows and roadsides. The following are rewarding ground cover or border plants, providing they have good, moist soil and are sheltered from sun and wind, which can bruise the leaves.

Tovara virginiana 'Painter's Palette', also listed as *T. filiformis* 'Painter's Palette', *T. filiformis* or *T. virginiana filiformis*, is bushy, clump-forming and well branched. Its large oval, pink-tinged leaves, marbled green and ivory white, are marked with a dark red-brown, central 'V'-shape. The insignificant flowers appear in late summer.

T. virginiana 'Variegata', also known as *Persicaria virginiana* 'Variegata' and *Poly-*

Top: Tricyrtis hirta 'Miyazaki Gold'

Above: Trifolium repens 'Purpurascens Quadrifolium'

Above: A close-up of Tovara virginiana 'Painter's Palette'

Right: Tovara virginiana 'Painter's Palette'

gonum virginianum 'Variegatum', is very similar but its leaves lack the pink tinge and 'V' marking.

Protect with a winter mulch the first season after planting, and thereafter in harsh winters. They start into growth relatively late in spring, so don't despair prematurely if they fail to appear after a bad winter. Propagate by division of established plants in autumn or spring, or by taking cuttings of non-flowering shoots in midsummer.

TRICYRTIS HIRTA 'MIYAZAKI GOLD'

Family: Liliaceae

Height: 60-75cm (24-30in)

Spread: 60-90cm (2-3ft)

Flowering time: Early to mid autumn

Aspect: Partial to deep shade

Soil: Moist and well drained, high organic content

Minimum temperature: −29°C (−20°F)

This cultivar, also known as 'Variegata', is the variegated form of the hairy toad lily *Tricyrtis hirta*. Growing to 60cm (2ft) or more high and wide, the plants have a graceful, arching habit. The hairy leaves are narrowly oval and pointed, mid green distinctly margined with yellow. They are arranged alternately on the arching stems, with the leaf bases clasping the stem. Clusters of open, star-like flowers, near-white heavily spotted with lilac-purple and with purple stamens and stigmas, are borne in profusion at the leaf axils along the stems in early to mid autumn.

'Miyazaki Gold' is well suited to borders and mixed plantings, ideally in a position where the detail of the flowers can be seen. It enjoys a position in partial shade or even deeper shade, in well-drained, moisture-retentive soil high in organic matter. Unlike the species, it will not come true from seed and must be propagated by division or cuttings.

TRIFOLIUM REPENS

Trifolium repens 'Susan Smith'

The generic name for clover, *Trifolium*, means three leaves, but the compound leaves can have up to six leaflets.

Most clovers are considered weeds, but an ornamental form of white clover, *Trifolium repens* 'Purpurascens Quadrifolium', is grown for its bronzy brown, evergreen or semi-evergreen foliage, edged in sharp green. A vigorous, prostrate spreader, it roots from the leaf nodes as it grows, making it potentially invasive and unsuitable for rock gardens, where it can swamp slower-growing subjects. In large areas, however, where it can roam at will, it is good ground cover, and ideal for underplanting with spring bulbs. Its typical white clover flowers, carried in summer, are immensely attractive to bees and butterflies.

T. repens 'Susan Smith' is an unusual, relatively new form, identifiable as clover more from its typical flowers than its elegant, elongated leaflets, finely veined in yellow. Useful as ground cover in full sun and well drained soil, it grows only 5cm (2in) high, but forms a carpet 45cm (18in) across.

A clover planting needs initial weeding, until it becomes established.

Family: Leguminosae

Height: 5-10cm (2-4in)

Spread: 45-60cm (18-24in)

Flowering time: Summer

Aspect: Sun

Soil: Ordinary, well drained

Minimum temperature: −29°C (−20°F)

TULIPA

Family: Liliaceae

Height: 20-40cm (8-16in)

Spread: 15cm (6in)

Flowering time: Mid-spring

Aspect: Sun

Soil: Rich, well drained

Minimum temperature:
−23°C (−10°F)

One of the few naturally variegated plants, the species *Tulipa greigii* was introduced from Turkestan in the late 1870s, grown for its large flowers of dazzling vermilion with a yellow-edged, black basal blotch. The hybrids and varieties derived from the species have metallic grey-green, often wavy-edged leaves, marbled or striped with brownish-purple. Popular forms include 'Red Riding Hood' and 'Oriental Beauty', both with red flowers; the yellow and red 'Yellow Dawn' and 'Cape Cod'; 'Plaisir', large red flowers with a golden yellow base; 'Dreamboat', salmon pink flushed with amber; 'Zampa', yellow flushed red, with a bronze base; and the rose red, white-edged, bronze-centred 'Bento'.

Two other tulip species provide interesting variegated forms. *T. kauffmanniana* 'Heart's Delight' has foliage similar to that of *T. greigii*, and pink blooms with a golden yellow base. *T. praestans* 'Unicum' has unusual creamy-edged, grey-green, ribbed leaves and bright red flowers, several to each stem.

The *greigii* hybrids are available as dormant bulbs and, unusual for tulips, as pot plants in bud or bloom, for instant infill for window boxes, rock gardens and front of borders. Plant bulbs in autumn, burying them in the soil to three or four times their own depth. Deadhead after flowering and, once the leaves die back, lift, dry off and store until the following autumn, then replant.

Tulipa praestans 'Unicum'

Tulipa greigii 'Plaisir' (left) and Tulipa kauffmanniana 'Heart's Delight' (right)

VERONICA GENTIANOIDES 'VARIEGATA'

A useful mat-forming plant which, though less vigorous than the species, contributes pleasing colour contrast in the glossy, dark green leaves splashed with creamy white. The basal rosettes are randomly marked and the variegation is best and most obvious on the smaller leaves carried on the stems, which may be clearly margined with pure white. Racemes of pale blue flowers 20cm (8in) long are borne at the tops of the stems in spring and early summer.

This makes a good front-of-border plant or rock garden subject. Plant in full sun or light shade, especially in warm areas, in soil that is well drained but moisture-retentive. Remove flower spikes as they fade and support stems with twigs if grown in an exposed position. Propagate by division in spring.

Family: Scrophulariaceae

Height: 30-60cm (12-24in)

Spread: 60-90cm (2-3ft)

Flowering time: Spring to early summer

Aspect: Full sun or light shade

Soil: Moist, well drained

Minimum temperature:
−29°C (−20°F)

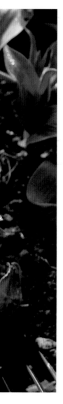

VINCA

Family: Apocynaceae
Height: 5-60cm (2-24in)
Spread: 90-120cm (3-4ft)
Flowering time: Spring
Aspect: Sun or shade
Soil: Well drained
Minimum temperature: −29°C (−20°F)

Periwinkle, like ivy, is undervalued because of its omnipresence and its toughness, especially in dry shade. While the plain-leaved species of greater and lesser periwinkle, *Vinca major* and *V. minor* respectively, have modest foliage, variegated forms are worth garden space and more favourable growing conditions. The clear, distinctive hue of their mainly lavender-blue flowers is an added bonus. These appear in spring but may also be carried, to a lesser extent, in summer, autumn, and occasionally into winter.

'Variegata', or 'Elegantissima', is the main variegated form of *V. major*, also called common periwinkle or blue buttons. Technically an evergreen, self-rooting shrub, it is often included among perennials in garden centres. It has barren, long, trailing stems and shorter, erect flowering stems 30-60cm (1-2ft) high. The glossy green leaves are boldly margined with creamy yellow when young, later fading to white. 'Surrey Marble', also known as *V. major* 'Maculata', has central yellow blotches on its dark green leaves.

Greater periwinkle is exuberant and invasive, with a fountain-like growth habit; the variegated forms are only slightly less invasive than the species. They are safest grown in large areas in isolation, such as on banks, beneath the crowns of tall trees, along woodland walks or rocky ground, or cascading over retaining walls. Nearby plants must be equally strong, such as large hostas or *Bergenia cordifolia*, or they will be swamped.

The variegated forms of lesser periwinkle, or trailing myrtle, are altogether smaller scale and more ground-hugging than arching. Though much less vigorous than the all-green species, they can still grow up into and strangle shrubs many times their own height, and work their way into rock garden crevices, or into the middle of other subjects, where they are impossible to eradicate. They are, however, hardier than greater periwinkle and ideal for thickening the botton of a bare hedge, or enlivening the base of a wall.

Vinca minor 'Argenteovariegata', also sold as 'Variegata', is 15cm (6in) high and has light greeny grey leaves, blotched, edged and streaked with creamy yellow, later fading to white. The flowers are pale blue. The similar sized 'Aureovariegata', also sold as 'Variegata Aurea', has green leaves margined and striped with yellow, and blue flowers. 'Alba Variegata' also known as 'Alba Aureovariegata', has light yellow edges to its leaves and white flowers. 'Ralph Shugert' is a recent American introduction with glossy, dark green leaves uniformly margined in white or creamy white, and numerous, large, deep lilac flowers.

Periwinkles flower best in full sun, and variegated forms need more light than all-green ones, but very hot, dry conditions are unsuitable. Though the plants are tolerant of poor, acid and limy soils, rich soil gives the most luxuriant foliage. Cut back annually in later winter or early spring, for tidy, dense growth and profuse flowers. Slugs can be troublesome, especially with *V. major* and its forms.

Periwinkles root from the nodes, wherever they come into contact with the soil, and propagation is simply a matter of detaching rooted sections of stem and planting them elsewhere, or dividing and replanting old clumps. To encourage newly planted *V. major* forms to root, peg or weight down the shoots. Because of their spread, they are planted widely spaced apart, and need mulching to keep weeds under control until they knit together.

Flower arrangers value the arching stems and bold variegations of *V. major* 'Variegata', for adding a sense of movement to floral displays and breaking the horizontal line of the container rim. Put the ends of cut stems in boiling water for a few seconds, then submerge the stems completely in cool water for several hours.

Vinca major 'Variegata' and Lamium maculatum 'Roseum'

GRASSES

UNLIKE LAWN GRASS, the natural form of ornamental grasses, whether upright, arching or spreading, is featured, not suppressed. Though some are used *en masse* in woodland or meadow drifts, or as ground cover, ornamental grasses are also planted as individual clumps. Giant ornamental grasses, such as bamboos, can be treated as specimen shrubs, surrounded by lawn or low ground cover, or may act as screens, boundary hedges or windbreaks.

Visually, their main value is the linear contrast they provide to broader-leaved perennials, shrubs and trees; the transitional link they provide between lawn and ornamental planting; and the relief their subtle palette offers to the heavy, strident colours of some flowers and foliage. All but two of the grasses listed below are vertically striped, which further emphasizes their linear quality. Many are evergreen, and some deciduous types retain a ghostly winter presence.

Sophisticated planting schemes can be based solely on ornamental grasses set in gravel, but it is usually better not to confine them to single beds, where they can look muddled. Contrasting foliar shapes, such as hostas, bergenias and, on a larger scale, rheums and gunneras, make better partners. Other striking juxtapositions include ornamental grass and water; ornamental grass and hard paving; and even ornamental grass and tightly clipped lawn. Many grasses are also attractive grown in terracotta containers.

Spring planting is safest, and waiting until spring to cut back dwarf types gives winter protection. Paradoxically, although many grasses can be impossible to eradicate once established, young plants can be difficult to establish, so pot-grown subjects are best.

Technically, grasses are flowering plants, but are pollinated by wind, not insects, so their flowers need neither colour, scent nor arresting form. Most are modest, but those carried well above the leaves often create a delicate, soft haze. For drying, pick them just before the seed heads ripen; those that ripen fully on the plant tend to shatter when picked. Spread them flat to dry, as a single layer on newspaper, and turn every few days; or place upright in small containers, so the weight of the seed heads creates gracefully curving stems. To use grasses fresh in cut-flower displays, dip the cut ends in boiling water for a few seconds, then submerge completely for an hour or more.

Although some of the plants in this section are not strictly speaking grasses, they are so grass-like in appearance and use in the garden, that it makes sense to include them here.

ALOPECURUS PRATENSIS 'AUREOMARGINATUS'

Family: Gramineae

Height: 20-45cm (8-18in)

Spread: 20-45cm (8-18in)

Flowering time: Summer

Aspect: Sun or light shade

Soil: No special requirements

Minimum temperature: −23°C (−10°F)

Also sold as *Alopecurus pratensis* 'Aureus' and *A.p* 'Aureovariegatus', the variegated form of golden foxtail is a deciduous, tuft-forming perennial, which takes its common name from its bushy, foxtail-like seed head, carried well above the plant. Its strappy, initially upright, later arching leaves have gold edges that meet at the tips. It makes good ground cover, accent or edging, and is best cut back just before flowering in late spring, to produce bright, strongly colourful new growth.

ARUNDO DONAX 'VARIEGATA'

Family: Gramineae

Height: 1.2m (4ft)

Spread: 60cm (2ft)

Flowering time: Autumn

Aspect: Sun, shelter from wind

Soil: Rich

Minimum temperature: −12°C (10°F)

Sometimes listed as *Arundo donax* 'Versicolor', the variegated form of the giant reed is half the size of the species, which originates in southern Europe and inhabits damp places and streamsides. Noble and dignified in spite of its reduced stature, 'Variegata' has bamboo-like canes that carry imposing broad, drooping, blue-grey leaves, boldly striped with white. The leaves are borne alternately and are widely spaced, creating a striking architectural pattern.

If grown outdoors, 'Variegata' needs the protection of a heavy mulch in winter. It can be grown in containers in a cool greenhouse or conservatory, and moved outdoors for the summer, perhaps at a pool's edge, where it would associate well with rheums and gunneras. It also tolerates dry soil, where it could partner ornamental seakale (*Crambe maritima*) and acanthus. Exposure to wind or hot sun can cause scorching.

Cut back the canes in spring; if left *in situ* they sprout masses of crowded side shoots, but the effect is less graceful. It is difficult to propagate by division, but cuttings of side shoots taken from old stems root easily. The

Alopecurus pratensis 'Aureomarginatus'

upright, dense plumes of creamy white flowers rarely appear in cool temperate climates. The cut foliage makes good filler material, especially in all-foliage arrangements, although the leaves tend to curl when cut, and need regular replacement.

CAREX

Family: Cyperaceae
Height: 5-60cm (2-24in)
Spread: 20cm (8in)
Flowering time: Summer
Aspect: Light shade
Soil: Moist, lime-free
Minimum temperature: —18°C (0°F)

Although not a grass, sedge is included here for its grassy, graceful appearance. The old adage 'sedges have edges and rushes are round' refers to the triangular stem in cross section, which distinguishes sedges from the round-stemmed rushes. (Another key to identification is that sedges have unjointed stems, while those of rushes are jointed.) Sedge is a tuft-forming evergreen, with arching, long, narrow leaves and insignificant flower spikes.

The species inhabit marshy and other damp areas, in acid soil, their decomposed roots being one of the main components of peat. In the garden, the following variegated cultivars are ideal in cool, light shade.

Carex conica 'Variegata', also called *C. c.* 'Marginata', is a beautiful clump-forming sedge up to 20cm (8in) high. The slender, curving leaves have narrow silver edges, giving each clump an overall silvered effect. Although it prefers moist soil, it tolerates lack of moisture if grown in rich soil and light shade.

C. oshimensis 'Aureovariegata', the Japanese sedge, is also sold as *C. o.* 'Evergold' and *C. morrowi* 'Aureovariegata'. It grows 30cm (12in) high and wide, making an exuberant mound of narrow, yellow-striped leaves, radiating from a tight centre. The form *C. o.* 'Variegata', also sold as 'Expallida', has white-striped leaves. Both make colourful edging and ground cover and, if regularly and generously watered, excellent container plants.

C. phyllocephala 'Sparkler' is a striking recent introduction to America of oriental origin. Its strong, rigid leaves are arranged in whorls around a main stem. Leaves are white-

Carex oshimensis 'Aureovariegata'

Arundo donax 'Variegata'

margined, lime green or dark green, and sheathed in purple at the base; white streaks may appear down the inner green areas. Each leaf lasts about two years; as the foliage dies off, the main stem is gradually bared. Plants, grow to 60cm (24in) high, but older stems can be cut back to ground level, causing new shoots to form.

C. *riparia* 'Variegata', 60cm (2ft) high and wide, is a stunning variegated version of greater pond sedge, whose specific name refers to its preferred riverside habitat. Its narrow, arching leaves have broad central white stripes, thinly edged with green; some are nearly all white. It is potentially invasive, especially in the cool, moist conditions it likes, but makes a good specimen plant.

C. *siderostricta* 'Variegata', 30cm (12in) high and wide, is a rare form with relatively wide, green and white striped leaves, pink-tinged at the base.

C. *firma* 'Variegata' is a tiny form, 5-10cm (2-4in) high, with leaves margined in creamy yellow, useful for container gardens or alpine pans.

Carex riparia 'Variegata'

CORTADERIA SELLOANA

Family: Gramineae
Height: 1.5m (5ft)
Spread: 1.2m (4ft)
Flowering time: Late summer to early autumn
Aspect: Sun, shelter
Soil: Well drained, ordinary or rich
Minimum temperature: −12°C (10°F)

Variegated forms of pampas grass are somewhat smaller than the species, but still make eye-catching clumps of arching foliage above which rise heavy crops of typical silky flower plumes.

'Gold Band', also sold as *Cortaderia selloana* 'Aureolineata', has narrow, grassy foliage initially bordered in yellow, gradually fading at the end of the season to a uniform orange. It grows to 1.5m (5ft) high, slightly less across, and the silvery plumes appear in early autumn. It is evergreen in mild climates, otherwise deciduous, although the dead leaves persist over winter.

'Silver Comet' is of similar size, with narrow, sharp-edged foliage margined prominently in silver-white. The leaf bases are a pleasing pale purplish-blue. Its cream-coloured plumes are produced in late summer.

Pampas grass requires a sheltered position, but is suitable for coastal planting, as it is unaffected by salty air. It prefers deep, rich, loamy or sandy soil, but does not tolerate wet soil, especially in cold climates. Mulch annually and protect in cold winters; tying up the old foliage to form a protective crown is traditional. Cut or burn the old foliage in mid-spring: the young, new growth arises, phoenix-like, from the ashes. Wear gardening gloves to protect your hands from the razor-sharp leaf edges.

These make good accent plants, set in gravel, in a small lawn, or among all-foliage schemes. 'Gold Band' blends well in a green and yellow border, with goldenrod (*Solidago*), achillea and big yellow daisies, such as rudbeckia, coreopsis and perennial or annual sunflowers. Alternatively, site near sumachs, maples or deciduous azaleas, which provide strong autumn colour, or near equally architectural plants, such as yucca, New Zealand flax (*Phormium tenax*) and kniphofia. For a grouping of grasses, fountain grass (*Pennisetum setaceum*) and varieties of *Miscanthus sinensis* are visually and physically strong enough to hold their own near pampas grass.

GLYCERIA MAXIMA 'VARIEGATA'

Family: Gramineae
Height: 60-90cm (2-3ft)
Spread: 60cm (2ft)
Aspect: Full sun
Soil: Damp, or shallow water
Minimum temperature: −23°C (−10°F)

Known as variegated manna or sweet reed grass, and sometimes sold as *Glyceria aquatica* 'Variegata' or *G. spectabilis* 'Variegata', this highly invasive, weedproof, rhizomatous spreader needs its roots confined in buried or submerged pots in all but the largest-scale planting schemes. It tolerates dry soil but its variegations tend to fade as the season progresses; it is seen at its best in damp or waterlogged soil. It also thrives in up to 20cm (8in) of water, making it ideal for pots on planting ledges of artificial pools.

The semi-evergreen or deciduous,

Far left: *Cortaderia selloana 'Aureolineata'*
Left: *Cortaderia selloana 'Silver Comet'*

Glyceria maxima 'Variegata'

arching, broad, strap-shaped leaves are evenly and boldly striped and suffused with ivory white, creamy yellow and green. The young growth is flushed pink and again, late in the season, pink-purple. Taller plumes of greenish flowers that turn brown appear in late summer. It does not come true from seed, and must be propagated by divison, which, done regularly, renews the stock's vigour.

Suitably bold waterside partners include *Gunnera manicata*, rodgersias and the larger astilbes.

HAKONECHLOA MACRA 'ALBO-AUREA'

A relatively recent introduction, and also sold as *Hakonechloa macra* 'Variegata' or *H. m.* 'Aureola', its peculiar generic name is a combination of Hakon, its native habitat in Japan, and the Greek word for grass, *cloa*. The plant makes a mound of densely overlapping, narrow, shiny, yellow leaves, randomly and occasionally striped with thin bands of green. It retains its bright colour all through the

Family: Gramineae
Height: 30-40cm (12-16in)
Spread: 45-60cm (18-24in)
Flowering time: Late summer
Aspect: Sun or light shade
Soil: Humus-rich
Minimum temperature: −23°C (−10°F)

Hakonechloa macra 'Albo-Aurea'

HOLCUS MOLLIS 'ALBO·VARIEGATUS'

The variegated form of creeping soft grass is useful rather than beautiful, being tolerant of fairly dry soils and shade. Also listed as 'Variegatus', it is a good 'last resort' carpeting plant for quick ground cover, but can be invasive, with a hugely extensive root system. A close relative of *Holcus lanatus*, also known as velvet grass, 'Albo-Variegatus' has green and white striped, densely hairy leaves, especially velvety when young. The overall effect from a distance is shimmery white. It forms tight clusters and spreads by rooting runners, which carry new clusters at the tips; sparse purple flowers are insignificant. If kept under firm control, it makes effective edging.

Family: Gramineae
Height: 25-45cm (10-18in)
Spread: 25-45cm (10-18in)
Flowering time: Summer
Aspect: Sun or shade
Soil: Ordinary, acid, dry or poor
Minimum temperature: −23°C (−10°F)

season, but is showiest in late summer and early autumn, when it produces rich purple flower panicles on arching stalks. Cold weather turns the foliage russet, after which it dies back, leaving no visible presence The plant is rhizomatous but non-invasive, spreading slowly below ground. A sunny site with moist soil produces the strongest colour contrast; in shade, it is less vivid. Propagate by division, since it does not breed true from seed.

Single clumps look like endearing, shaggy sheepdogs, in the open ground or in large pots, while linear plantings make good edging. In ground-cover schemes, it combines well with pulmonarias and epimediums. Where space allows, *Veratrum nigrum*, with its pleated leaves, and the huge, gold and green *Hosta sieboldiana* 'Frances Williams' or grey *H. sieboldiana* are suitable partners. For an oriental vignette, plant it with the compact *Arundinaria humilis* under a cut-leaved Japanese maple.

LUZULA SYLVATICA 'MARGINATA'

The variegated form of the great wood rush, also sold as *Luzula maxima* 'Variegata' and *L. sylvatica* 'Aureomarginata', has evergreen leaves, with creamy yellow margins. It prefers cool, moist, acid soil and woodland conditions, and is especially valuable for clothing steep banks that would be difficult or dangerous to mow. Less invasive than the species but still a strong surface spreader, it roots as it goes, and is best kept away from choicer, slower-growing plants. The plant bears open, brown flower spikes in late spring to summer. The great English gardening writer Gertrude Jekyll recommended adjacent patches of wood rush, Solomon's seal (*Polygonatum*) and trilliums for leafy, mossy soil in light woodland.

The generic name *Luzula* is said to derive from the Italian word for glow-worm, *lucciola*, referring to the plant's shiny, almost glowing appearance when covered with dew or after rainfall.

Family: Juncaceae
Height: 30cm (12in)
Spread: 60cm (2ft)
Flowering time: Late spring to summer
Aspect: Light shade
Soil: Lime-free, moist
Minimum temperature: −23°C (−10°F)

Holcus mollis 'Albo-Variegatus' in a mixed planting

MISCANTHUS SINENSIS

This was formerly *Eulalia japonica*, named after the sound it was said to make in the wind, and commonly called silver grass, because of its pale midribs. The species forms stately clumps of upright growth, fountain-like at the tips, robust but not invasive. It carries its wiry, towering stems of feathery flower sprays, pink at first, turning beige, relatively late in the season, (sometimes not at all, after cold summers), and they remain statuesque through winter. The graceful blooms are often depicted in Japanese art.

As with many plants, the variegated forms are less hardy than the species; protect their crowns with a deep mulch in winter, and cut back the old, dead foliage in spring. Though tolerant of dry soil, they prefer a moist site, and colour best in sun.

Miscanthus sinensis 'Variegatus', also sold as *M. s. foliis striatus* and *M. s.* 'Vittatus' or 'Univittatus', has leaves striped in white and creamy yellow. It is dramatic against a dark background or as a foil for the dark foliage of cannas. For a softer, more subtle effect, plant with pale pink phlox, foxgloves (*Digitalis*) and astilbes.

M.s 'Zebrinus', the zebra or tiger grass, has horizonatal stripes in alternating wide bands of green and narrow bands of yellow-ish white. The contrast increases as the season progresses, and is strongest in sun, though growth is more luxuriant in shade. One form is rather lax; 'Zebrinus Strictus', or porcupine grass, is hardier, denser and dram-atically stiffer. Either combines well with *Nicotiana* 'Lime Green' and nerines, in a sunny border, or as contrast to bergenias.

Two American forms are outstanding for drought-tolerance and easy, low-mainten-ance cultivation. *M. s.* 'Cabaret' has broad mid-green leaves with yellow variegation appearing as solid central bands or heavy stripes, which retain their brilliance through-out the growing season. The flower spikes produced in late summer, up to 2.4m (8ft) tall, are pale bronze. *M. s.* 'Morning Light', known

Family: Gramineae
Height: 90-150cm (3-5ft)
Spread: 60cm (2ft)
Flowering time: Autumn
Aspect: Sun or light shade, shelter
Soil: Deep, moist or dry
Minimum temperature: −18°C (0°F)

Top: Miscanthus sinensis 'Zebrinus'
Above: Miscanthus sinensis 'Variegatus'

as the silver variegated maiden grass, is a graceful and elegant recent introduction from Japan. The narrow, arching, light green leaves have creamy margins and midribs. The plant eventually reaches 1.5m (5ft) high, forming a dense, fountain-like effect. In late summer, it bears a profusion of tall red-bronze flower spikes that age to creamy white. These stay on the plant through winter and form a spectacular effect with the foliage, which fades to an overall pale brown.

MOLINIA CAERULEA 'VARIEGATA'

Family: Gramineae
Height: 30-90cm (12-36in)
Spread: 30cm (12in)
Flowering time: Early autumn
Aspect: Sun or light shade
Soil: Neural or acid, moist
Minimum temperature: −23°C (−10°F)

The variegated purple moor grass, or Indian grass, is among the most strikingly white of all variegated grasses. It makes neat, dense, tidy tufts of green leaves, 30-60cm (1-2ft) long but arching from the middle, with creamy white stripes. Leaves are often more white than green when young. The foliage turns soft orange in autumn, then parchment after the first frost, and remains a winter presence until flattened by snow or wind. In autumn, it produces airy, purple-brown flower spikes on creamy stalks, twice the height of the leaves.

An effective weed-suppressing ground cover, it is ideal in an all-green scheme, with dwarf pines and other dwarf conifers; or with variegated perennials, such as *Hosta undulata*, or *Salvia officinalis* 'Icterina'.

PHALARIS ARUNDINACEA

Family: Gramineae
Height: 60-150cm (2-5ft)
Spread: 60cm (2ft)
Flowering time: Summer and autumn
Aspect: Sun or light shade
Soil: Moist
Minimum temperature: −29°C (−20°F)

Phalaris arundinacea 'Picta', or 'Elegantissima', is the traditional gardener's garters, or ribbon grass, of cottage gardens. Its green and white striped foliage is handsome, especially in late spring and early summer, but the plant can be invasive. It is often dismissed as little more than a weed, but does make good, weed-proof ground cover itself,

Molinia caerulea 'Variegata'

tolerant of all but heavy clay soils, though it prefers soil that does not dry out. Planting in bottomless buckets or buried vertical drainpipes helps control root spread.

The foliage turns pale ivory beige in winter, and is cut down in early spring to make way for the new growth. A second trim in midsummer, as the flower heads form, encourages bright new growth; otherwise, the foliage becomes dull and untidy. Lifting, dividing and replanting every two years in enriched soil ensures a robust, dense display.

Rarer cultivars include 'Feesey's Form', whiter and more striking but less vigorous than 'Picta'; 'Aureovariegata' or 'Luteopicta', with creamy yellow stripes; 'Streamlined',

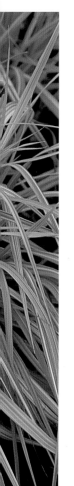

with white-edged, green leaves; and 'Tricolor', with purple-tinged young growth. All are good with dark green or purple foliage, such as *Rhus typhina* or one of the purple berberis or cotinus; or with boldly contrasting plants, such as hostas or bergenias. Its young spring growth makes a perfect setting for hybrid Greigii tulips and, in autumn, for *Sedum* 'Autumn Joy' and *Ricinus communis* 'Gibsonii'.

PHYLLOSTACHYS AUREA 'VARIEGATA'

Family: Gramineae
Height: 3m (10ft)
Spread: 2m (6ft)
Flowering time: Summer
Aspect: Sun or light shade
Soil: Well drained
Minimum temperature:
—18°C (0°F)

Also known as 'Albovariegata', the variegated form of the golden bamboo is a graceful, outsized member of the grass family. Like other bamboos, it has woody stems and an unusual life cycle, taking approximately 15 years to flower, after which flowering canes die. New shoots eventually grow from the base.

The canes, relatively straight for this genus, which normally produces zig-zag growth, are green when young, then golden brown. Branching starts from the base and occasional stems have interesting, knobby basal forms where the lower stem joints are crowded. Beneath each joint is a swollen band, unique to the species and its cultivars. The canes form slow-spreading clumps, harvested commercially for umbrella handles.

The narrow, evergreen, pointed leaves are unevenly striped with white, and glaucous beneath. Variegation is at its best as new growth starts in late spring, when the plant looks almost white. The variegation fades as the foliage matures and by late summer the effect is much reduced.

Bamboo provides an excellent background for low-growing, glossy evergreens, such as box (*Buxus*) or any of the sarcococcas. It is suitable for container growing, but should be moved into a cold greenhouse where winters are harsh.

Phalaris arundinacea 'Picta'

Phyllostachys aurea
'Variegata'

PLEIOBLASTUS

Family: Gramineae
Height: 60-120cm (2-4ft)
Spread: 90-180cm (3-6ft)
Flowering time: Summer
Aspect: Sun
Soil: Moist
Minimum temperature:
−23°C (−10°F)

Bamboo nomenclature is a nightmare, with some species being sold under four or five different names, although only one is 'correct'. Unless you are dealing with a specialist supplier, it may be safer to buy plants by going to view them, rather than relying on the vagaries of nurserymen's catalogue descriptions.

Pleioblastus variegatus, also sold as *Arundinaria variegata, Arundinaria fortunei* and *Bambusa variegata*, grows 60-120cm (2-4ft) high, forming slow-spreading thickets. It grows most strongly and rapidly in moist soil. Its very slender stems branch near the plant base and carry narrow evergreen leaves heavily striped with creamy white, sometimes more white than green. Unlike many bamboos, which look worn out and dishevelled by winter, this is attractive until mid-winter, and is considered by many to be the best white-striped hardy bamboo.

P. auricomus, also sold as *P. viridistriatus, Arundinaria viridistriata* or *A. auricoma*, and formerly called *Bambusa fortunei aurea*, is one of the brightest gold-variegated garden plants. Growing 90-120cm (3-4ft) high, it produces non-invasive clumps of slender, dark purple canes carrying broader leaves than those of *P. variegatus*, unevenly striped gold and green, often with only pencil lines of green between gold. It colours best in full sun, but dislikes dry soil. It can be cut down annually, in mid-spring, to promote fresh young growth with much larger leaves than those produced by older canes. If, however, the canes are strong and height is required, cut them back by only half.

Bamboo as cut foliage can be tricky, as the leaves tend to curl. Placing the cut ends in boiling vinegar for a couple of minutes, following a long drink in warm water, is the traditional antidote.

Top: Pleioblastus variegatus

Above: Pleioblastus auricomus

SASA VEITCHII

Family: Gramineae
Height: 30-120cm (1-4ft)
Spread: 60-120cm (2-4ft)
Flowering time: Summer
Aspect: Sun or light shade
Soil: No special requirement
Minimum temperature:
−23°C (−10°F)

Variously known as *Bambusa veitchii, Arundinaria veitchii, A. albomarginata* and *Sasa albomarginata*, this is not strictly a variegated form. Every year its large, dark green leaves, glaucous beneath, gradually die back irregularly from the edges, which become first yellow then parchment, creating a variegated effect. This is unique among bamboos; some people dislike the idea of half-dead leaves, but they are very effective seen *en masse*,

Sasa forms vast thickets of branching, purple stems, difficult to eradicate once established, and is probably better placed in a wild or woodland garden than where space is at a premium.

SCIRPUS LACUSTRIS TABERNAEMONTANI

Family: Cyperaceae
Height: 60-150cm (2-5ft)
Spread: Spreads indefinitely
Flowering time: Summer
Aspect: Full sun to light shade
Soil: Moist, or shallow water
Minimum temperature:
−23°C (−10°F)

The grey rush is a sub-species of the true bulrush, *Scirpus lacustris*, once used in the making of rush mats and chair seats. (The cigar-shaped flower spike commonly known as bulrush is that of *Typha*, or reedmace.) It is found in rich, silty soil in ditches, bogs, streams and ponds, and is tolerant of brackish water. Its two variegated forms need similar conditions, growing in up to 20cm (8in) of water and ideal for small ornamental pools.

'Zebrinus', also called *S. zebrinus* or *Schoenoplectus tabernaemontana* 'Zebrinus', and commonly known as zebra rush, has unique spiky, leafless stems, like porcupine quills, that are horizontally banded green and white. 'Albescens' also sold as *S. albescens*, has longitudinally striped stems and sparse foliage. The effect is largely white, with occasional broken green lines. Both plants are evergreen, with insignificant flowers.

Lift and divide regularly in spring, to maintain healthy growth. Remove any all-green shoots as soon as seen, especially in 'Albescens', or the plant is liable to revert.

Above: *Spartina pectinata* '*Aureomarginata*'

Above right: *Scirpus lacustris tabernaemontani* '*Zebrinus*'

Right: *Sasa veitchii*

SPARTINA PECTINATA 'AUREOMARGINATA'

Also sold as *Spartina pectinata* 'Aureo-variegata' and *S. michauxiana* 'Aureomarginata', variegated cord grass is a rhizomatous, potentially invasive herbaceous perennial. Its arching, ribbon-like, light green leaves are edged and centrally striped with yellow, turning russet in late autumn. It makes a good specimen and waterside plant, even in brackish water, and is also eminently suitable for maritime planting. The narrow flower spikes with dangling purple stamens are effective when used for dried flower displays.

Family: Gramineae
Height: 1.2-1.8m (4-6ft)
Spread: 90cm (3ft)
Flowering time: Summer
Aspect: Sun or light shade
Soil: Moist
Minimum temperature: −23°C (−10°F)

CLIMBERS

CLIMBERS HAVE POTENTIALLY more impact per leaf than any other type of plant. An ivy covering a wall, for example, is basically one leaf thick, each leaf playing a part in creating a two-dimensional wallpaper of foliage. Climbers also provide the best value for available ground space, with a relatively small pocket of soil capable of supporting a substantial plant. In small or paved urban gardens, climbers are especially useful, since they can visually soften the overwhelmingly hard appearance of brick, concrete or rendered walls, and form the basis of 'vertical' gardening. Free-standing fences, arches, pergolas and trellises can also support climbers, or, more modestly, you can use tripods of bamboo canes. Where no open ground is available, climbers are suitable for container growing, a large terracotta pot or urn adding to the visual interest of the featured plant. A row of such climber-filled pots, with trellis or bamboo canes inserted for support, can make a garden wall or outdoor room divider, defining a seating area, for example, or concealing a clothes-drier or washing-line.

Many climbers also make good ground cover, suppressing weeds and clothing the soil with attractive foliage. However, rampant climbers used as ground cover need isolating from shrubs or other low-growing plants, since the former's natural inclination to climb or cling can result in strangulation of the latter. The bare ground under a large tree is ideal for fast-growing, shade-tolerant climbers used as ground cover.

As with any other type of plant, the quality and proportion of the variegation affects how the plant 'reads' across a garden. Green-leaved climbers with subtly contrasting edging or veining need close observation, while large-scale or startling variegations such as those of *Actinidia kolomikta* or *Hedera helix* 'Gold-heart', can 'colour' an entire garden.

The prunings from variegated climbers make first-class material for flower arranging, adding both colour and a sense of movement, and helping to conceal the rigid line of the vase rim. A vase or bowl generously filled with variegated foliage alone makes an attractive arrangement in its own right. Woody-stemmed climbers need the bottom 2.5-5cm (1-2in) of stem slit to facilitate the uptake of water; both woody and soft-stemmed climbers benefit from standing for several hours in a deep container of water before being arranged.

As well as the straightforward climbers included in the following section, certain plants in other categories may be trained as climbers. Please see the index under Climbers for individual entries.

ACTINIDIA KOLOMIKTA

Family: Actinidiaceae
Height: 6m (20ft)
Spread: 6m (20ft)
Flowering time: Early summer
Aspect: Sun, shelter
Soil: Well drained, rich loam
Minimum temperature:
−29°C (−20°F)

A striking relative of the kiwi fruit, *Actinidia chinensis, A. kolomikta* is a robust, twining climber with large, heart-shaped leaves. These start the season green, with a purple tinge, and later develop irregular, wide bands of white and pink. Variegation spreads from the pink tip backwards, occasionally colouring entire leaves. Young plants do not develop full colour, nor do those grown in shade, and some inexplicably prove disappointing in spite of ideal conditions. Plants can also be slow to get started, then, once established, grow vigorously. Small, fragrant, white, cup-shaped flowers appear in midsummer, followed by large, yellowish fruits on female plants, if a male plant is grown in proximity.

A good plant for training up a wall, pergola, arch, pole, or even an old tree, it can also be grown as a wide-spreading specimen shrub; in either case, it needs initial support. The foliage is vulnerable to late spring frosts; chalky and poorly drained soils are unsuitable.

AMPELOPSIS BREVIPEDUNCULATA 'ELEGANS'

Family: Vitaceae
Height: 9m (30ft)
Spread: 6m (20ft)
Flowering time: Summer
Aspect: Sun or light shade, shelter
Soil: Well drained, acid or neutral loam
Minimum temperature:
−23°C (−10°F)

The generic name of this plant is Greek for 'resembling the grape', and its former name was *Vitis heterophylla*, indicating its close relationship with the grape family. It is also sold as *A. heterophylla* 'Elegans', *A. elegans* 'Variegata', *A. e.* 'Tricolor' and *Cissus brevipedunculata*. A vigorous, twining deciduous, climber, clinging by means of tendrils, it carries pink young shoots and three- or five-lobed, hop-like leaves with a heart-shaped base, strikingly mottled white and pink. The grape-like, porcelain blue fruits are only produced in a mild autumn following a hot summer.

In cool climates, it benefits from the

Actinidia kolomikta

Family: Araliaceae
Height: 3-30m (10-100ft)
Spread: 3-30m (10-100ft)
Flowering time: Autumn
Aspect: Sun or shade
Soil: Well drained
Minimum temperature: −18°C (0°F)

protection of a wall in full sun, but can be trained up a pergola or tree, or over a hedge. It can also be trained on free-standing posts, with the uppermost shoots allowed to drape freely from the top, and pruned back annually.

HEDERA

Ivies include some of the richest, most valuable variegated plants, for striking impressions or subtle detail. A few, however, have variegation that confuses the shape of individual leaves and their orderly overlap.

Ivies vary enormously in leaf size and shape, hardiness and growth rate, and in general impression from lacy to densely solid foliage patterns. The plants have two forms of growth. The familiar sterile, juvenile form consists of lax, creeping or climbing stems with self-clinging aerial roots and leaves arranged on a single flat plane. The adult, non-clinging, bushy, branching form is produced once the top of the support is reached. It carries umbels of modest green flowers, much loved by wasps, flies and bees, usually followed by black, or more rarely yellow or orange, berries. The adult leaves often vary from the juvenile ones, being narrow, unlobed and wavy edged, and carried spirally on the branches. Adult shoots of 'tree ivy' are propagated from cuttings or grafted, to make shrubby, free-standing bushes up to 1.5m (5ft) high.

Ivy is a Jack-of-all-trades, climbing on trees, buildings and garden walls; making weed-proof ground cover, especially under trees; or trained over frames for topiary-like effect. The Victorians were especially fond of its rustic, romantic connotations and trained it over furniture, both indoors and out. Ivy is thought to harm its supports, but it can safely clamber up mature trees provided it does not overgrow the leafy shoots and compete for light. Likewise, ivy keeps walls warm and dry, and often holds together old, lime-mortar garden walls. It should, however, be kept

away from gutters and roof tiles. For ground cover among shrubs, choose less vigorous types, or the ivy can quickly festoon and overrun its neighbours.

Many ivies are slow growing initially, and need help in becoming attached to the support, but once established, grow away quickly. Newly planted ground-cover ivy needs weeding for at least two growing seasons, until the foliage mats up, and frequent pinching out of the growing tips to encourage branching.

Ivies tolerate shade, urban and industrial conditions, and almost any soil that is not waterlogged, but they dislike hot, dry soils. Enriching the soil at planting time and annual mulching repay the effort. Ivies are ideal for shady walls, or wandering along the base of hedges, though variegation tends to fade in deep shade. Old plants can be cut back hard, to encourage fresh shoots and colourful young foliage. They are popular house plants for cool, bright rooms, and are often trained up canes or around hoops.

Ivies may suffer from ugly fungal leaf spots, which often appear pale and translucent; spray with an appropriate fungicide, if necessary. Heavily variegated types can be disfigured by frost.

Nomenclature is confused, partly as a result of the standard Victorian book *The Ivy*, in which the author Shirley Hibberd renamed many variegated forms, according to personal whim! Today, there are over 300 cultivars for sale, many virtually identical but sold under several names, and any listing of ivies is bound to be contentious.

Hedera canariensis, Canary Island ivy, also grows in North Africa, hence its synonym, *H. algeriensis*. 'Gloire de Marengo', its popular variegated form, is also sold as *H. a.* 'Variegata'. It is a handsome, strong plant, with variable, shield- or diamond-shaped, grey-green leaves, plain green along the veins and irregularly edged in silver and white. The leaves are carried on maroon stems, and in winter become tinged with crimson at the edges, purply brown in the

Top: Hedera colchica
'Dentata Variegata'

Middle: Hedera colchica
'Sulphur Heart'

Bottom: Hedera helix
'Cavendishii'

Top: Hedera helix
'Sagittifolia Variegata'

Above: Hedera helix
'Glacier'

Right: Hedera helix
'Marginata Major'

central green area. Avoid exposure to cold winds or draughts; young leaves are especially vulnerable.

Persian ivy, *H. colchica*, has the largest leaves of all. 'Dentata Variegata', or 'Dentata Aurea', is tougher and less glossy than *H. canariensis*. Its large, polished, slightly heart-shaped and toothed green leaves have painterly, creamy yellow edges on young leaves, creamy white on mature ones, and broad intermediate zones of grey-green; some leaves are all yellow. *H. colchica* 'Sulphur Heart', or 'Paddy's Pride', has large, ovate leaves, with uneven, dark green margins and fresh green and yellow central splashes. (See photographs on p. 125.) 'Gold Leaf' is similar, if not identical; some books list it as a form of *H. canariensis*.

The common or English ivy, *H. helix*, provides the bulk of the variegated cultivars. 'Adam' is slow-growing and slightly tender, with dainty, grey-green leaves edged in white. 'Cavendishii', a Victorian form, has small, angular leaves, mottled grey and broadly edged in creamy white, flushed pink in cold weather. (See photograph on p. 125.) 'Chicago Variegata' resembles the species, but is edged in creamy white and tinged bronze-purple. 'Clotted Cream' has crinkled foliage boldly edged in creamy white. 'Discolor', also sold as 'Marmorata Minor' or 'Minor Marmorata', has tiny triangular green leaves sharply veined and stippled white, tinged with pink in winter. 'Eva' has small, grey-green leaves, with broad, irregular but strongly angular white margins.

H. h. 'Glacier' has shallow, blunt-lobed, grey-green leaves, brokenly edged with white; it is moderately vigorous, and easily controlled. 'Goldheart', also called 'Golden Jubilee' or 'Jubilee', is immensely popular, with its central blotches of rich yellow on the dark green, glossy, leaves, and red young stems. It needs plenty of light to colour well, and is especially vulnerable to reversion.

One of the more uncommon cultivars is the handsome *H.h.* 'Marginata Major' which has a large medium green, almost triangular-shaped leaf edged with deep cream. It is quick-growing with prominent yellow flowers in late autumn. It does well in sun or light shade.

H. h. 'Ivalace', also called 'Green Gem', 'Minigreen' or 'Little Gem', has small, glossy, undulating, dark green leaves with prominent pale green veins – perhaps not technically variegated but worthy of inclusion. 'Little Diamond' has small, diamond-shaped, grey-green and white leaves, and is good for trailing.

'Luzii', sometimes sold as 'Marmorata', has small leaves speckled and blotched with creamy white; some are predominantly white, others half plain green, creating a disconcertingly broken overall effect. 'Marginata Elegantissima' sometimes sold as 'Tricolor' or 'Marginata Rubra', is a moderate grower with small, triangular, grey-green leaves margined with creamy white, flushed carmine in winter. 'Silver Queen' is similar, with a less pronounced pink winter tinge and sparse leaf coverage. 'Midas Touch' is a new introduction, with gold-splashed foliage. 'Sagittifolia Variegata' has dainty, deeply cut, arrow-shaped leaves suffused with creamy white, creating a lacy effect. The foliage is vulnerable to hard frosts, though the plant is hardy.

Above: Hedera helix 'Luzii'
Left: Hedera helix 'Goldheart'

JASMINUM OFFICINALE

The common white jasmine, summer jasmine or poet's jessamine, is a traditional cottage garden climber, introduced to the West from Asia centuries ago. Though deciduous, its dense tangle of green young stems appear verdant even in winter, and its ferny, pinnate leaves are as attractive as its terminal clusters of fragrant flowers. It climbs by twining or pushing up through its support, and can be trained up a tree or against a wall or pergola. Hard pruning annually in spring results in new growth up to 1.8m (6ft) long, bearing top-quality leaves but fewer flowers.

Family: Oleaceae
Height: 6-9m (20-30ft)
Spread: 6-9m (20-30ft)
Flowering time: Summer
Aspect: Sun or light shade
Soil: Well drained
Minimum temperature: −6°C (20°F)

Given a warm soil and shelter, it is tolerant of sun or shade. The two variegated forms are 'Argenteovariegatum', or 'Variegatum', with delicate green leaves broadly variegated creamy white and tinged with pink; and 'Aureum', or 'Aureovariegatum', with leaves irregularly blotched and suffused yellow, and the new spring foliage flushed orange. The latter produces a piebald effect overall.

LONICERA JAPONICA 'AUREORETICULATA'

This valuable semi-evergreen, twining climber was introduced from the Far East in the mid-nineteenth century. Its leaves, oak-leaf-shaped on old wood, oval on trailing new growth, are permanently netted and veined in bright yellow. Its sweetly fragrant, small flowers are sparse, except in long, hot summers. They are white at first and, like most honeysuckles, mature to a rich Chinese yellow.

Honeysuckle can scramble over shrubs and tree stumps, up trees, or through balustrades, or may be trained against a wall or over a pergola. It can be grown as ground cover in large spaces, or trained on a 1.2-1.5m (4-5ft) support and allowed to cascade downward, forming a loose, wide-spreading shrub. 'Aureoreticulata' is vulnerable in cold winters, dying back completely, but usually sprouting again from ground level. Hard pruning in spring gives the best display of foliage. Aphids can be troublesome, if the soil is dry.

The graceful trailing stems are much appreciated by flower arrangers for adding a sense of movement to a design.

Family: Caprifoliaceae

Height: 3-6m (10-20ft)

Spread: 3-6m (10-20ft)

Flowering time: Summer to autumn

Aspect: Sun or light shade

Minimum temperature: −29°C (−20°F)

Lonicera japonica 'Aureoreticulata' with Cornus alba 'Spaethii'

PARTHENOCISSUS HENRYANA

Family: Vitaceae
Height: up to 9m (30ft)
Spread: up to 9m (30ft)
Flowering time: Spring
Aspect: Light shade, shelter
Soil: Well drained, neutral or limy
Minimum temperature: −18°C (0°F)

Formerly listed under *Vitis*, the Virginia creeper and related species, including Boston ivy (*P. tricuspidata*). are ornamental vines of great beauty and, often, vigour. *P. henryana*, an elegant climber up to 9m (30ft) high, was introduced at the turn of the century from China. It is self-clinging by means of sucker-like discs attached to tendrils. The leaves, composed of three to five leaflets, are rich velvety green or bronze, with prominent silvery white veining, sometimes tinged pink. The variegation is most striking in shade, and in autumn the silvery markings remain visible as the leaves turn rich red. The insignificant flowers are carried in spring, followed only after hot summers by small, blue-black, ornamental grapes.

It may take a couple of growing seasons to become self-clinging, and is not reliably hardy, so best grown against a sheltered wall in cold climates. In favoured areas, it could be used as ground cover or allowed to scramble up a pergola or up and through a dark tree such as yew.

Well drained, neutral or limy soil is best. For flower arranging, use mature foliage, singe or boil the cut ends, and submerge in lukewarm water for several hours. Even then, it is short lived and must be replaced after a day or two.

SCHIZOPHRAGMA HYDRANGEOIDES 'MOONLIGHT'

Family: Hydrangeaceae
Height: 15m (50ft)
Spread: 12m (40ft)
Flowering time: Summer
Aspect: Sun or light shade
Soil: Rich, organic, well drained
Minimum temperature: −12°C (10°F)

The variegated hydrangea vine is a recent introduction from Japan, an excellent addition to the range of variegated climbers. It is deciduous and has broadly ovate, strongly serrated leaves, carried on long reddish leaf stalks, heavily tinged with silvery white between the veins. The silvery appearance is strongest early in the year as the leaves emerge, but remains distinct to late summer. Large, drooping, flat-topped white flower-heads are borne in summer.

This self-clinging vine prefers some light shade, but the more sun it receives, the brighter the colouring appears. It is vigorous and can achieve a height of 15m (50ft); grown against a wall or large tree, the base stems form a pleasing and intricate tracery. Well-drained soil enriched with plenty of organic matter is ideal.

TRACHELOSPERMUM JASMINOIDES 'VARIEGATUM'

Family: Apocynaceae
Height: 3m (10ft)
Spread: 3m (10ft)
Flowering time: Mid to late summer
Aspect: Sun, shelter
Soil: Well drained, acid
Minimum temperature: −12°C (10°F)

The variegated form of Confederate, Chinese or star jasmine (actually related to periwinkle) is a slow-growing, twining climber, with lustrous, dark, evergreen leaves, splashed and edged in creamy white and suffused with crimson in winter. The very fragrant, white, jasmine-like flowers are carried in mid to late summer and become cream with age.

The plant is slow growing to start with, but can eventually become quite large. In cool climates, it does best against a sunny, sheltered wall, especially since young growth is vulnerable to frost. It can also be grown as a conservatory plant.

Parthenocissus henryana

TREES AND SHRUBS

Any tree or shrub needs careful choice and siting. Its cost and lifespan are greater than those of herbaceous plants, and the risk of moving it, once established, also greater. Depending on size, a tree or shrub can have considerable visual impact from a distance, whether in a small walled garden or large parkland setting.

Positioning of variegated trees and shrubs may need special forethought. Those with subtle colour contrasts, such as green leaves with narrow white or yellow edging or leaf tips, usually 'read' as plain-leaved except when seen up close; but trees or substantial shrubs with showy or startling variegations, especially if combined with large leaves, can visually commandeer an entire garden. Those with a high proportion of red, purple or bright yellow are especially arresting and potentially disruptive. Several such trees and shrubs dotted about in a confined space can compete for attention and create a restless effect, as the eye darts from one to another. A pair of identical variegated trees or shrubs, however, can set up a pleasing symmetry suitable for a formal layout, and a variegated hedge can provide a stunning feature. Evergreen variegated trees and shrubs are especially valuable, providing winter foliage cover and year-round colour.

A well-placed variegated tree or shrub can become the focal point of a lawn, a mixed planting or shrub border, or enliven a dim, shady corner. Some variegations look less natural than others, and such sophisticated variegations are excellent in the equally sophisticated setting of an urban paved garden, divorced from the native flora. The impact is even greater with plants that have an architectural growth habit – yucca, for example.

For use in flower arrangements, mature foliage is longer-lasting than young growth, although the latter often shows the best variegations. To condition woody-stemmed foliage, split, do not crush, the bottom 2.5-5cm (1-2in) of stem and, if possible, scrape the bark from this portion. Place stems immediately in water for several hours so that the foliage becomes fully turgid. Flagging foliage can sometimes be revived by recutting the tip, dipping it in boiling water for thirty seconds, then soaking in warm water.

ABELIA × GRANDIFLORA

Family: Caprifoliaceae
Height: 90-180cm (3-6ft)
Spread: 90-180cm (3-6ft)
Flowering time: Midsummer to mid-autumn
Aspect: Sun, shelter
Soil: Open, well drained, loam
Minimum temperature: −12°C (10°F)

This lax, graceful, semi-evergreen or evergreen hybrid, also known as glossy abelia, is prized mainly for its late-season flowers, which are tubular, pale pink and slightly fragrant, and the persistent coppery bracts which remain long afterwards. There are two reliable forms that also have interesting foliage colour: 'Variegata' has pale green, oval leaves, blotched and streaked with dark green loosely following the midrib and veins; 'Francis Mason' has bronzy yellow young shoots and yellow-edged and tinged, dark green leaves.

Although relatively hardy, the variegated cultivars can still be cut back to ground level in hard winters, after which they usually shoot again from the base. A sunny, sheltered spot is best; trained against a wall, the shrub achieves greater height.

ACANTHOPAX PENTAPHYLLUS 'VARIEGATUS'

Family: Araliaceae
Height: 1.8m (6ft)
Spread: 2.4m (8ft)
Flowering time: Early summer
Aspect: Sun or light shade, shelter
Soil: Light loam
Minimum temperature: −29°C (−20°F)

Also sold as *Acanthopax sieboldianus* and, correctly, as *Eleutherococcus sieboldianus*, this deciduous shrub is related to ivy and fatsia. Introduced from China in Victorian times, the species was originally grown in cool greenhouses for its elegant growth habit and foliage. It produces many erect, thorny stems and arching branches, carrying clusters of deeply lobed or compound, palmate leaves. In 'Variegatus' the leaflets are irregularly edged with a wide band of creamy white. The insignificant, dull flowers are followed by ivy-like berries.

Protect from cold winds. Although hardy, it does best where hot summers can ripen the wood.

ACER

Family: Aceraceae
Height: 1.8m-10m (6-32ft)
Spread: 1.8m-10m (6-32ft)
Flowering time: Spring
Aspect: Sun or light shade
Soil: Well drained
Minimum temperature: −23°C (−10°F)

The maples are an immense genus, with several worthwhile variegated forms. None is as quick-growing as the species, which in the case of the Japanese maple (*Acer palmatum*) is slow-growing itself. All carry a modest display of spring flowers.

Acer negundo, the North American box elder, makes a large, open, spreading tree, ideal for specimen planting, and relatively tolerant of wind, drought and a wide range of soil types. Its compound leaves have three to nine leaflets, bright green with pale undersides. 'Variegatum', formerly 'Argenteovariegatum', has leaflets unevenly edged in white, occasionally all-white. It tends to throw out plain green shoots and will revert totally if these are not regularly removed. It is less popular than formerly; in Victorian times it was often trained as a small standard or half-standard house plant for cool rooms.

A. n. 'Aureomarginatum' is similar, with yellow-edged leaves that are brightest in spring and slowly fade. 'Elegans', originally sold as 'Elegantissimum' or *A. n. aureomarginatum elegans*, also has bright yellow margins and downy, white young shoots. 'Flamingo' has pink young leaves, maturing to green with pink and white variegations. All can be cut back to form multi-stemmed shrubs.

The Japanese maple, *A. palmatum*, makes a low, domed shrub or wide-spreading, small tree, with five- or seven-lobed, palmate leaves. 'Butterfly' has delicate, pale green foliage edged with pink-tinged creamy-white. 'Kagirinisiki', or 'Roseomarginatum', has light green leaves unevenly edged with pink, but is liable to revert. The rare 'Karasugawa' has brilliant shrimp-pink young foliage, gradually deepening in colour to red, with white splashes. 'Ukigomo', which means 'passing cloud' in Japanese, has deeply lobed leaves mottled and edged with pink and white. All need moist but well-drained, leafy, peaty soil and shelter from cold winds and late frosts.

A. platanoides, the Norway maple, is large, upright, handsome and vigorous,

Acer palmatum 'Butterfly'

**Above: Acanthopax
pentaphyllus 'Variegatus'
Left: Abelia × grandiflora
'Francis Mason'**

Acer negundo 'Variegatum'
(right) and Acer negundo
'Flamingo' (left)

Acer platanoides
'Drummondii'

tolerant of most soils. 'Aureomarginatum' has long, pointed, three-lobed leaves, edged in yellow. 'Drummondii' has pale yellow-green leaf edges, but tends to revert.

The sycamore, *A. pseudoplatanus*, is a fast-growing ultimately large tree considered a weed in some places, but the variegated forms are handsome. 'Leopoldii' has yellowish-pink young leaves, later turning green, speckled and splashed with yellow, pink and purple. 'Tricolor' and 'Simon Louis Frères' have similar colouring: pink young leaves, green and white streaked when mature, with green undersides. The leaves of 'Nizetii' are heavily marked with yellow and white, and have pinkish-purple undersides. The foliage of 'Prinz Handjery' is suffused with pinkish-yellow when young, turning gold, then finally green above, purple underneath.

Japanese maples are too slow-growing to cut for large-scale flower arrangements and their mature foliage wilts unless frequently misted. Variegated forms of *A. negundo* are excellent for pedestal displays.

Above: Acer pseudoplatanus 'Tricolor'

Left: Acer negundo 'Flamingo'

ARALIA ELATA

The Japanese angelica tree is usually a suckering shrub, with thick, pithy, spiny young shoots. Its tropical-looking, doubly pinnate leaves, up to 1.2m (4ft) long and 60cm (2ft) wide, are dark green in the species, with pale undersides, and carried in ruffle-like clusters at the stem tips. Huge panicles of tiny white flowers appear in late summer or early autumn.

'Aureovariegata' has leaves unevenly and broadly edged in yellow, gradually fading to white by the end of the season. 'Variegata', or 'Albomarginata', has white-margined leaves, sometimes more than half white, which remain bright. They make good lawn specimens or focal points, especially against a dark background and underplanted with bergenia.

Cutting the stems back to ground level, or stooling, produces the largest leaves, but

Family: Araliaceae

Height: 1.8-3m (6-10ft)

Spread: 1.8-3m (6-10ft)

Flowering time: Late summer, autumn

Aspect: Sun, shelter

Soil: Ordinary or poor, well drained

Minimum temperature: −18°C (0°F)

the plants are fairly impressive grown naturally. Variegated forms are increased by grafting onto the species, which is difficult and makes them expensive. Avoid digging round the roots, which encourages the rootstock to sucker, eventually overtaking the cultivar.

Both variegated forms are hardy, but best in mild climates and relatively poor soil; rich soil encourages soft growth. In Victorian times they were grown as cool greenhouse plants, kept compact by very firm potting in loamy soil with a high sand content.

green stems and pale yellow leaf margins, which tend to revert in shade.

Aucubas, slow-growing initially, tolerate hard pruning, and can be cut back heavily in spring to reduce height and spread. They grow happily in containers; though perfectly hardy, they were used by the Victorians as cool greenhouse plants, hand-pollinated to ensure fruiting, and moved outdoors in summer. The berried branches, stripped of leaves, are effective in flower arrangements, whether the berries are green, red, or the transitional dusky orange.

AUCUBA JAPONICA

Family: Cornaceae
Height: 1.2-2.4m (4-8ft)
Spread: 1.2-2.4m (4-8ft)
Flowering time: Summer
Aspect: Sun or shade
Soil: Well drained
Minimum temperature: −18°C (0°F)

Spotted laurel, or gold dust plant, is the Cinderella of the garden. Too tolerant for its own good of dry, urban soils, dense shade, even under trees, and polluted atmosphere, it is often neglected, and sad specimens result. Being so common also detracts from its undoubted value, and it is generally underrated.

The plants are either male or female, and a male must be grown near females for pollination to occur, resulting in a berry crop. (Nurserymen and growers often disagree about the sex of certain clones, one catalogue listing a cultivar as male, another listing that same cultivar as a free-fruiting female. The similarity between the clones helps explain the confusion.)

The common female form 'Variegata', sometimes sold as 'Maculata', has leathery, evergreen, pointed leaves, irregularly spotted and splashed with yellow. There are various selections, the most dramatic of all being 'Crotonifolia', or 'Crotonoides', a male form with leaves boldly splashed with yellow; 'Mr Goldstrike' similarly has heavy splashes of gold. 'Gold Dust' is a female form with leaves conspicuously blotched, spotted and speckled yellow; 'Picturata' is a male form, with leaves centrally blotched with yellow; and the female 'Sulphur', or 'Sulphurea', has sea-

AZARA MICROPHYLLA 'VARIEGATA'

Family: Flacourtiaceae
Height: 5m (16ft)
Spread: 3m (10ft)
Flowering time: Late winter
Aspect: Sun, shelter
Soil: Well drained, loam
Minimum temperature: −6°C (20°F)

The species is a native of Chile, and the hardiest of a rather tender genus. 'Variegata' is a slow-growing, graceful evergreen shrub or small tree, with small, shiny, bright green leaves, irregularly and broadly edged in creamy white, carried on fan-like branches. Clusters of tiny, intensely vanilla-scented, petal-less flowers with deep yellow stamens are borne on the twig undersides in late winter, followed by violet or red berries. Though visually insignificant, the flowers are wonderful for scenting a room.

This plant needs the protection of a sunny, sheltered wall; young growth is vulnerable in severe winters.

BERBERIS THUNBERGII

Family: Berberidaceae
Height: 90-180cm (3-6ft)
Spread: 90-180cm (3-6ft)
Flowering time: Spring
Aspect: Sun or light shade
Soil: Well drained, ordinary or poor
Minimum temperature: −29°C (−20°F)

The Japanese barberry is a fiercely thorny, deciduous species, tolerant of poor soil and dry shade. It is much used in hedging and barrier planting, and as ground cover. It has arching sprays of tiny spoon-shaped leaves, brilliant red in autumn, and red-tinged yellow flowers in spring. The variegated forms, of which there are several, tend to be more compact, and the purple-leaved types

Berberis thunbergii 'Rose Glow'

Above: Aucuba japonica 'Gold Dust'

Right: Aralia elata 'Aureovariegata'

Aralia elata 'Variegata'

perform best in full sun.

'Gold Ring', or 'Golden Ring', is among the strongest growing, up to 1.8m (6ft) high. Its purple-tinged leaves are thinly edged in pale green, and turn brilliant red in autumn.

'Rose Glow' has a graceful, arching habit, and grows 90-120cm (3-4ft) high. Young foliage is purple-bronze mottled with silver and pale pink, darkening to red-purple as the season progresses. Cutting back annually in spring produces the best colour; left unpruned, the leaf colouring takes on a more uniform coppery bronze.

'Harlequin' is similar, but overcast with yellow, and slightly larger growing. 'Tricolor', 1.5m (5ft) high, has a pale green base colour streaked with pink and white, and rich red autumn foliage. It thrives in light shade.

BUDDLEIA DAVIDII

Family: Loganaceae
Height: 1.5-2.4m (5-8ft)
Spread: 1.5-2.4m (5-8ft)
Flowering time: Summer
Aspect: Full sun
Soil: Well drained
Minimum temperature: −23°C (−10°F)

The butterfly bush, originally from north-western China, is an enormously tough and quick-growing, multi-stemmed shrub. Its orange-eyed, pale purple, heavily scented flowers are very attractive to butterflies, and it is widely planted for this reason. 'Harlequin', the most popular variegated form, is more compact than the species, with leaves heavily splashed with creamy white, and dark red-purple flowers. 'White Harlequin' is similar, with white flowers. 'Variegata' and 'Variegated Royal Red' are older, inferior forms, nowadays largely replaced by 'Harlequin'.

Hard-prune annually in spring and remove any all-green shoots. Perfect drainage is essential, which explains the species' preferences for self-seeding on railway embankments or urban wasteground, and even inserting itself into chinks in walls and cornices.

Buddleia davidii 'Harlequin'

BUXUS SEMPERVIRENS

The box, common box or tree box, is a slow-growing, long-lived native of western Asia and North Africa. It can make an elegant, slender-stemmed tree with graceful feathery branches, but is more often grown as a shrub. Its glossy, leathery leaves have year-round value, if little seasonal interest. Traditionally clipped as formal edging, hedging or topiary (*Buxus sempervirens* 'Suffruticosa' is a mainstay of knot and parterre gardens), box is also ideal for container growing and, in the larger forms, for specimen planting. There are several variegated forms, all valuable for maintaining their variegations in shade, which is unusual among yellow-variegated shrubs.

'Marginata', also sold as 'Aurea Marginata', is upright, coarse, open and strong, growing steadily to 3m (10ft) high. Its slightly puckered leaves are irregularly edged with yellow, surrounding an olive green central zone which becomes glaucous if the plant is grown in shade. It tends to revert if grown in lush conditions.

'Aureovariegata', up to 1.8m (6ft) high and wide, has smooth green leaves irregularly streaked with yellow, in linear markings that run parallel with the leaf veins. 'Aurea Pendula' is similar in colour, but develops weeping secondary branchlets.

'Elegantissima' is dainty, dome-shaped and compact, eventually 90cm (3ft) high and 60cm (2ft) wide, with grey-green, puckered leaves edged in creamy white, smaller and narrower than those of the species.

'Gold Tip', also listed as *B. s.* 'Notata', with yellow-tipped leaves on the terminal shoots, is a subject of controversy. Some authorities identify it as a distinct cultivar; others consider that it is the species, showing yellow tips as a temporary symptom of stress or nutrient deficiency.

'Latifolia Maculata' has relatively large leaves, butter yellow when young, gradually streaked with green as the season progresses. It remains bright through winter, even in shade.

Family: Buxaceae
Height: 90cm-3m (3-10ft)
Spread: 60cm-3m (2-10ft)
Flowering time: Flowers insignificant
Aspect: Sun or light shade
Soil: Well drained
Minimum temperature: −23°C (−10°F)

'Variegata' forms a flattened rather than dome-shaped shrub, 60cm (2ft) high and spreading. The long leaves are silvery green with white edges.

Box is tolerant of any well-drained soil, but thrives on chalk and limestone. It roots easily from semi-ripe cuttings, taken in summer and pushed into the ground. Clipping to shape is also done during the summer months.

Variegated box is good in winter cut-flower displays; left to stand for several weeks in a container of half glycerine, half water, it turns a delicate creamy white, fully preserved but flexible.

CAMELLIA SASANQUA 'VARIEGATA'

Family: Theaceae
Height: up to 1.8m (6ft)
Spread: up to 1.8m (6ft)
Flowering time: Autumn, winter, early spring
Aspect: Sun, shelter
Soil: Well drained, acid
Minimum temperature: −18°C (0°F)

This is a rare variegated form of a species immensely popular and hybridized in Japan, that was introduced relatively late to the West.

The fragrant, modest flowers, slightly hidden by the leaves, are single, blush white tipped with pink and with a bold central yellow boss. They appear in autumn, winter and early spring, when other blooms are scarce. Though the plant is hardy, the flowers are easily damaged by frost and it needs a sheltered, sunny spot. The pale green, relatively narrow leaves are irregularly splashed with dark centres.

The species can grow to 6m (20ft) or more high and wide in ideal conditions – California or Italy, for example – but is usually half that size, or less, and 'Variegata' is more compact still. In favourable climates it can also be grown as a hedge. Like all camellias, it prefers well drained, leafy, acid soil. If necessary prune after flowering, although prunings during flowering are delightful displayed indoors. Interestingly, the oil pressed from the seeds of C. *sasanqua* was used by the Japanese as fuel in lamps.

Camellia sasanqua 'Variegata'

Buxus sempervirens 'Elegantissima'

CEDRUS DEODARA 'SNOW SPRITE'

Family: Pinaceae
Height: 3.5-4.5m (12-15ft)
Spread: 4.5-2.4m (15-18ft)
Flowering time: Non-flowering
Aspect: Sun or light shade
Soil: Well drained, dry
Minimum temperature: −23°C (−10°F)

This recently introduced, diminutive selection of the deodar cedar at first forms a mound, but after a few years develops a main leader, reaching about 1.2m (4ft) tall and wide after 10 years. It can eventually become a graceful, pendulous-branched tree 3.5-4.5m (12-15ft) high. The evergreen, light green needles are ivory white at the tops of the branches. This striking colour contrast is maintained as the tree matures. 'Silver Mist' and 'White Imp' are similar.

With its compact growth habit, this is a useful, attractive conifer where space is restricted. It requires a dry location, in full sun or light shade, and protection from cold wind and hard frost.

CHAMAECYPARIS

Family: Cupressaceae
Height: 30cm-2.4m (1-8ft)
Spread: 30cm-1.5m (1-5ft)
Flowering time: Non-flowering
Aspect: Sun, shelter from cold winds
Soil: Moist, well drained, deep loam
Minimum temperature: −23°C (−10°F)

False cypresses range from huge forest trees grown for timber to miniature cushion- or dome-shaped shrubs, popular for ornamental gardening. All have leaves made of small, overlapping scales, which form fan-like, flattened sprays. The dwarf forms below are ideal for rock or container gardens, or in association with heathers (*Erica*, *Calluna* species and cultivars); the rest are slow-growing, taking 10-15 years to reach 1.8m (6ft) in height, and good subjects for mixed shrub plantings.

Variegated forms of *Chamaecyparis lawsoniana*, Lawson cypress, include the dwarf 'Pygmaea Argentea', also sold as 'Backhouse Silver'. A Victorian favourite, it makes a slow-growing, rounded or conical bush, 30-45cm (12-18in) high and wide, with blue-green foliage tipped with creamy white. The whole bush has a charming white appearance in spring. The yellow-green, creamy white-flecked columnar 'Silver Threads' is taller, at 90-120cm (3-4ft); 'Snow White' is blue-green with white-tipped young growth and attains a height of 1.2-1.5m (4-5ft) after 15 years,

ultimately 2.4m (8ft). It has a wide base and multiple stems, rather than a single leader. 'Summer Snow' with cream tips on the new shoots, forms a broad-based conical shape, 1.8m (6ft) high after 15 years. 'White Spot', silver-grey with white tips on new growth, reaches 1.8m (6ft) in 10-15 years.

C. nootkatensis 'Aureovariegata', a variegated form of the Nootka or yellow cypress, makes a hardy medium-sized, narrowly conical tree. It has strong-smelling foliage, duller green than that of *C. lawsoniana* and speckled with deep yellow. It is more tolerant of indifferent soils.

C. pisifera 'Nana Aureovariegata', a dwarf form of Sawara cypress, makes a perfect flat-topped globe of golden-tinged foliage, 30-45cm (12-18in) high. 'Gold Dust', a recent Canadian introduction, is virtually identical. 'Nana Variegata' and the very similar 'Silver Lode' are white-flecked versions of 'Aureovariegata'. 'Snow', or 'Squarrosa Snow', is a tiny bun-shaped shrub with white-tipped, blue-grey, feathery foliage, which turns green in winter. It needs protection from cold wind or hot sun. 'White Pygmy' is a Japanese bun-shaped form, 30cm (12in) high and wide, green with white-tinged growing tips which remain bright all year round.

All prefer a moist climate and loamy soil, and need watering in dry weather. Protect young plants from wind and hard frost.

CORNUS

Family: Cornaceae
Height: 90cm-6m (3-20ft)
Spread: 90cm-6m (3-20ft)
Flowering time: Winter, spring or summer
Aspect: Sun or light shade
Soil: Varies according to type
Minimum temperature: −29°C (−20°F) to −23°C (−10°F)

Variegated dogwoods, or cornels, are valued not only for their foliage but for attractive growth habits, colourful bark, flower-like bracts, fruits and autumn leaf colour. They range from suckering shrubs to magnificent, elegant specimen trees. Cultivation needs vary, since the plants come from habitats ranging from the Far East to the eastern United States and Siberia.

The several variegated forms of *Cornus*

Above: Cornus alba 'Elegantissima'

Far left: Chamaecyparis lawsoniana 'Pygmaea Argentea'

summer sun without scorching, and keeps its bright yellow colour as the season progresses. *C. a.* 'Variegata' has grey-green, white-edged leaves and a vigorous constitution.

The cultivars are excellent in damp places, but equally tolerant of dry conditions, in sun or light shade. They are traditionally partnered with the yellow-barked dogwood *C. stolonifera* 'Flaviramea', white-stemmed *Rubus cockburnianus* and yellow- or red-stemmed willow. The more rampant forms of *C. alba* can be used as isolated lawn specimens, filling an island bed of their own and kept rigorously in check by mowing. All are easily propagated from hardwood cuttings, stuck two-thirds of their length into the ground in autumn.

C. alternifolia 'Variegata', also sold as *C. a.* 'Argentea' and sometimes called the pagoda dogwood, makes a 3m (10ft) high, flat-topped, spreading shrub with an elegantly tiered branch system – a truly 'architectural' plant. Most dogwoods have paired leaves, but in 'Variegata' the leaves grow alternately up the stem. They are narrow ovals of green edged in white, with occasional pink overlay, followed by rich red autumn tints. The shrub is usually grafted and needs strong sunlight and shelter to thrive.

C. controversa 'Variegata', the giant dogwood or wedding-cake tree, is a tiered, wide-spreading shrub or small tree, up to 6m (20ft) high and wide, with horizontal layers of regularly forked branches and red young wood. Its long, narrow, slightly irregular, lance-shaped, alternate leaves have uneven light yellow margins, and turn red and purple in autumn. In mature plants, small blue-black fruits follow the profuse, creamy white flower clusters. Provide shelter from cold winds and late spring frosts.

C. florida, the flowering dogwood from eastern North America, grows up to 6m (20ft) high in cultivation, larger in the wild. Its late spring 'flowers' are four heart-shaped bracts surrounding the visually insignificant botanical flowers. These are followed, in dry, sunny climates, by brilliant red fruits.

alba, the red-barked or Tartarian dogwood, all make multi-stemmed, suckering, thicket-forming shrubs. The erect stems can reach 3m (10ft) high, but are usually half that. The specific name *alba* refers to the white fruits, tinted blue, that follow the modest flat heads of creamy white flowers produced in late spring or early summer.

'Elegantissima', the variegated Westonbirt dogwood, has the most brilliant red bark, but is the least robust of the *C. alba* forms described here. The leaves are grey-green at the centre, with creamy white edges spreading over half of the leaf, and can be slightly pink-tinged in autumn. *C. a.* 'Sibirica Variegata' is similar, but with darker green leaves. *C. a.* 'Spaethii', often considered the most effective variegated dogwood, has green-centred leaves broadly margined with yellow. It is especially valuable in that it tolerates hot

Unsuitable for poor or chalky soils, this tree is vulnerable to spring frosts, and lack of strong, continuous summer sun prevents the wood from ripening and diminishes flowering. The best autumn foliage colour – a rich, rosy red – also comes after hot, sunny summers. 'Cherokee Sunset', a recent American introduction, has spectacular foliage colour and bright red bracts. New leaves have pinkish red tips, maturing to green with a broad, irregular yellow margin; full leaf colouring is finally a combination of yellow, pink, red and purple. 'Welchii', also sold as 'Tricolor', has leaves irregularly margined in creamy white, with pink tinges, turning to bronzy purple edged with rosy red in autumn. Slow-growing, it reaches half the height of the species, and carries typical white flowers. The white-flowered 'Rainbow' makes a dense, upright shrub, with dark green leaves edged in deep yellow, in autumn turning to deep red-purple edged in scarlet.

C. *kousa*, the Japanese or Kousa dogwood, is a large shrub valued for its dense, glossy foliage and the large, creamy white bracts that appear in spring. In 'Gold Star', a recent Japanese introduction, the dark green leaves have a broad, irregular central blotch of deep butter yellow, maintained until leaf fall. 'Snowboy' has pale grey-green leaves regularly and broadly margined with white; occasionally paler grey-green or yellow-green splashes appear along the edge of the darker green centre. Leaf tips are often reddish, as are leaf bases on new shoots and young twigs. 'Snowboy' needs a shady position, as leaves may scorch in hot sun. Moist but well-drained, neutral or acid soil is best.

C. *mas*, the Cornelian cherry, is a large, wide-spreading shrub or small tree, with red, cherry-like acidic fruits that were once used to make syrups. Its buttercup yellow, small, spidery flowers appear on leafless stems in late winter or early spring. 'Aurea Elegantissima', also sold as 'Elegantissima' or 'Tricolor', is a slow-growing, medium-sized shrub, its shiny leaves broadly edged with yellow and tinged with pink. It needs light

Above: Cornus alba 'Variegata' in autumn at Kiftsgate Court, Gloucestershire.

Far left: Cornus alternifolia 'Argentea'

Left: Cornus controversa 'Variegata'

shade. The slow-growing 'Variegata' has bright green leaves broadly and irregularly margined with white. The foliage, which turns red-purple in autumn, and flowers of both these cultivars look good against dark evergreens, such as holly (*Ilex*) or yew (*Taxus*). Provide shelter, especially when young.

C. *stolonifera*, or C. *sericea*, is an invasive, suckering shrub, which forms dense thickets up to 1.8m (6ft) high. 'Silver and Gold' is a recent American introduction with striking golden yellow stems, turning greener in summer, and leaves distinctly bordered in creamy white. 'White Gold', or 'White Spot', is another attractively marked form with red stems.

Coloured-bark dogwoods are often grown as pondside planting, their stems reflected in the water. They should be pruned every other year, which also encourages the showiest foliage. Cut back one-third of the oldest shoots to within 15cm (6in) of ground level in early spring, to gradually renew the shrub; total renewal in one go weakens the plant and limits its height.

bees, stud the branches in summer. The scarlet berries that follow are equally attractive to birds but sparser than those of the species.

Tolerant of all but waterlogged soils, it is useful for planting on dry banks. It does well in sun or light shade, ideal for a sunless wall or a site that receives morning sunlight, and particularly effective planted at the top edge of a retaining wall, from which it can cantilever out, or where it can sprawl over a rock.

The leaves turn rich mahogany when preserved in glycerine. A light coating of hairspray or polyurethane retards shrivelling of the berries on stems cut for vases.

CRATAEGUS LAEVIGATA 'GIREOUDII'

Also sold as C. *oxycantha* 'Gireoudii', this relatively rare variegated form of hawthorn makes a sharply spiny, widespreading, mounded large shrub or small tree, with young leaves mottled white and pink.

Family: Rosaceae
Height: 4.5m (15ft)
Spread: 6m (20ft)
Flowering time: Mid-spring
Aspect: Sun or light shade
Soil: Well drained, including limy
Minimum temperature: −34°C (−30°F)

COTONEASTER HORIZONTALIS 'VARIEGATUS'

Family: Rosaceae
Height: 30-180cm (1-6ft)
Spread: 1.2m (4ft)
Flowering time: Early summer
Aspect: Sun or light shade
Soil: Well drained
Minimum temperature: −23°C (−10°F)

The fishbone cotoneaster is unique, with its splayed, herringbone branching system and tiny leaves. Usually seen as spreading ground cover, perhaps 30cm (12in) high, both the species and its dainty, dwarf variegated form can also grow vertically. Given wall support, tied in and pruned, they can reach 1.8m (6ft) or more, creating a cascading, layered effect.

The grey-green, white-edged leaves of the slow-growing 'Variegatus' are suffused pink in autumn and, though deciduous, generally remain on the plant until early winter, with new growth appearing early in spring. Small pink flowers, much loved by

× CUPRESSOCYPARIS LEYLANDII 'SILVER DUST'

The dense, columnar Leyland cypress is a bigeneric hybrid between *Cupressus macrocarpa* and *Chamaecyparis nootkatensis*, combining the rapid growth and wind-tolerance of the former with the hardiness of the latter. Tolerant of hard pruning, it is a popular but mercurial hedging plant, liable to die off inexplicably. The American 'Silver Dust', like the species, can grow up to 90cm (3ft) a year; its variegated foliage, green splashed and flecked with creamy white, is perhaps better displayed as a specimen plant than as hedging.

Family: Cupressaceae
Height: 6m (20ft)
Spread: 3cm (10ft)
Flowering time: Non-flowering
Aspect: Sun
Soil: Well drained
Minimum temperature: −18°C (0°F)

Cotoneaster horizontalis
'Variegatus'

Crataegus laevigata
'Gireoudii'

DAPHNE

Family: Thymelaeaceae

Height: 15cm-1.8m (6in-6ft)

Spread: 60cm-1.8m (2-6ft)

Flowering time: Winter to summer, according to type

Aspect: Sun or light shade, shelter from cold winds

Soil: Moist, well drained loam

Minimum temperature: −29°C (−20°F) to −18°C (0°F)

The variegated daphnes are as valuable for the heavy scent of their waxy flowers as for their foliage, although they are liable to be short-lived. *Daphne* × *burkwoodii* 'Variegata', or 'Carol Mackie', forms a dense, rounded hummock up to 1.2m (4ft) high and wider across. It has green-grey, semi-evergreen leaves with narrow creamy yellow margins, becoming white. The thick clusters of pale pink, fragrant blooms form at the shoot tips in late spring and early summer, occasionally with a second, smaller flush in autumn, and are followed by red berries. With age, the plant is liable to become bare and leggy at the base.

D. cneorum 'Variegata', a vigorous form of the prostrate, slow-growing daphne known as garland flower, carries cream-edged, laurel-shaped evergreen leaves and profuse, rosy pink, heavily fragrant flowers in spring, followed by brownish-yellow berries. Its trailing shoots, usually under 30cm (12in) high, are easily layered by weighting them down with stones. A suitable subject for rock gardens, it can be difficult to establish. In Victorian times it was trained vertically as a wall shrub in camellia greenhouses, to provide the scent that camellias lack.

D. odora 'Aureomarginata', sometimes sold as *D. o.* 'Variegata', makes a loose, open, spreading shrub, up to 1.8m (6ft) high and wide. Hardier and easier to grow than the species, which originated from China and Japan, it still appreciates the shelter of a sunny wall, or warm slope of a rock garden. Its shiny, oval, evergreen leaves are very thinly and subtly edged in cream – from a distance, it does not 'read' as variegated. Purple buds open into heavily fragrant, waxy pinky white flowers, appearing from mid-winter to early spring. This, too, can be grown as a cool greenhouse plant, and the cut branches are excellent for forcing.

Sandy or peaty loam, mulched annually with leaf mould, is ideal; old gardening books suggest mixing equal parts by bulk of road

Daphne × burkwoodii 'Variegata'

sand, leaf mould and loam in the planting holes, and warn against very rich, wet or dry soils. The plants' small root systems resent disturbance; it is safest to buy young pot-grown specimens. To keep the roots cool and conserve soil moisture in summer, cover the ground beneath the shrub with stones or roofing slates. In hot climates, light summer shade is also appreciated. Daphnes rarely need pruning. These plants, especially their berries, are poisonous.

ELAEAGNUS

Family: Elaeagnaceae
Height: 1.5-4.5m (5-15ft)
Spread: 1.2-3m (4-10ft)
Flowering time: Autumn
Aspect: Sun or light shade
Soil: Moist, well drained
Minimum temperature: −18°C (0°F)

The genus includes one of the most popular and spectacularly variegated broad-leaved garden evergreens, *Elaeagnus pungens* 'Maculata', but also more subtle and, to many, more pleasing variegated forms. Their small, silvery, bell-shaped flowers appear in autumn – not much to look at, but sweetly vanilla-scented.

E. × ebbingei is a vigorous garden hybrid, up to 4.5m (15ft) high and wide, with large grey-green leaves, silvery beneath. 'Gilt Edge', which has bright yellow leaf margins, is half that size, with an upright growth habit. The similar-sized 'Limelight' has leaves centrally blotched with acid green-yellow. In bad winters these plants can lose their leaves, although new foliage normally appears in spring.

E. pungens is vigorous, with slightly spiny branches and dark, shiny leaves. 'Dicksonii', sometimes sold as 'Aurea', is a slow-growing, more compact, erect form, up to 1.5m (5ft) high, with light-green leaves that have wide, irregular, rich yellow margins, entirely covering the upper third of some leaves. It prefers light shade. The Dutch 'Goldrim' has gold edges to its dark green leaves.

E. p. 'Maculata', also sold as 'Aureo-variegata', is the most familiar variegated form and moderately quick-growing. Its dark green, shiny leaves are centrally splashed and

Elaeagnus × ebbingei 'Gilt Edge'

striped in vivid gold, with pale green between that and the dark green edge. It is especially effective in winter if sited where the sun's rays can strike it directly, but is also good in light shade. Its flowers are said to have a gardenia-like scent. 'Frederici' is similar, but with cream-splashed, slightly smaller leaves and a more compact growth habit.

E. p. 'Variegata', sometimes listed as 'Argenteovariegata', makes a large, robust shrub with thin, creamy white margins to its grey-green leaves.

Although slow to establish and in need of frost protection when newly planted, these eventually make good hedging and shelter belt plants, and are favourite coastal shrubs. In most gardens, however, they are grown in informal mixed or shrub borders. They do well in containers and can also be trained as formal standards. Most thrive in sun or light shade and in all soils except shallow chalk. They are more tolerant of drought and heat, than wet, cold conditions. Remove any reverted all-green shoots as soon as seen.

Euonymus fortunei 'Silver Queen' at Stancombe Park, Somerset.

Euonymus fortunei 'Emerald 'n' Gold'

EUONYMUS

Family: Celastraceae

Height: 30cm-3m (1-10ft)

Spread: 30cm-3m (1-10ft)

Flowering time: Late spring, early summer

Aspect: Sun or shade

Soil: Well drained

Minimum temperature: −23°C (−10°F)

Although this genus comprises deciduous and evergreen species, the best variegated cultivars are evergreen, and Japanese in origin. They subdivide easily between the ground-hugging, mounding or climbing *Euonymus fortunei radicans*, and the shrubby, large-scale *E. japonicus*, much used in seaside and urban planting. Both tolerate a wide range of conditions, including poor or chalky soils, seaside and urban sites; waterlogged soils are unsuitable. They do well in sun or shade, though white-variegated forms produce the best contrast in shade, and the pink autumn or winter tints are strongest in sun. Their greenish flowers are insignificant, and fruiting is modest, compared to the brilliantly colourful seeds of the deciduous species.

E. fortunei radicans, also sold as *E. radicans*, has leathery, slightly toothed, oval leaves. On the flat, it makes trailing evergreen ground cover, up to 45cm (18in) high and 60cm (2ft) across, rooting from the nodes as it goes. Against a wall, it becomes a self-clinging, ivy-like climber, up to 4.5m (15ft) high, clinging by means of aerial roots. Its juvenile, creeping or clinging stems are sterile; only the mature, erect, shrubby growth produces flowers and fruits. Some variegated forms are propagated from adult growth, and naturally maintain a shrubby habit.

'Emerald 'n' Gold' is a dense, shrubby type that has green-centred yellow leaves, which take on purplish tints in winter, especially in exposed positions. 'Emerald Charm' has deep green leaves veined with white. 'Emerald Gaiety' is a slow-growing, upright form, up to 90cm (3ft) high, with broad, round leaves edged in creamy white. 'Emerald Surprise' forms a mounded shrub up to 75cm (30in) high and wider-spreading, and has leaves variegated green, gold and creamy white.

'Harlequin' is a striking, recent Japanese introduction with a climbing or trailing habit, excellent as ground cover in partial shade. Its broad, mid-green leaves have pure white, narrow margins and profuse speckling of white and yellow-green. Some shoots or stem tips may be all-white, and occasional young green stems are striped or banded with white.

'Silver Pillar', also sold as 'Versicolor Albus', is upright, with narrow leaves broadly margined with white. 'Silver Queen', an old Victorian form, is slow-growing when young, eventually making a small, compact shrub 60cm (2ft) high by 90cm (3ft) across. Its creamy yellow new leaves gradually turn to green widely margined with creamy white.

'Sunspot', a relatively new introduction, has dark green leaves splashed with creamy white and bright yellow at the centre, and tinged red in winter. It grows 30-45cm (12-18in) high, slightly more across. 'Variegatus', also sold as 'Gracilis', 'Argenteo-marginata' or 'Silver Edge', is a trailing or climbing juvenile form. Its oval, bright green young leaves are margined with creamy white, and mature to grey-green and white, flushed pink in winter. There are many forms in cultivation under this name, with minor variations.

These forms look good with purple foliage, like that of the dainty *Viola labradorica* 'Purpurea', or as underplanting for purple-leaved berberis, phormium, weigela or cotinus. On a lightly shaded wall, combine them with clematis or the perennial climbing nasturtium, *Tropaeolum speciosum*.

As well as ground cover and climbers, the shrubby cultivars are useful as edging or clipped into a low hedge. In the north-eastern United States, euonymus is a substitute for ivy (*Hedera*), where low temperatures preclude use of the latter. Trim plants occasionally in early spring to keep them compact and encourage fresh growth. Propagation is easy, from cuttings or by layering.

E. japonicus, the Japanese spindle, makes a large, densely branched shrub or tree up to 6m (20ft) high and wide. Its leaves are shiny, leathery and rounded or blunt at the tips. Often clipped as hedging, when grown naturally it produces attractive red, winged fruits. The variegated forms are much smaller than the species, and also less hardy than *radicans* varieties and very vulnerable to mildew and caterpillars. They are often grown as pot plants, for cool rooms indoors or in the greenhouse, where they need maximum light and ventilation. Ideally, they should be taken outdoors for the summer.

'Albomarginatus', or 'Pearl Edge', has narrow white leaf margins. 'Aureopictus', also sold as 'Aureus', has narrow yellow leaves with thin green margins, and pale yellow young stems. It needs shelter in exposed positions, and tends to revert.

'Duc d'Anjou', sometimes sold as 'Viridivariegatus', has dark green leaves with yellow and grey-green broad edges. 'Macrophyllus Albus', variously sold as 'Latifolius Variegatus' and 'Latifolius Albomarginatus', is one of the most striking variegated forms. Its large yellow-green leaves have broad white leaf margins, yellow when young, flushed pink in autumn. It is vulnerable to spring frosts.

'Microphyllus Pulchellus', or 'Microphyllus Aureus', is an upright, dense-growing, compact form, 45-60cm (18-24in) high, half that across. Its very small, narrow leaves are predominantly yellow. It is relatively tender. 'Microphyllus Variegatus', or 'Microphyllus Albovariegatus', is similar, but with white leaf margins. Both are excellent in sheltered rock gardens.

'Ovatus Aureus', sometimes sold as 'Aureovariegatus,' is a popular form, but needs a sunny position to do well. The young growth is the most colourful, with broad, irregular, creamy yellow leaf margins, blending into green centres. 'Ovatus Albus' is similar, but with leaves edged in white.

× **Fatshedera lizei**

FAGUS SYLVATICA 'TRICOLOR'

This is one of the most distinct and attractive forms of the European purple-leaved beech. It is relatively slow-growing and eventually forms a dense, pyramidal to oval tree, branching low to the ground. The leaves are purple, edged with an irregular border of pale pink to rose. The variegation, which can be unstable, is best in spring to early summer. The appearance of the smooth grey branches after leaf fall provides a spectacular feature of the winter landscape.

It requires partial shade, as the pale leaf borders easily scorch in hot, dry weather. Grow in moist, well-drained soil.

Family: Fagaceae
Height: 15-18m (50-60ft)
Spread: 12m (40ft)
Flowering time: Flowers insignificant
Aspect: Semi-shade
Soil: Moist, well drained
Minimum temperature: −23°C (−10°F)

× FATSHEDERA LIZEI

This is a bigeneric hybrid, a cross between *Fatsia japonica* 'Moseri' and *Hedera helix hibernica*, the Irish ivy. It is commonly known as the ivy tree or, informally, as fat-headed Lizzy. The form 'Variegata' has ever-green, leathery, shiny, five-lobed leaves, 10-25cm (4-10in) across, glossy-green with an irregular white margin, tinged crimson or bronze in winter. The leaves of 'Annamieke' have a dramatic, bright yellow-green central splash. The sterile clusters of small, pale cream flowers are produced in autumn.

From ivy, the plants inherit unbranched, thin, leaf-covered stems. These are erect initially, but later need the support of a wall, trellis or poles to remain upright and reach full height. Unsupported, the stems sprawl, and plants can be used as ground cover, spaced 90-120cm (3-4ft) apart, or allowed to tumble over banks or retaining walls. Frequent pinching out of the growing tips encourages bushiness and a slightly more compact habit.

The variegated forms tolerate light shade (deep shade reduces colour contrast), maritime exposure, urban pollution, and almost

Family: Araliaceae
Height: 90cm-3m (3-10ft)
Spread: 90cm-1.8m (3-6ft)
Flowering time: Late autumn, winter
Aspect: Sun or light shade
Soil: Well drained
Minimum temperature: −12°C (10°F)

Fatsia japonica 'Variegata'

any soil, provided it is well drained. They are ideal for container growing and, like fatsia, especially effective in the hard setting of a patio or courtyard. For a dense effect, several plants can be potted in one large container.

Both are also grown as greenhouse or house plants, in cool, bright, airy conditions. They need frequent watering and regular misting in hot weather; cool temperatures and restrained watering in winter. Aphids, scale insects and red spider mites can be troublesome.

FATSIA JAPONICA 'VARIEGATA'

This is commonly known as Japanese aralia, fig leaf plant or false castor oil plant, the 'true' castor oil plant being the tender *Ricinus communis*. Introduced to the West from Japan in the 1830s, fatsia is a self-supporting shrub. Its thick, sparsely branching stems each end in a huge rosette of long-stalked, palmate, seven- or nine-lobed shiny leaves, up to 45cm (18in) across. In 'Variegata', these have irregular, creamy white margins and broadly splashed white tips. Panicles of milky white flower heads appear in autumn, followed by clusters of ivy-like black berries, which self-seed readily.

Like × *Fatshedera*, it is also grown as a greenhouse shrub or house plant, for cool, bright airy conditions, and is ideal for seaside and urban gardens. The leaves, the largest of all hardy broad-leaved evergreens, create a sub-tropical effect, in spite of their relative toughness. They are long-lasting in flower arrangements, and excellent for glycerining, which turns them varying shades from rich chestnut brown to black. Ferns, ivies, *Tiarella cordifolia* and hostas, such as *H. undulata*, make good underplanting for this and × *Fatshedera*.

Family: Araliaceae
Height: 1.5-3m (5-10ft)
Spread: 1.5-2.4m (5-8ft)
Flowering time: Autumn
Aspect: Sun or light shade
Soil: Well drained
Minimum temperature: −12°C (10°F)

Fuchsia magellanica gracilis 'Variegata'

FUCHSIA MAGELLANICA

Family: Onagraceae

Height: 45cm-1.8m (18in-6ft)

Spread: 45cm-1.8m (18in-6ft)

Flowering time: Summer, autumn

Aspect: Sun or light shade, shelter

Soil: Well drained but moisture-retentive

Minimum temperature: −12°C (10°F)

The beauty of fuchsia blooms is undeniable, but the plain green leaves are dull; variegated forms provide foliage as well as floral interest. All are quick growing, the heights given below being reached in a single season.

There are several variegated forms. The rare 'Alba Aureovariegata', 45cm (18in) high, has white flowers and gold and green variegated leaves. *F. m. gracilis* 'Variegata', variously sold as *F. g.* 'Variegata' or *F. m.* 'Variegata', grows 60-90cm (2-3ft) high, its small green leaves heavily margined in creamy white and tinged with pink. It has small scarlet and purple flowers, and red young shoots. *F. m.* 'Versicolor', also sold as *F. m. g.* 'Versicolor' or 'Tricolor', is stronger growing, with arching, spreading stems 90-180cm (3-6ft) high. Its new leaves are tinted rose and ash grey, then pinky green, and when mature are irregularly variegated creamy white and grey-green. In spring and autumn, when a second crop of new shoots often forms, the overall effect from a distance is dusky plum purple. Plants are apt to revert, so remove all-green shoots as they appear in spring, and check regularly during the growing season. Colour contrast is greatest in full sun.

F. m. molinae 'Sharpitor', also sold as *F. m.* 'Sharpitor' and *F. m.* 'Alba Variegata', makes a compact shrub, 60cm (2ft) high, with bright creamy white and pale green, small leaves, and sparse, slender, palest pink and lilac flowers.

These fuchsias are generally hardy and in mild climates can make evergreen hedges. They still benefit from deep planting, with the crowns 5-8cm (2-3in) below soil level, and annual winter mulching with leaf mould, bracken or straw, especially in the first season after planting. (Coal ash was a favourite Victorian mulch, and helped keep slugs at bay.) In cold climates plants often die back to ground level over winter, like herbaceous perennials, shooting from the base in spring and flowering in midsummer. In any case, the best foliar and floral display is produced on young wood, so pruning back hard, or even to ground level in spring is standard practice. Tender forms are covered on page 36.

Fuchsias need a steady supply of moisture in the growing season, especially in sun; dry soils are unsuitable. Soft cuttings taken in late summer root easily, and are best overwintered under glass. All look good with the blues of late-flowering hebes, cerato-stigmas, perovskias and agapanthus; or the brilliant cerise of *Lychnis coronaria*.

GINKGO BILOBA 'VARIEGATA'

Family: Gingkoaceae
Height: 1.8-3m (6-10ft)
Spread: 1.8-3m (6-10ft)
Flowering time: Summer
Aspect: Sun, shelter
Soil: Rich, deep, well drained
Minimum temperature: −23°C (−10°F)

The maidenhair tree is, surprisingly, a deciduous conifer, and the only survivor of a family that grew in many parts of the world almost 200 million years ago. Ginkgo is a sacred tree in the Buddhist religion, and frequently planted near temples. Its common name comes from its leaves' similarity to those of the maidenhair fern; they are fan-shaped, with radiating veins and a central split running from the top edge nearly to the base. They turn bright butter yellow before

falling, and in the rare 'Variegata' are randomly streaked with creamy white.

Like the species, 'Variegata' is very slow-growing, but tends to form a multi-stemmed shrub rather than a single-leader tree. It also tends to revert, and therefore needs careful watching.

GRISELINIA LITTORALIS

Family: Cornaceae
Height: 1.2-2.4m (4-8ft)
Spread: 1.2-2.4m (4-8ft)
Flowering time: Flowers insignificant
Aspect: Sun, shelter
Soil: Light, well drained
Minimum temperature: −6°C (20°F)

The species, originally from New Zealand, makes a dense, leafy shrub or small tree with thick, smooth, glossy, apple green leaves and shoots. The fresh colour is retained all year round, and is especially cheerful in winter. The flowers are inconspicuous, male and female being carried on separate plants, and the ivy-like berries are rarely produced in cool temperate climates. An archetypal sea-side shrub, it tolerates salt-laden winds in maritime climates but is less hardy inland. The variegated forms are vulnerable particularly to frost damage.

'Bantry Bay', an Irish cultivar 1.2-1.5m (4-5ft) high, is randomly and generously splashed with yellow. 'Dixon's Cream', a sport of 'Variegata', is splashed with creamy white. 'Gold Edge' is self-descriptive. 'Variegata' has yellow-rimmed, bright green young leaves, maturing to central splashes of grey-green and dark green with irregular creamy white margins. Occasional branches have reversed variegation, with green edges and pale centres.

Well-drained soil is essential; griselinia tolerates chalky and sandy soils, but not heavy clay. Spring planting is best, and any pruning, usually confined to plants grown as hedging, is also sensibly done in mid-spring. Check regularly for reverted shoots, and remove them when seen.

Griselinia littoralis 'Bantry Bay'

HEBE

Family: Scrophulariaceae

Height: 30cm-1.8m (1-6ft)

Spread: 30cm-1.8m (1-6ft)

Flowering time: Late spring, summer or autumn

Aspect: Sun

Soil: Light, well drained

Minimum temperature: −6°C (20°F)

These sun-loving, evergreen shrubs, sometimes called shrubby veronica or shrubby speedwell, come mostly from New Zealand. Traditional seaside plants, they also tolerate urban and industrial conditions, but may need protection in cold areas. In general, the smaller the leaf, the hardier the hebe.

'Amanda Cook', 45-60cm (18-24in) high and 90cm (3ft) across, has creamy white leaves with narrow green centres, flushed violet in spring and again in winter. The flowers are bright purple.

Hebe × *andersonii* 'Variegata' is one of the most striking and tender variegated hebes, growing up to 1.8m (6ft) high in a favourable situation, such as against a sunny wall. Its long, large, glossy leaves, soft and almost leathery, are grey-green and dark green, broadly margined and splashed with creamy white, sometimes tinged pink. Long racemes of lavender-blue flowers, fading to white, appear in late summer and early autumn. It was traditionally grown annually from cuttings, used as dot plants or edging in summer bedding, and as greenhouse decoration.

H. 'Carnea Variegata', 1.2m (4ft) high, has narrow, grey-green leaves striped creamy white and flushed pink in winter. Long racemes of deep pink flowers, fading to white, are carried from late spring to late summer.

H. × *franciscana* 'Variegata', also sold as *H. elliptica* 'Variegata', is relatively tougher but less spectacular than some of the tender forms. A reliable hedging and window-box plant, it makes a 60cm (2ft) high, dense, dome-shaped shrub. The oval leaves are broadly edged in creamy white; the sparse, mauve flowers appear in summer.

H. 'Glaucophylla Variegata', sometimes listed as *H. darwiniana* 'Variegata', is one of the hardiest variegated hebes. It makes a small, tidy, upright shrub, 45cm (18in) high and 60cm (2ft) wide, with slender, wiry shoots and modest white flowers. Its greyish-green leaves are edged creamy white.

H. 'Lopen' is an outstanding variegated

Hebe × **franciscana 'Variegata'**

form, growing 1.2m (4ft) high and wide. Its leaves, which have purple undersides when young, are broadly margined with creamy yellow. Fuchsia-pink flowers are carried from midsummer to early winter.

H. 'Purple Tips', also sold as 'Tricolor' or *H. speciosa* 'Variegata', grows 90cm (3ft) high and wide, or wider. The leathery, grey-green leaves are broadly margined with yellow; young leaves are tinged and narrowly edged in red. The long spikes of magenta-purple flowers appear in summer and autumn.

H. 'Red Edge', sometimes sold as 'Pink Edge', forms a dense, dwarf, round shrub, 30cm (12in) high and twice as wide. Upright stems carry four rows of rigidly ordered, pointed leaves, glaucous grey and edged in pale red, with the contrast most noticeable in summer and autumn. Short spikes of white flowers appear in early and midsummer.

H. salicifolia 'Snow Wreath', 90-120cm (3-4ft) high, has long, pale grey-green leaves generously splashed with white, and white or pale lilac-tinged flowers. *H. s.* 'Variegata' is similar, but with creamy white leaf margins.

Most well-drained soils are fine, even poor soil, but hebes dislike extended drought. They associate well with heathers (*Erica, Calluna* species and cultivars), dwarf conifers and Mediterranean plants. Pruning is not usually needed, but plants can be cut back after flowering to encourage bushiness; lank, leggy plants can be hard-pruned back to 15cm (6in) above ground in mid-spring.

HOHERIA POPULNEA 'ALBA VARIEGATA'

The variegated form of lace bark, a rather tender, New Zealand evergreen, makes a large shrub or small tree with narrow, glossy, oval, dark green leaves, edged in creamy yellow. Its dense clusters of white flowers, like cherry blossom, appear in late summer and early autumn. Except in very favourable climates, it needs the protection of a wall.

Family: Malvaceae

Height: 1.8-3m (6-10ft)

Spread: 1.8-3m (6-10ft)

Flowering time: Late summer, autumn

Aspect: Sun, shelter

Soil: Well drained

Minimum temperature: −6°C (20°F)

or basic soil, blue on acid soil. 'Variegata', or 'Maculata', is a strong-growing form with grey-green leaves edged in cream and pale pink lacecap flowers.

Hydro is Greek for water, and hydrangeas need continually moist but well-drained soils; they resent dryness at the roots, especially in full sun. Lacecap types also need cool conditions, and are good companions for rhododendrons, camellias and lilies in light woodland. Avoid planting in frost pockets, since the young growth is vulnerable to spring frosts. Protect in cold winters; in spring, mulch and remove old, weak and frost-damaged branches.

HYPERICUM

This genus includes herbaceous plants as well as shrubs, both valued for their profuse yellow flowers in summer and autumn. The shrubs are semi-evergreen, but deciduous in hard winters, when stems may die back to ground level. Otherwise, cut back stems by a third in early spring.

Hypericum androsaemum 'Variegatum', also sold as 'Mrs Gladys Brabazon' is a relatively new Irish introduction. It forms clumps of semi-woody stems with slightly angled shoots, branching at the top. Its young leaves, the largest of the hardy hypericums, are marked white and pink and often tinged red. Its clusters of small, pale yellow flowers with conspicuous anthers are followed by red, later black, berries.

H. × *moserianum* 'Tricolor' makes a dwarf, tufty shrub 60cm (2ft) high and slightly wider. Its arching red stems carry green leaves edged with pink and pale yellow; clusters of yellow flowers with conspicuous red anthers develop at the stem tips. It needs shelter, and often dies back to ground level in winter, with new shoots appearing in mid-spring. Nonetheless, it makes excellent ground cover.

Family: Hypericaceae
Height: 60-90cm (2-3ft)
Spread: 60-90cm (2-3ft)
Flowering time: Late summer or autumn
Aspect: Sun or light shade, shelter
Soil: Well drained, moist loam
Minimum temperature: −23°C (−10°F)

Hypericum × *moserianum* 'Tricolor'

Hydrangea macrophylla 'Variegata'

Family: Hydrangeaceae
Height: 90-150cm (3-5ft)
Spread: 90-150cm (3-5ft)
Flowering time: Summer or autumn
Aspect: Light shade, shelter
Soil: Rich, moist but well drained
Minimum temperature: −18°C (0°F)

HYDRANGEA MACROPHYLLA

The macrophylla group of hydrangeas is largely grown for its showy flowers, either dense, globular mopheads or flat lacecaps, and not its foliage, which is dull green, deciduous, toothed and ovate. The variegated forms below have attractive lacecap flowers, but also very beautiful leaves.

H. *macrophylla* 'Quadricolor', also sold as H. *hortensis* 'Quadricolor', has leaves splashed with grey-green, yellow and creamy white, with an irregular dark green centre. Its white lacecap flowers are comprised of tiny fertile flowers surrounded by an outer showy ring of sterile florets, pink-tinged on neutral

Ilex aquafolium 'Golden King' at
Barnsley House,
Gloucestershire.

Ilex aquifolium 'Ferox
Argentea'

ILEX

Family: Aquifoliaceae
Height: 90cm-9m (3-30ft)
Spread: 90cm-4.5m (3-15ft)
Flowering time: Spring
Aspect: Sun or light shade
Soil: Well drained
Minimum temperature: −18°C (0°F)

The variegated hollies listed below are broad-leaved evergreens, potentially stately specimen trees but more often grown as hedges. In this form, their dense, often spiny, leaves create an effective barrier and their variegations provide a splendid mosaic effect. Berries are another feature, though regular pruning removes much of the one-year-old, fruiting wood. The tiny male and female flowers are usually borne on separate plants; for berries to develop a male should be within 30m (100ft) of one or more females, or a male branch can be grafted onto a female plant.

Nomenclature is confused, with the original eighteenth-century names, such as painted lady holly, fine Phyllis holly and glory of the east holly, replaced by unwieldy, descriptive Latin names when the latter became fashionable. It is safest to choose plants on sight.

Ilex × altaclarensis comprises a group of vigorous large shrubs or small or medium-sized trees, excellent for hedges. 'Camelliifolia Variegata', a free-fruiting female form, has lustrous, spineless, dark green leaves, up to 15cm (6in) long, marbled light green and edged in yellow. Some leaves are half or all yellow; the berries are relatively large and dark red.

I. × a. 'Lawsoniana' has large, spineless leaves, edged in dark green and splashed bright green and canary yellow in the centre, and long-lasting, orange-red fruit. An old Victorian cultivar, it is very liable to revert. 'Maderensis Variegata', also listed as *I. aquifolium* 'Maderensis Variegata', is a male form, with reddish-purple stems and flat, spiny leaves, dark green with an irregular central splash of bright green and gold. 'Silver Sentinel', 'Perado Variegata' or 'Belgica Aurea', is a vigorous, upright, female clone. Its long, flat, almost elliptic, sparsely spiny leaves are deep, rich green, shading to pale green and grey, with an irregular, creamy white or yellow edge.

I. aquifolium, English or European holly, is a well-known common, native British species, hardier than *I. × altaclarensis*. If left to grow naturally, the upper part of the tree bears relatively spineless leaves. There are many attractively variegated forms.

'Argentea Marginata', the broad-leaved silver holly, has both male and female forms with white-margined leaves and green young shoots. 'Argentea Marginata Pendula', also sold as 'Argentea Pendula' and 'Perry's Weeping Silver Holly', makes a small, mushroom-shaped tree with weeping purple branches carrying white-margined leaves and heavy crops of berries.

'Ferox Argentea', the silver hedgehog holly, is a dwarf, very slow-growing male, curious rather than attractive. Its small leaves, carried on purple twigs, are margined creamy white. They are spiny-edged and spiny on the upper surfaces, creating a pimply, puckered effect. 'Ferox Aurea', the gold hedgehog holly, is also male, with leaves splashed deep yellow or yellow-green at the centre.

'Golden King', sometimes sold as *I. × altaclarensis* 'Golden King', has broad, almost spineless, smooth-edged leaves, with bright yellow margins. It is female, in spite of its name, and a good cropper. The male 'Golden Milkboy', also sold as 'Aurea Medio-picta Latifolia', and the female 'Golden Milkmaid', or 'Aurea Medio-picta', both have large, flat, spiny-edged leaves, splashed with gold, but tending to revert. The surprisingly named male, 'Golden Queen', or 'Aurea Regina', has young shoots tinged red or green, and broad, spiny, dark green leaves shaded pale green and grey, with a wide yellow edge. Some leaves are predominantly yellow or all-gold.

'Golden van Tol' has almost spineless leaves, margined in yellow, and makes a broadly pyramidal tree. The female 'Handsworth New Silver' has purple stems and relatively long, spiny leaves, mottled deep green and grey, with broad, creamy white margins.

The Victorian 'Madame Briot' has

Ilex aquifolium 'Madame Briot'

Ilex × altaclarensis
'Lawsoniana'

The young foliage is tinted pink.

As well as being immensely tolerant of pruning, hollies withstand urban conditions, pollution and maritime exposure. They like moist but well-drained soil and dislike extreme drought or wet; variegations are best in sun. They are slow growing, at least initially, and as a general guide, the more yellow or white on a leaf, the slower it is. Boldly variegated types look good against dark backgrounds, such as yew (*Taxus*), laurustinus or Portugal laurel (*Prunus lusitanica*). Damp, warm spring or autumn weather is best for planting, and pot-grown plants are safer than root-balled ones, since holly does not transplant well. Reversion is a problem, especially with variegated forms having a central, rather than marginal variegation. Prune, if necessary, in spring and again, if required, in summer. Holly-leaf miner and aphids can be troublesome.

Like ivy, holly was thought to have the power to keep witches at bay, and its red berries were a special protection against evil. So strong were these ancient beliefs that they were absorbed into Christianity: the white blossom became a symbol of the birth of Christ, the red berries, prickly leaves and thorns represented the crown of thorns and Christ's blood.

purple young stems and very spiny leaves, edged and mottled deep yellow, with occasional all-yellow leaves or whole sprigs. It bears heavy crops of berries. The male 'Myrtifolia Aureomaculata' is a dense, compact form, with purple young bark and small, spiny, dark green leaves, shaded pale green and irregularly splashed in gold. The male 'Ovata Aurea' has unusually thick, short-spined, leathery leaves edged in gold, and deep purple twigs. The male 'Silver Milkboy', or 'Argentea Medio-picta' has dark green spiny leaves, with a central splash of creamy white. 'Silver Milkmaid' is similar; some catalogues list them as synonymous. The male 'Silver Queen', or 'Argentea Regina', has dark purple young shoots and dark green leaves marbled grey and broadly edged in white.

JUNIPERUS

Junipers are tough, hardy and tolerant of drought and lime, making them especially valuable on chalk soils. Growth habit and size vary enormously, from tall and narrowly columnar to prostrate, according to species and cultivar. The three variegated forms listed below are low and widespreading, ideal for overhanging paving, a sunny bank, rock garden or retaining wall.

The foliage has two forms: large, tapered and pointed juvenile leaves and scale-like or linear adult leaves. Sometimes adult and juvenile are carried on the same plant. The

Family: Cupressaceae
Height: 60cm-1.5m (2-5ft)
Spread: 1.5-1.8m (5-6ft)
Flowering time: Flowers insignificant
Aspect: Sun
Soil: Well drained
Minimum temperature: −18°C (0°F)

foliage has a characteristic, pungent aroma when crushed. The grey-green berries produced on female plants if pollinated by a nearby male plant are used to flavour gin.

Juniperus davurica 'Expansa Variegata', the variegated Dahurian juniper, is also sold as *J. chinensis* or *J. squamata* 'Expansa Variegata' and *J. c.* or *J. s.* 'Parsonii'. It is a dwarf, wide-spreading, mounded shrub, 60cm (2ft) high, with thick, ascending branches of grey-green, coarse adult and fine juvenile, foliage that is flecked creamy white at the tips. 'Expansa Aureospicata' is similar, but with yellow splashes. Both are vulnerable to winter frosts. *J.* × *media* 'Blue and Gold' is semi-prostrate, 1.2-1.5m (4-5ft) high, with upward arching sprays of blue-grey foliage splashed with creamy yellow. It is vulnerable to frost and hot sun.

Mid-spring, shallow planting is best, and after hard frosts, check and re-firm the root-ball, if necessary. In winter shake heavy snow off the branches, to prevent them breaking under the snow's weight.

Juniperus davurica 'Expansa Variegata'

KERRIA JAPONICA 'VARIEGATA'

Also sold as *K. j.* 'Picta', the variegated Jew's mallow forms a spreading, suckering mass of bright green, arching stems, clothed in pale, grey-green leaves deeply and irregularly margined in white. The single, pale yellow, buttercup-like flowers are carried all spring long on one-year-old wood. Though the shrub is deciduous, the bright green stems add a cheerful touch in winter.

The variegated form is less hardy than the green-leaved kerria, and in cold gardens benefits from the protection of a wall, which encourages taller growth. If necessary, thin out old flowered shoots after flowering.

Family: Rosaceae
Height: 60-90cm (2-3ft)
Spread: 90cm (3ft)
Flowering time: Spring
Aspect: Sun or light shade
Soil: Well drained
Minimum temperature: −18°C (0°F)

Right: Ligustrum ovalifolium 'Aureum' in a mixed planting

Top: Lavatera arborea 'Variegata'

Above: Leucothoe fontanesiana 'Rainbow'

LAVATERA ARBOREA 'VARIEGATA'

Family: Malvaceae

Height: 1.2-1.8m (4-6ft)

Spread: 60-90cm (2-3ft)

Flowering time: Summer

Aspect: Sun, shelter

Soil: Ordinary or light, well drained

Minimum temperature: −23°C (−10°F)

Tree mallow looks exactly like a small tree, with stout, erect, softwood stems, up to 5cm (2in) thick, carrying large, maple-like, densely felted leaves. In 'Variegata', the foliage is strikingly marked with white. The single, hollyhock-type, rose-purple flowers are veined in deeper purple, especially at the base, and carried on the upper 45-60cm (18-24in) of stem.

The species grows wild along sandy, rocky coasts of southern Europe, including Britain. Lavateras may be short-lived, but 'Variegata' can be easily propagated from cuttings.

LEUCOTHOE FONTANESIANA 'RAINBOW'

Family: Ericaceae

Height: 60-150cm (2-5ft)

Spread: 60-150cm (2-5ft)

Flowering time: Spring

Aspect: Light shade

Soil: Well drained, lime-free

Minimum temperature: −23°C (−10°F)

Formerly known as *Leucothoe catesbaei* and also commonly described as drooping leucothoe, the species is a graceful evergreen shrub, native of the south-eastern United States. Its arching, slightly zig-zagging branches carry long, tapering, leathery leaves and drooping racemes of white, lily-of-the-valley type flowers along the branches in spring. The variegated form, 'Rainbow', also known as 'Multicolor' or as 'Girard's Rainbow', after its American breeder, has leaves variegated creamy yellow and green. The young foliage is especially stunning, with pinky copper overtones, carried on crimson stems and leaf stalks. The mature foliage turns bronze-purple with the advent of cold weather in autumn.

Related to heather (*Erica*), leucothoe requires much the same conditions and looks good with heathers and other lime-hating members of the *Ericaceae* family, such as pieris, rhododendrons and kalmias. Spreading slowly by means of underground runners, it makes excellent but controllable ground cover in well-drained, moist, peaty soils, or sandy soils with leaf mould added. It is particularly effective planted above eye level, such as in a raised bed, so the flowers and elegant growth habit are more visible. Prune old stems back to ground level in early spring, from time to time, to rejuvenate.

It is long-lasting as cut foliage, and glycerines well.

LIGUSTRUM

Family: Oleaceae

Height: 1.8-9m (6-30ft)

Spread: 1.8-4.5m (6-15ft)

Flowering time: Late summer, autumn

Aspect: Sun or light shade

Soil: Well drained

Minimum temperature: −23°C (−10°F) to −12°C (10°F)

Privets are so tough and ubiquitous as quick-growing, twiggy suburban hedges, that they are undervalued for more ornamental uses. Left to grow naturally, many form handsome, large, loose shrubs or trees, with panicles of heavily scented white flowers in late summer and autumn, followed by blue-black berries. The scent, however, is not universally considered pleasant.

The oval foliage is evergreen or semi-evergreen, the latter usually lasting well into winter. The wax leaf privet, *Ligustrum lucidum*, a Chinese species, is considered the best evergreen privet, with large, glossy deep green leaves. It makes an erect, tall shrub, or an elegant, symmetrical tree up to 9m (30ft) high. The form 'Aureomarginatum' has leaves mottled and edged in strong yellow. The free-flowering 'Excelsum Superbum' has leaves margined and mottled with deep yellow and creamy white. 'Tricolor' has relatively narrow, pale and dark green leaves, which are thickly edged in white, tinged pink when young. It is very slow-growing and slightly tender, and does best in mild areas. The Chinese *L. sinense* 'Variegatum' is similar to but hardier than *L. lucidum* 'Tricolor', with creamy white-margined, light grey-green leaves and huge flower sprays.

The semi-evergreen Japanese oval-leaf privet, or California privet, *L. ovalifolium*, is the type commonly used for hedging. There are two variegated forms: 'Argenteum', with leaves margined with creamy white; and

Ligustrum lucidum 'Tricolor'

'Aureum', the golden privet, with green-centred, bright yellow leaves, occasionally all-yellow, but quick to revert.

Though privets tolerate poor soil and are often sited where little else will grow, such as under trees or in dark corners, they grow better, and retain their leaves better, in rich soil. They also tolerate hard-pruning, and can be used for topiary. Newly planted privet hedges should be cut back by half their height in spring, and thereafter new growth cut back by half annually in autumn, until the desired height is reached. Once established, hedges need several clippings per growing season.

Grafted forms need careful watching, to prevent all-green suckers taking over, and reversion among the top growth also occurs. Privets are among the easiest plants to propagate from stem cuttings, simply stripped of lower leaves and pushed into the ground.

LIQUIDAMBAR STYRACIFLUA

Family: Hamamelidaceae

Height: 15m (50ft)

Spread: 6m (20ft)

Flowering time: Spring

Aspect: Sun or light shade, shelter

Soil: Rich, moist, deep, lime-free

Minimum temperature: −23°C (−10°F)

The sweet gum, so called because of its fragrant resin, is not a tree for small gardens. Where space allows, however, this native of east-coast North America makes an impressive specimen tree, with a straight trunk and broadly columnar, slightly pyramidal crown. The brilliant purple, red and orange autumn leaf colouring is the main feature. The deeply lobed leaves are maple-like in appearance, but carried alternately, not opposite as with maples. The insignificant male and female flowers are carried on separate heads in spring. Variegated forms include 'Aurea', with yellow striped and mottled foliage; 'Golden Treasure', with yellow-margined leaves; and 'Variegata', or 'Silver King', with leaves margined creamy yellow, and flushed deep pink in late summer and autumn.

Sweet gum resents disturbance and can be difficult to establish; small, young container-grown plants are safest, but still need protection from late spring frosts and wind.

Liquidambar styraciflua 'Variegata'

Family: Magnoliaceae
Height: up to 18m (60ft)
Spread: 6m (20ft)
Flowering time: Summer
Aspect: Sun, shelter
Soil: Fertile, deep, moist, well drained
Minimum temperature: −29°C (−20°F)

Family: Myrtaceae
Height: 90cm-4.5m (3-15ft)
Spread: 90cm-3m (3-10ft)
Flowering time: Spring, summer or autumn
Aspect: Sun
Soil: Open, well drained loam
Minimum temperature: −6°C (20°F)

LIRIODENDRON TULIPFERA 'AUREOMARGINATA'

The variegated form of the North American tulip tree is smaller and slower growing than the stately species. Its unusual, square-cut, five-pointed, smooth leaves are broadly edged in yellow, deepening to yellow green as the season progresses and turning bright yellow in autumn before falling. Its yellowish green, tulip-shaped flowers, orange inside, are carried at a younger age than those of the species, which appear after ten or more years' growth. It dislikes root disturbance and is best planted in mid- or late spring.

MYRTUS

Myrtles are evergreen shrubs or trees, with glossy, aromatic foliage and fragrant white, sometimes pink-tinged flowers with prominent stamens. The flowers are carried singly or in small clusters, and much loved by bees. In favourable climates, flowers are followed by black, red or white berries, according to type.

Myrtus apiculata 'Glangleam Gold', also sold as *Luma apiculata* 'Glangleam Gold' or *Myrtus luma* 'Glangleam Gold', is the variegated form of a Chilean species, with foliage splashed and edged with yellow. The species eventually makes a considerable tree, with cinnamon-coloured outer, older bark flaking away to reveal creamy, inner, new bark, but 'Glangleam Gold' is more compact. Its flowers are carried in late summer or autumn, and followed by edible, sweet, red and black fruits.

M. communis, the common myrtle, is widespread in the Mediterranean and western Asia, its probable origin, and has long been cultivated. Its white flowers, with their central 'powder puff' of creamy white stamens, appear in late summer or early autumn, and are followed by black berries. The form 'Variegata', also sold as 'Tricolor', has grey-green foliage, finely edged with creamy white on older leaves, thickly and irregularly edged on younger leaves. *M. c. tarentina* 'Variegata', the variegated form of Tarentum myrtle, has smaller, narrower leaves, edged in white, and white berries. It is dainty and compact, rarely exceeding 90cm (3ft) high.

The variegated form of Chilean guava, *M. ugni* 'Variegata', is also sold as *Ugni molinae* 'Variegata' and *Eugenia ugni* 'Variegata'. It makes a small, slow-growing, erect shrub, up to 1.8m (6ft) high, with leathery leaves shaded grey and edged in creamy yellow. It flowers and fruits when relatively young; its waxy, pink bell flowers, carried in mid-spring, are followed by reddish-brown, highly scented, edible fruit, said to taste of wild strawberries. It is suitable for hedging.

Myrtles thrive in hot, sunny conditions and well-drained soil, though the Chilean forms dislike lime. They tolerate maritime exposure, but in cooler areas are best grown against a sunny, sheltered wall. Remove reverted shoots as soon as seen; in mid-spring, remove frost-damaged wood and prune hedges, pruning again as necessary.

The Victorians grew myrtle in tubs in cool greenhouses, moving the plants outdoors in summer, to ripen the wood. A sprig of myrtle, symbolizing love, was traditionally included in Victorian bridal bouquets; on arrival at her new home after the wedding, many a bride planted the sprig by the front door, in the hope that it would root and love would bless her marriage.

Top: Liriodendron tulipfera 'Aureomarginata'

Above: A close-up of Liriodendron tulipfera 'Aureomarginata'

OSMANTHUS HETEROPHYLLUS

Family: Oleaceae
Height: 1.5-1.8m (5-6ft)
Spread: 1.5-1.8m (5-6ft)
Flowering time: Autumn
Aspect: Sun or light shade
Soil: Well drained
Minimum temperature: —18°C (0°F)

This slow-growing evergreen shrub or small tree is Japanese in origin. It so resembles the holly that its common name is false holly and it was once classified as *Ilex heterophyllus*, though the genus is more closely related to the olive. The leaves are glossy and variable, some densely spiny, others smooth-edged; these are always carried in pairs, unlike holly leaves, which grow alternately on the branches. Clusters of small, fragrant, white flowers appear in the leaf axils in early autumn and are followed, in favourable climates, by olive-like fruits. Variegated forms include 'Aureomarginatus', also sold as 'Aureovariegatus' and 'Aureus', with deep yellow margins; 'Argenteomarginatus', or 'Variegatus', with creamy white margins; 'Goshiki', or 'Tricolor', with yellow, pink and green leaves; and 'Latifolius Variegatus', with broad, silver-variegated leaves.

Osmanthus prefers sun or light shade and well-drained soil. It stands clipping well and makes good hedging, as well as topiary, although flowering is much reduced as a result.

Osmanthus heterophyllus 'Argenteomarginatus'

PACHYSANDRA TERMINALIS 'VARIEGATA'

Family: Buxaceae
Height: 15-30cm (6-12in)
Spread: 40-60cm (16-24in)
Flowering time: Late winter or early spring
Aspect: Sun or light shade
Soil: Light, lime-free
Minimum temperature: —23°C (—10°F)

Although technically a dwarf shrub, this prostrate, soft-wooded evergreen is often placed with the herbaceous plants in garden centres. It is also known as *P. t.* 'Silver Edge', and its common name, Japanese spurge, refers to the spurge-like appearance of the leaf rosettes, which resemble those of *Euphorbia robbiae*. The rosettes are made up of diamond-shaped, toothed leaves, grey-green edged with creamy white, and are carried at the ends of the stems; the variegated form often has slightly twisted, puckered growth, absent in the species. Each rosette lasts two or three years, with a short

Philadelphus coronarius 'Variegatus'

length of bare stem growing between rosettes. The tiny, greenish-white or purple, lightly scented, petal-less flowers, female at the base of the flower spike, male above, are produced on the previous year's shoots, in late winter or early spring.

It spreads steadily by underground runners and its main use is as large-scale, carpeting ground cover, especially under trees. In many areas of the United States, it is so reliable that it is used as a substitute for grass. Though dry shade is tolerated, moist shade is better and young plants need a steady supply of moisture until established. Slugs can be troublesome.

It is valuable material in cut flower arrangements, and glycerines well.

PHILADELPHUS

Family: Philadelphaceae
Height: 1.5-2.4m (5-8ft)
Spread: 1.5-2.4m (5-8ft)
Flowering time: Early summer
Aspect: Light shade, shelter
Soil: Well drained
Minimum temperature:
—23°C (—10°F)

The mock orange is so-called for its sweetly scented white blooms, which briefly bridge the gap between spring and summer flowers. Confusingly, it has another common name, syringa, which is also the generic name for lilac. The foliage of plain green species is coarse and dull; the variegated forms are altogether more attractive, although the flowers are less visible against the backdrop of green and white.

Philadelphus coronarius 'Variegatus' is an old, heavily scented cultivar, one of the first to flower, that can eventually reach 2.4m (8ft) high and wide. The mid-green leaves are broadly edged and splashed with creamy white, with occasional bands of grey-green. Some leaves are all-white, creating a light, shimmery effect from some distance. *P. c.* 'Bowles Variegated' is so similar as to appear almost identical.

P. 'Innocence', sometimes sold as 'Innocence Variegatus', is one of many fine forms raised by the French nursery Lemoine, in the early 1900s. It grows 1.5m (5ft) high and wide. The small, dark green leaves are splashed and streaked with creamy yellow, and the profuse, single, creamy white flowers are highly scented.

Flowers are carried on short twigs on one-year-old shoots. To prune, every year or two remove the oldest, flowered branches after flowering, leaving the long, new shoots to provide next year's flowers. The growth habit of some forms is densely twiggy; thin the central twiggy growth in late summer or autumn, as necessary.

Any well-drained soil, including chalk, is fine, but variegated forms need shelter, water in dry weather and light shade; colours fade in deep shade, and full sun can cause leaf scorch. The young leaves are particularly vulnerable to frost, wind and spring drought.

The blossoms are traditional components of wedding floristry, but some people find the fragrance too sweet and overpowering, especially in a confined space indoors.

PHOTINIA GLABRA 'VARIEGATA'

Formerly sold as *Crataegus glabra* 'Variegata' and *Sorbus glabra* 'Variegata', and also known as 'Rosea Marginata' and 'Parfait', this Asiatic member of the rose family forms a medium-sized shrub with clusters of hawthorn-scented, pink-tinged, white spring flowers, followed in autumn by sparse red berries that turn to black. Its evergreen, oval leaves are dark green splashed with pink and pale yellow, and the young growth is pale green, rather like that of pieris.

'Variegata' is a valuable large shrub for a mixed or shrub border, providing colour and interest in winter. It is suitable for coastal planting, but is slow to establish and somewhat tender, and needs protection from cold winds.

Family: Rosaceae
Height: 3m (10ft)
Spread: 2.4m (8ft)
Flowering time: Late spring to early summer
Aspect: Sun or light shade, shelter
Soil: Warm, light
Minimum temperature:
—12°C (10°F)

Photinia glabra 'Variegata'

PICEA MARIANA 'AUREOVARIEGATA'

Most people know the spruce genus from the familiar Christmas tree, or Norway spruce, *Picea abies*. *P. mariana* 'Aureovariegata' is a dwarf variegated form of the black spruce, a native of east-coast North America. It slowly makes an erect, broadly triangular column of dense, silvery green needles tipped in gold. These are arranged spirally on the shoots, creating an all-over golden glow.

Provide cool, moist root conditions, shelter and full sun; it dislikes air pollution and shallow, limy soils. It makes a good focal point for a rock garden, or among a collection of dwarf conifers.

Family: Pinaceae
Height: 90cm (3ft)
Spread: 90cm (3ft)
Flowering time: Non-flowering
Aspect: Sun
Soil: Moist but well drained
Minimum temperature:
—34°C (—30°F)

white-variegated leaves, flushed pink when young. Ideal for a rock garden, its only drawback is its shyness to flower.

P. j. 'Variegata' is a larger, older form. Its relatively small, narrow, grey-green leaves are edged in white, especially near the apex, and flushed pink. Also slow-growing, especially when young, it eventually reaches 2.1m (7ft) or more in height.

Pieris is related to rhododendron, and needs much the same growing conditions: light shade and moist but well-drained, lime-free, peaty soil or loam enriched with leaf mould. Although the plant itself is hardy, the young spring growth can be damaged by frost and wind, so shelter is advisable.

Its oriental overtones invite plant partnership with rhododendrons, magnolias, camellias and bamboos, or just an under-planting of pachysandra. It is also a suitable specimen shrub for container growing, provided the growing medium never dries out. Pruning is rarely necessary but can be done as new growth starts.

Pieris japonica 'Variegata'

Family: Ericaceae
Height: 60cm-2.1m (2-7ft)
Spread: 60cm-2.1m (2-7ft)
Flowering time: Mid to late spring
Aspect: Light shade, shelter
Soil: Moist but well drained, lime-free
Minimum temperature: −23°C (−10°F)

PIERIS

Pieris is among the most popular of ever-green shrubs, furnished to the ground with branches of dense, narrow, glossy leaves, often pink or coppery when young. It carries cascades of sometimes scented, white or pink-tinged, lily-of-the-valley type flowers in spring, from pink buds formed in autumn.

The hybrid 'Flaming Silver', a sport of 'Forest Flame', is a new, dwarf Dutch intro-duction. The silver refers to its white-edged, narrow leaves; 'flaming' to the fiery red, young spring foliage which develops varie-gation as it matures. Very slow-growing, it may eventually reach 1.2m (4ft) high in ten years.

Pieris japonica 'Little Heath', another new introduction, is truly miniature. It makes a dense round shrub, up to 60cm (2ft) high and wide, with tiny, copper and creamy

PINUS DENSIFLORA 'OCULUS DRAGONIS'

The dragon eye pine makes a unique and eye-catching garden feature, one of the few variegated pines and certainly a treasure, although hard to obtain. The dark green, lustrous needles are each marked with two yellow bands – when seen from above, distinct yellow and green rings appear around a brown central bud or eye. The colouring is especially evident in summer and autumn, less clearly defined in winter.

It has a pleasing open habit, with trunk often leaning and crooked, branches spread-ing horizontally to form a broad, flat head; the bark colour is an attractive orange-red. It is relatively slow-growing. Well-drained, slightly acid soil is ideal, and an open, sunny position.

Family: Pinaceae
Height: 3m (10ft)
Spread: 3.5m (12ft)
Flowering time: Non-flowering
Aspect: Sun
Soil: Well drained, slightly acid
Minimum temperature: −29°C (−20°F)

PITTOSPORUM

Family: Pittosporaceae

Height: 1.2-6m (4-20ft)

Spread: 1.2-3m (4-10ft)

Flowering time: Spring

Aspect: Sun or light shade, shelter

Soil: Moist but well drained, light loam

Minimum temperature: −6°C (20°F)

These evergreen shrubs are slightly tender, some more so than others, and are grown mainly for their crisp, often wavy-edged foliage, with the scented flowers an added bonus. The cut foliage of *Pittosporum tenuifolium* is much used in floristry, often indiscriminately or as token greenery, which undervalues its real beauty. Pittosporums stand pruning well, and make good hedges or screens in mild or coastal gardens. In colder or exposed gardens, they are best grown as wall shrubs; they also make good container plants for patios and cool conservatories. They dislike badly drained soils and cold winds.

P. crassifolium 'Variegatum', the variegated form of New Zealand karo, eventually makes a dense, bushy shrub, 3-4.5m (10-15ft) high, slightly less across. Its attractive clusters of large, thick, leathery, green-grey leaves are edged in white and white-felted beneath. In cool climates, it definitely needs wall protection; its clusters of dark purple flowers, followed by white seed capsules, are only produced in favourable climates.

P. tenuifolium is a fast-growing New Zealand species, forming a broadly columnar shrub or tree up to 9m (30ft) or more in its native environment, less elsewhere. Its glossy, wavy-edged leaves have an attractive way of reflecting light, and contrast well with the black stems. In spring, tiny bell-shaped, purple-brown flowers emit a scent at night, variously described as unpleasantly rank or exquisitely honey-like. There are several variegated forms, all smaller than the species.

'Garnettii', raised in New Zealand, is often listed under *P. tenuifolium*, but is thought to be a hybrid. It is hardier than the similar 'Silver Queen' (see below) and its greeny grey leaves, edged in white and flushed pink in winter, are larger, broader and tougher, with a more distinct white margin. Its seedling progeny, 'Saundersii', is virtually identical.

P. t. 'Abbotsbury Gold' is a new introduction, with yellow-centred, green-margined leaves most effective on young growth. It is compact, growing 1.8-2.4m (6-8ft) high, less across. *P. t.* 'Irene Patterson', a very compact form up to 1.2m (4ft) high, has creamy white young foliage, marbled green and white when mature, and tinged pink in winter. *P. t.* 'Silver Queen' is an old, tall cultivar from the famous Slieve Donard Nursery, County Down, Ireland. Its pale, grey-green leaves have irregular white edges. *P. t.* 'Wendell Channon' is a recent introduction, with wavy-edged, green leaves edged in creamy white, tinged purple in winter. It has an open, loose habit and an expected height of 6m (20ft). It needs more shelter than most.

P. tobira 'Variegatum' is the variegated form of Japanese pittosporum, with tight, terminal whorls of large, leathery, polished, grey-green leaves, edged with silver. Showy clusters of conspicuous, creamy white flowers, becoming yellow with age, are carried in late spring or early summer; they have a heavy, orange-blossom scent. 'Variegatum' is on the borderline of hardiness and in cool climates makes a dome-shaped shrub; in Mediterranean regions and warmer areas of Australia and the United States, it can reach tree-like proportions, up to 6m (20ft) high. It is often grown as hedging, valuable for its drought resistance. In cold climates it makes a good greenhouse or conservatory shrub, put outdoors through summer to ripen the wood, and given full light all year round. Grown under glass, it flowers in winter.

Pittosporum tenuifolium 'Saundersii'

Pittosporum tenuifolium 'Silver Queen'

POPULUS CANDICANS 'AURORA'

Family: Salicaceae

Height: up to 9m (30ft)

Spread: 1.8-3m (6-10ft)

Flowering time: Flowers insignificant

Aspect: Sun, light shade

Soil: All except shallow chalk

Minimum temperature: −23°C (−10°F)

Prunus laurocerasus 'Variegata'

Family: Rosaceae

Height: 1.8-3m (6-10ft)

Spread: 2.4-3.5m (8-12ft)

Flowering time: Spring or early summer

Aspect: Sun or light shade

Soil: Well drained

Minimum temperature: −18°C (0°F) to −12°C (10°F)

Formerly *P. candicans* 'Variegata', this all-female form of Ontario poplar or balm of Gilead is one of the more popular variegated woody plants. It makes a broad-headed, suckering tree with upright branches, but can be pollarded hard annually, in late winter or early spring, to form a columnar shrub, with more intense, concentrated colouring. Left to grow naturally, variegation tends to occur mainly at the top of the tree. The young, heart-shaped leaves, downy grey and conspicuously veined beneath, vary enormously. Some are all green, others are brightly edged or marbled creamy white and pink, and others still are all white. They gradually turn green as the season progresses, in contrast to later new growth.

The sticky, yellow resinous bud scales are heavily balsam-scented in spring, when the leaves, narrow at first, are unfolding and the tree or shrub continues to scent the air through summer.

It is easy to grow, in any soil in sun or light shade, but vulnerable to canker. Like all poplars, it is best kept well away from house foundations, soakaways and drainpipes, especially on clay soils.

PRUNUS

Evergreen members of the *Prunus* genus tend to take second place to the deciduous flowering cherries, popularly grown for their showy blossoms. Nonetheless, they are valuable foliage shrubs or small trees. Both evergreen species have smaller, denser and slower-growing variegated forms.

Prunus laurocerasus, commonly called the cherry laurel or English laurel, has large, glossy, oblong leaves, bright green but darkening with age. In 'Variegata', also sold as 'Marbled White' and 'Castlewellan', the leaves are smaller, and are mottled and

Populus candicans 'Aurora'

edged in grey and creamy white, some being almost entirely white. The rare 'Taff's Golden Gleam' has yellow-splashed leaves. Though eye-catching from a distance, both yellow- and white-variegated forms are curious, rather than beautiful. The candlestick-like, erect racemes of dull white flowers are carried in the leaf axils in mid-spring, and are followed by purple-black fruits. Shallow, chalky soil is unsuitable, causing chlorosis.

P. lusitanica 'Variegata', a variegated form of the Portugal laurel, is much more subtle, and hardier. Its pointed, oval, dark green leaves have thin white margins with transitional patches of grey-green, set off in winter by a rose-pink overall tint, rich red stems and leaf stalks. Its erect racemes of small, white, hawthorn-scented flowers are carried in early summer. It prefers warm, well-drained soil, and tolerates chalk. Prune if necessary after flowering.

Both forms of laurel glycerine well for inclusion in dried flower arrangements.

PYRACANTHA

Family: Rosaceae
Height: 60cm-2.4m (2-8ft)
Spread: 1.2-2.4m (4-8ft)
Flowering time: Spring
Aspect: Sun or light shade, shelter
Soil: Well drained
Minimum temperature: −18°C (0°F)

Pyracanthas are evergreens closely related to cotoneaster, but are easily identified by their thorns (the common name is firethorn) and toothed leaves. Their profuse crops of colourful berries and tolerance of hard pruning make the green-leaved forms among the most popular wall-trained shrubs, but only one of the variegated cultivars below, 'Mohave Silver', is vigorous enough to be used in this way, and to fruit reliably.

'Harlequin' has leaves edged and splashed in creamy green, flushed pink in cold weather, and sparse, red-orange berries. It slowly reaches a height of 1.8m (6ft). 'Mohave Silver' is the hardiest variegated cultivar, with white splashed leaves, a strong growth habit, and orange-red berries. 'Sparkler' forms a sprawling plant, 60cm (2ft) high, and twice that across. Its leaves are heavily splashed with white, again sometimes

Left: Prunus lusitanica 'Variegata'

Quercus cerris 'Variegata'

tinged pink in autumn and winter. So far, it has proved shy to flower and fruit and is fairly tender.

Warm, light or ordinary, well-drained soil and shelter are ideal; heavy soils are unsuitable. All dislike root disturbance, and are best planted as young, pot-grown specimens. Shorten the new season's growth after flowering, if pruning is necessary. Fruit crops are likely to be taken by birds.

QUERCUS CERRIS 'VARIEGATA'

Family: Fagaceae
Height: 9m (30ft)
Spread: 4.5m (15ft)
Flowering time: Spring
Aspect: Sun or light shade
Soil: Well drained, including chalk
Minimum temperature: −18°C (0°F)

This is a slow-growing sport of the quick-growing Turkey oak; the creamy white leaf margins are variable in width, sometimes extending to the centre of the leaf. It is prone to reversion and must be watched carefully, but makes a handsome specimen tree on a lawn.

RHAMNUS ALATERNUS 'ARGENTEOVARIEGATA'

Family: Rhamnaceae
Height: 3m (10ft)
Spread: 2.4m (8ft)
Flowering time: Spring
Aspect: Sun
Soil: Ordinary or poor, warm
Minimum temperature: −12°C (10°F)

Few members of this genus have any garden merit, but the variegated form of Italian buckthorn, *Rhamnus alaternus* 'Argenteovariegata', does. It forms a rounded shrub with small, narrow, evergreen leaves, conspicuously edged in creamy white, and marbled grey and green. They are glossy on both sides and occasionally puckered. The tiny, yellow-green flowers are inconspicuous but are followed by red berries that later turn black.

The species is Mediterranean in origin, found on rocky terrain, especially limestone. These plants are good for seaside planting and tolerant of most well-drained soils, and of pollution, but are unsuitable for cold, windy inland areas. They dislike root disturbance and only young, pot-grown specimens should be used. They are rapid growing and hard pruning causes no harm.

RHODODENDRON

Family: Ericaceae
Height: 1.2-1.8m (4-6ft)
Spread: 1.2-1.8m (4-6ft)
Flowering time: Mid to late spring
Aspect: Sun or light shade
Soil: Well drained, acid
Minimum temperature: −18°C (0°F)

Evergreen rhododendron foliage is largely so dull that its inclusion may seem odd, but there are three interesting variegated forms. One is the variegated form of pontic rhododendron, the bane of English gardeners, foresters and conservationists. Introduced to Britain in the mid-eighteenth century and once planted as game covert, *Rhododendron ponticum* became firmly naturalized, especially on light, acid soil or where the native vegetation was once disturbed by fire or supplanted by large-scale conifer crops. It was also used as rootstocks for grafting, and with its vigorous, suckering habit, often overtook the named varieties altogether. Self seeding and impervious to hard pruning, it is almost impossible to eradicate.

R. p. 'Variegatum' is much more polite. Its smaller, narrower and tidier leaves are dark green with creamy white margins,

suffused rich red-purple in winter. As in the species, its lilac-pink flower clusters appear in late spring. The form 'Aucubifolium', with yellow-spotted leaves, seems to have disappeared from cultivation.

R. 'President Roosevelt' is a slow-growing, open cultivar, eventually reaching 1.8m (6ft) high and wide. Its lax, drooping branches carry dark green leaves randomly streaked with yellow, and bell-shaped, frilly pink flowers in mid to late spring. Reversion is a problem.

R. 'Silver Sword', a member of the *R. kaempferi*, or hybrid azalea, group, has deep green leaves irregularly margined with creamy white, and bright rosy scarlet flowers. It is semi-evergreen in cold climates, and somewhat slow-growing. Provide moist but well-drained soil, light shade and shelter.

Rhododendron ponticum 'Variegatum'

RIBES AMERICANUM 'VARIEGATUM'

Family: Grossulariaceae
Height: 90-120cm (3-4ft)
Spread: 90-120cm (3-4ft)
Flowering time: Spring
Aspect: Sun or light shade
Soil: Well drained
Minimum temperature: −23°C (−10°F)

The variegated form of American black-currant, a native of the eastern United States, has three-to-five-lobed, coarsely toothed, deciduous leaves, mottled pale creamy white and green and colouring well in autumn. Glands on the leaf undersides produce the characteristic, heavy, musky odour. Racemes of insignificant yellow flowers are followed by black fruit.

If necessary, thin out old wood in spring, after flowering. It is vulnerable to aphids and, in the US, to white pine blister rust; cultivation is forbidden in certain areas.

Rhamnus alaternus 'Argenteovariegata' in a parterre planting at the Royal Botanic Gardens, Kew.

ROSA WICHURAIANA 'VARIEGATA'

Family: Rosaceae
Height: 15cm (6in)
Spread: 3.5m (12ft)
Flowering time: Late summer
Aspect: Sun or light shade
Soil: Well drained, sandy
Minimum temperature: −23°C (−10°F)

The species, a vigorous, semi-evergreen rambler, is the parent of numerous rambler hybrids, including 'Albertine', 'American Pillar', 'Dorothy Perkins' and 'Alberic Barbier'. Its long, almost thornless, lax stems carry highly polished leaves made of five, seven or nine, round to oval leaflets, and small conical clusters of single, white, richly scented flowers in late summer, followed by tiny, round, red hips. Often used as quick-growing ground cover, especially on dry banks or sandy soil, in the United States it is known as the 'memorial rose', for its popularity as grave planting. It can also be trained up trees or over a pergola or trellis.

'Variegata' is almost as vigorous, with new shoots creamy white, tinged pink. As the leaves expand, they become green, markedly splashed and edged in creamy white. Foliage on older stems becomes dull and untidy; and hard pruning, annually or even twice annually, produces the showiest colour, but much reduces the plant's value as ground cover.

A close-up of Rubus fruticosus 'Variegatus'

Family: Rosaceae
Height: 15cm-1.8m (6in-6ft)
Spread: 1.8m (6ft)
Flowering time: Summer
Aspect: Light shade
Soil: Well drained, rich
Minimum temperature: −18°C (0°F)

RUBUS FRUTICOSUS 'VARIEGATUS'

Bramble or blackberry is a tenacious weed, but ornamental forms include the self-descriptive 'Parsley-leaved' and 'Variegatus', with graphic white edges to the dark green leaflets. 'Variegatus' can be trained against a wall as a climber or allowed to scramble as tidy 15cm (6in) high ground cover in a wild or woodland garden. Cut back older canes in autumn, to encourage formation of young shoots with fresh foliage; replace old plants with node- or tip-rooted shoots. Any well drained soil suffices, but light shade is necessary, to keep the margins from scorching.

RUTA GRAVEOLENS 'VARIEGATA'

Family: Rutaceae
Height: 60cm (24in)
Spread: 60cm (24in)
Flowering time: Flowers insignificant
Aspect: Full sun
Soil: Light, well drained, dry
Minimum temperature: −29°C (−20°F)

The evergreen species, usually represented by the steely blue 'Jackman's Blue', is almost universally admired for its mounds of lacy, rounded, pinnate compound leaves. 'Variegata', 60cm (2ft) high and wide, has random, creamy white variegation, especially on young growth, to some eyes, disrupting the natural sense of order of the already intricate, filigree foliage. The variegation fades as the season progresses.

Light, dry, well-drained soil, ideally chalky or sandy, suits it best; heavy clay soils are deadly. It also prefers full sun. Grow in herb gardens, container gardens, open beds and borders, and as an edging plant or low hedge. It associates equally well with grey-, golden- and purple-leaved subjects, especially those with bold, chunky or sword-shaped leaves.

Cut back hard every spring, to encourage compact, fresh-coloured growth; old plants tend to get woody, straggly and leafless at the base. Nip out the insignificant, greenish-yellow flowers that appear in early or mid-summer, to keep the plant compact. Propagate from cuttings. An ancient herb, it was once used to keep witches and infection away, and the bitter-tasting leaves were used medicinally. The sap can cause skin rashes.

SALIX

Family: Salicaceae
Height: 1.2-2.4m (4-8ft)
Spread: 1.2-2.4m (4-8ft)
Flowering time: Spring
Aspect: Sun or light shade
Soil: Ordinary, moist
Minimum temperature: −23°C (−10°F)

Most willows are useful and reliable rather than showy garden plants. The variegated forms are not spectacular, but worth considering if space allows. Willows are deciduous trees that bear male and female flowers on separate plants.

Salix caprea 'Variegata' is a rare form of great sallow or goat willow, common in European woods and hedgerows. The male form is also called 'palm' and collected for decorating homes at Easter, when its large, yellow cat-

Salix integra 'Albo Maculata'

grafted onto a 1.5m (5ft) stem to form a standard, enchanting but expensive. Provide shelter and light shade if the soil is dry.

SAMBUCUS NIGRA

The hardy, deciduous common elder, a native of Europe, North Africa and western Asia, is a coarse but characterful shrub or small tree. Its leaves are composed of three, five or seven leaflets and its flat heads of heavily fragrant white flowers, 10-15cm (4-6in) across, are followed by dense clusters of shiny black berries.

Golden-leaved elders are the most popular cultivars, but there are three variegated options, all attractive against dark backgrounds. 'Albomarginata', 'Albovariegata' and 'Marginata' are different names for the same form, with leaves irregularly edged in creamy white. 'Aureovariegata', or 'Aureomarginata', has irregular, bright yellow leaf margins. The less vigorous 'Pulverulenta' produces white new shoots, heavily dotted with green. The leaves mature to green, splashed, striped and mottled with white; as is sometimes the case with this type of variegation, leaves can be puckered.

Elders tolerate most aspects and soil types, but need to be well supplied with moisture where grown in hot sun. For the lushest-looking foliage, prune annually before growth starts, cutting back lateral branches a little above the previous year's growth.

Elder flowers are much visited by insects and used in the making of wine and eye and skin lotions; the berries, much loved by birds, are also used to make wines, jellies and medicinal syrups, and taken as herbal remedies for colds. In folklore, elder wood is both evil and a talisman against evil. Cradles were never made of elder wood, for example, or fairies would snatch the infant; but hearse drivers used elder-wood handles for their horse whips, to keep away evil spirits associated with the dead.

Family: Caprifoliaceae
Height: 2.4-3m (8-10ft)
Spread: 2.4-3m (8-10ft)
Flowering time: Early summer
Aspect: Sun or light shade, shelter
Soil: Ordinary, moist
Minimum temperature: −23°C (−10°F)

Sambucus nigra 'Pulverulenta'

kins are out; the female is the familiar pussy willow, with silvery catkins. 'Variegata' has grey-green leaves margined in creamy yellow, with woolly undersides; it retains its variegations through summer. It grows 1.8-2.4m (6-8ft) high, less across. In sun, it needs moist soil.

S. cinerea 'Variegata', or 'Tricolor', is a form of grey sallow. Its grey-green oval leaves, hairy beneath, are blotched yellow and white and tinged pink; the colouring, combined with a puckered leaf texture, can look rather unnatural. It makes a spreading shrub, 1.8-2.4m (6-8ft) high and wide.

S. integra 'Albo Maculata', or 'Hakuro-nishiki', has polished, slightly drooping branches carrying pale pink young shoots in late spring. The shoots open into green and silvery white leaves, the variegations lasting through summer. It grows 1.2-1.8m (4-6ft) high, but for the most colourful foliage can be stooled annually, cut down to within 15cm (6in) of ground level in spring. It is sometimes

SPIRAEA

Family: Rosaceae

Height: 90cm-1.5m (3-5ft)

Spread: 1.2-1.5m (4-5ft)

Flowering time: Spring or early summer

Aspect: Sun

Soil: Ordinary, moist

Minimum temperature: −23°C (−10°F)

Stachyurus chinensis 'Magpie'

These hardy deciduous shrubs are largely grown for their starry flowers, which produce a glorious but brief spring show. The plain green forms are dull for months thereafter, but the variegated forms, both relatively recent introductions, provide interest well into late autumn, when their leaves finally fall. Once established, prune away oldest and weakest stems after flowering.

Spiraea thunbergii 'Mount Fuji' eventually grows 90cm (3ft) high, 120cm (4ft) wide. Like the species, it has a twiggy, bushy habit, and flowers before the leaves appear. These are small and narrow; some are all-white, a few are all-green and most are misted, mottled or banded with white.

S. × *vanhouttei* 'Pink Ice', also listed under *S. japonica* 'Pink Ice', has white spring shoots suffused with pink, which turn creamy white and then develop into green leaves heavily mottled with white and tinged pink. Clusters of white flowers appear all along the arching branches in late spring or early summer. The dense thickets of wiry stems make an excellent hedge, 90-150cm (3-5ft) high and wide. Like the species it can be grown in pots in a greenhouse for gentle forcing.

STACHYURUS CHINENSIS 'MAGPIE'

Family: Stachyuraceae

Height: 1.5m-1.8m (5-6ft)

Spread: 1.5-1.8m (5-6ft)

Flowering time: Late winter to early spring

Aspect: Sun or light shade, shelter

Soil: Rich, acid

Minimum temperature: −18°C (0°F)

Like the more popular witch hazel (*Hamamelis*) and corylopsis, *Stachyurus chinensis* is grown for its yellow flowers carried on two-year-old leafless stems. The translucent, cowslip-like flowers, which hang in racemes up to 15cm (6in) long, are remarkably weather-resistant, though not scented. The brown buds form in autumn, and lengthen and swell visibly during mild spells in autumn and winter.

'Magpie' came from the famous English

Symphoricarpos orbiculatus 'Variegatus'

nursery Hillier, in the 1940s. It has shiny, ovate, grey-green leaves, splashed light green and tinged rose, with irregular, creamy white, serrated edges.

Rich, acid soil is ideal, but neutral or slightly alkaline ones can be made acceptable by adding plenty of leaf mould or peat. The shrub has a spreading habit and can be trained against a sheltered wall, to protect the young growth from spring frosts. It needs a steady supply of moisture in summer if grown in full sun.

STRANVAESIA DAVIDIANA 'PALETTE'

Family: Rosaceae
Height: 1.8-2.4m (6-8ft)
Spread: 1.8-2.4m (6-8ft)
Flowering time: Early summer
Aspect: Sun or light shade, shelter
Soil: Fertile, well drained, light
Minimum temperature: −23°C (−10°F)

Also sold as *Photinia davidiana* 'Palette', this erect-growing evergreen displays vivid seasonal changes. The bright, reddish-pink young shoots develop into lance-shaped, leathery leaves brightly splashed with green, pink and creamy white. In autumn, the oldest leaves turn brilliant red and remain on the tree over winter, contrasting well with the young, green foliage. Hawthorn-like white flowers in early summer can be followed by clusters of round, vermilion berries, which last until the first hard frost, but it can be shy to fruit.

It tolerates atmospheric pollution and chalk, but dislikes prolonged or severe wind and frost. On dry soil, provide some shade.

SYMPHORICARPOS ORBICULATUS

Family: Caprifoliaceae
Height: 90-150cm (3-5ft)
Spread: 90-120cm (3-4ft)
Flowering time: Late summer
Aspect: Sun or light shade
Soil: No special requirement
Minimum temperature: −23°C (−10°F)

The Indian currant or coralberry is less well known than *Symphoricarpos albus*, or snowberry, so called from its marble-like, long-lasting white fruits. *S. orbiculatus* has flowers insignificant for display, though they are rich in nectar and much-loved by bees; its rosy purple berries are very small, almost bead-like, and produced in clusters along the

wiry, arching stems, following hot summers. A hardy, deciduous North American native, *S. orbiculatus* has two variegated forms, neither as fruitful as the species but both more attractive in leaf.

'Variegatus', also sold as 'Aureovariegatus' or 'Foliis Variegatis', is more common. Its dainty, oval leaves are smaller than those of the species and irregularly edged in yellow. 'Argenteovariegatus', also sold as 'Albovariegatus' or 'Taff's Silver Edge', is similar, but with white-edged leaves. Both grow in almost any soil, even among tree roots, and in sun or light shade, but reversion is a problem in shade. For the freshest-looking growth, prune back hard in early spring, to 30cm (12in) above ground. The plants rarely sucker, but self-layering sometimes occurs.

Syringa emodi 'Variegata'

SYRINGA

Lilacs have notoriously dull foliage but there are two exceptions. The old, rare, variegated form of *Syringa vulgaris* has fragrant, double, mid-lilac blooms and centrally blotched, lime-yellow foliage, edged in green. It throws up suckers but these are also variegated.

The equally rare, variegated form of the vigorous Himalayan lilac, *S. emodi* 'Variegata', has oval, pale green leaves up to 20cm (8in) long, with irregular dark green central patches and silvery undersides. Its flowers are white, opening from pale lilac buds, unpleasantly scented and appearing later than those of *S. vulgaris* and its cultivars.

Both dislike cold, heavy soils. If practical, and as for all lilacs, remove the faded flowers before they set seed, and thin tangled growth then as well. Pruning in late winter or early spring is counter-productive, as flowers form on the previous year's wood.

Family: Oleaceae
Height: 1.8-2.4m (6-8ft)
Spread: 1.8-2.4m (6-8ft)
Flowering time: Summer
Aspect: Sun, shelter
Soil: Well drained, fertile, including chalk
Minimum temperature: −18°C (0°F)

TAXUS BACCATA

Family: Taxaceae
Height: 1.5-4.5m (5-15ft)
Spread: 1.8-2.4m (6-8ft)
Flowering time: Flowers insignificant
Aspect: Sun or light shade
Soil: Well drained
Minimum temperature: −23°C (−10°F)

The common or English yew is usually grown as a hedge, invaluable as a dark setting for paler or more colourful plants. A slow-growing, long-lived evergreen, it is tolerant of most soils and aspects, including heavy shade. Plants are usually either male or female; seeds and foliage are both poisonous. None of the following variegated forms is suitable as hedging, but all make excellent rock-garden subjects or focal points in a lawn or shrub border, according to size.

'Argentea Minor', or 'Dwarf White', is a very slow-growing female with drooping branches. The foliage is narrowly margined in white. After thirty years, it may reach a height and spread of 1.5m (5ft). 'Elegantissima' is a popular golden yew, Victorian in origin. It forms a large, dense shrub, 3m (10ft) or more high, 1.8m (6ft) across, with ascending branches. The young foliage is yellow, but later becomes green-centred with straw yellow margins.

'Fastigiata Aureomarginata' is a male, golden-variegated form of Irish yew, narrowly columnar when young but eventually forming a broad column up to 4.5m (15ft) high, 1.8-2.4m (6-8ft) wide, of densely packed, upright branches. The foliage is margined bright yellow, but becomes dull with age.

In ancient English folklore, yew was assigned powerful, protective powers and planted next to many a farmhouse and cottage, to protect its occupants from evil.

*Teucrium scorodonia
'Crispum Marginatum'*

TEUCRIUM

Family: Labiatae
Height: 23-30cm (9-12in)
Spread: 23-30cm (9-12in)
Flowering time: Summer
Aspect: Sun
Soil: Light, well drained
Minimum temperature: −23°C (−10°F)

Germanders include herbaceous plants as well as woody ones. Sub-shrubs, such as the evergreen variegated forms below, are intermediate between the two.

Teucrium chamaedrys, or wall germander, is a sub-shrub with a woody base, herbaceous top and creeping rootstock. The form 'Variegatum' has aromatic, deep green, polished leaves edged and splashed in creamy white, and rosy purple, lipped flowers in summer. It makes good edging, especially in a formal herb garden.

T. scorodonia 'Crispum Marginatum', the variegated wood sage or wood germander, makes dense tufts of small, wrinkled, suede-textured leaves, with ruffled, parsley-like edges beaded in white. In winter, the leaves take on purple overtones. Spikes of tiny, creamy white flowers appear in midsummer on 30cm (12in) high stems. The plant is slow-spreading and ground-hugging, and makes good ground cover on sunny banks or around shrubs. It also enjoys much the same conditions as heathers (*Erica*), and contrasts well with their spiky forms.

Both forms are sun-loving and thrive in light, even poor, warm well-drained soil.

THUJA PLICATA

Family: Cupressaceae
Height: 6m (20ft)
Spread: 3m (10ft)
Flowering time: Non-flowering
Aspect: Sun, shelter
Soil: Well drained
Minimum temperature: −34°C (−30°F)

Plants of this genus are also known as arbor vitae. They usually form dense, conical trees with flattened, fan-shaped sprays of foliage which has a distinct, fruity aroma when bruised or crushed. *Thuja plicata* is known as giant arbor vitae or western red cedar, from its origins in western North America. The species and its two variegated cultivars, among the tallest golden conifers, are narrowly conical trees, excellent as specimens on a lawn, but needing shelter from cold winds.

T. p. 'Irish Gold' has sprays of green foliage banded and flecked with deep yellow

Taxus baccata 'Fastigiata Aureomarginata'

on the current year's shoots, when grown in full sun. 'Zebrina', or 'Aureovariegata', is a similar but older Victorian form, with creamy yellow variegations. In both, the variegations are so pronounced that the trees look yellow from a distance.

Provide shelter from winds; young plants are vulnerable to sun scorch.

TSUGA CANADENSIS

The following, slow-growing variegated forms of eastern hemlock are good candidates for a rock garden or mixed planting of dwarf conifers. 'Dwarf Whitetip' makes a small, widely conical shrub. Its new spring shoots are brilliant white, but eventually fade to green in late summer. 'Gentsch White' forms a flattened globe, 1.2m (4ft) high and wide, with glossy dark green foliage, but young tip growth is a striking silvery white, which is maintained throughout the year. Colouring is improved by light pruning as new growth begins in early spring.

They thrive in full sun, but tolerate light shade, and in moist but well-drained, loamy soil. Some shelter is desirable; they are not suited to an open, windswept site.

Family: Pinaceae
Height: 90-150cm (3-5ft)
Spread: 90-150cm (3-5ft)
Flowering time: Non-flowering
Aspect: Sun or light shade, shelter
Soil: Rich, moist, well drained
Minimum temperature: −29°C (−20°F)

ULMUS

Elms are noted for their hardiness and ability to thrive in most soils and exposed positions. The Chinese elm, *Ulmus parvifolia*, is relatively disease-resistant, and provides two variegated forms. Their shiny, doubly toothed, leathery leaves remain well into winter or, in mild climates, until new shoots appear.

The form 'Frosty' is a slow-growing shrub, up to 90cm (3ft) high and wide, with tiny, toothed leaves densely packed on the shoots. The leaves start the season white-edged, but the variegation gradually shrinks

Family: Ulmaceae
Height: 90cm-35m (3-100ft)
Spread: 90cm (3ft) or 15m (50ft)
Flowering time: Spring or autumn
Aspect: Sun or light shade
Soil: Well drained
Minimum temperature: −23°C (−10°F)

Ulmus parvifolia 'Frosty'

VIBURNUM TINUS 'VARIEGATUM'

Viburnum tinus, also called laurustinus, is a broad-leafed evergreen, Mediterranean in origin. Long cultivated and a familiar component of mixed shrub plantings, the species is worthy rather than beautiful, tolerant of urban and maritime exposure, indifferent to limy soil and shade, and useful where rhododendrons and other evergreen lime-haters will not grow. It has dense, oval, dark green leaves; flat heads of small white flowers, opening from pink-tinged buds, appear from late autumn to early spring. The flowers are followed, after hot summers, by shiny metallic blue-black fruits.

'Variegatum' has showy yellow splashes and edges to the two-toned, pale green leaves. It is slower growing and more tender than the species, and benefits from the shelter of a warm wall; the leaves are liable to turn brown in extreme cold.

Family: Caprifoliaceae
Height: 1.2-1.8m (4-6ft)
Spread: 1.2-1.8m (4-6ft)
Flowering time: Autumn to spring
Aspect: Sun or light shade
Soil: Ordinary
Minimum temperature: −12°C (10°F)

until only the teeth remain white. 'Geisha' is similar, with dainty, toothed leaves, edged in silver. It forms an elegant low mound, and is also available grafted onto 1.5m (5ft) high stems.

U. minor var. vulgaris 'Argenteovariegata', or 'Foliis Variegata' formerly U. procera, is a variegated form of English elm, cultivated since the eighteenth century. It makes a large, stately tree, up to 30m (100ft) high, 15m (50ft) across. Its green leaves are splashed and blotched with white and silver-grey, and turn yellow in autumn before falling. Inconspicuous flowers appear in spring.

WEIGELA

These flowering shrubs, among the most popular for general garden planting, are reliable and easy to grow, even in urban locations. The leaves are fairly coarse in the species, but smaller, more pointed and attractive in variegated forms. Though deciduous, they remain on the shrub until well into autumn, often to midwinter, before finally falling.

Weigela florida 'Variegata', 'Aureovariegata' or 'Variegata Aurea', 90-150cm (3-5ft) high and as much across, carries slender, upright and arching sprays of light green leaves edged in deep creamy yellow when young, gradually turning creamy white, tinged with pink at the base in autumn. Some leaves have narrow, even variegations, while others have broadly irregular ones. It occasionally throws up strong vertical water shoots of bolder leaves, useful for flower

Family: Caprifoliaceae
Height: 90-180cm (3-6ft)
Spread: 90-180cm (3-6ft)
Flowering time: Late spring or early summer
Aspect: Sun, shelter
Soil: Well drained, fertile
Minimum temperature: −23°C (−10°F)

Above: Weigela florida
'Variegata'

Left: Viburnum tinus
'Variegatum'

Left: Weigela praecox
'Variegata'

Right: Yucca filamentosa
'Variegata' behind
variegated euonymus

Yucca filamentosa
'Variegata'

arrangers. The tubular, pale pink, foxglove-like flowers, shaded deeper pink, are carried in clusters on year-old wood. 'Variegata Compacta' and 'Variegata Nana' are similar but smaller and more wide-spreading. In Victorian times, W. *florida*, then known as W. *rosea*, and its forms were grown as cold greenhouse plants, and the blooms gently forced for bouquets and table decorations.

W. *praecox* 'Variegata' is larger, with an upright growth habit and large, honey-scented, rosy pink flowers in late spring. It has creamy white leaf edges when grown in a sunny spot, yellow in shade. 'Rubigold', 'Olympiade' or 'Briant Rubidor', is a recent French introduction with gold-splashed leaves, some all yellow, and ruby-red blossom. It is more tolerant of sun than other varie-gated weigelas.

To prune thin out the old flowering shoots to within a few centimetres of old wood immediately after flowering. Leave the young shoots intact, to produce next year's flowers. The flowers are liable to brown if exposed to drought or winds, so a sheltered spot in moisture-retentive soil is best.

YUCCA

Family: Agavaceae
Height: 90cm-3m (3-10ft)
Spread: 90cm (3ft)
Flowering time: Late summer
Aspect: Hot sun
Soil: Well drained, dry, sandy loam
Minimum temperature: −29°C (−20°F) to −18°C (0°F)

These stately, slow-growing, rosette-forming evergreens combine a tropical appearance with a surprising degree of hardi-ness. The narrow, usually rigid, sword-like leaves are particularly attractive when the plants are grown in containers or surrounded by paving. The panicles or racemes of bell-shaped, pendant blooms, carried on imposing spikes appear only in suitably hot, sunny conditions.

Yucca filamentosa, one of the hardiest species, comes from the coastal plains of the south-east United States. It forms dense, stemless clumps or rosettes of lance-shaped, narrow leaves up to 75cm (30in) long and edged with curly white threads. Creamy white flowers on panicles 90-120cm (3-4ft)

high appear in mid to late summer, even in young plants. Variegated forms, unfortun-ately less reliable in flowering, include 'Bright Edge', with narrow yellow margins; 'Starburst', with leaf borders attractively striped creamy yellow, and tinged with pink in cold weather; and 'Variegata', with dark green leaves streaked with narrow pale green lines and broadly edged in creamy white, becoming duller with age. Some leaves are more white than green. This was a popular Victorian greenhouse plant; under glass the leaves grew luxuriantly and the contrast between green and white was more brilliant.

Y. flaccida 'Golden Sword' is another stemless, clump-forming cultivar, spreading by suckers. Its lance-shaped, less rigid, leaves, up to 60cm (2ft) long and edged in white, thread-like fibres, have wide central bands of creamy yellow margined with soft green. The creamy yellow flowers are carried on short stalks, up to 60cm (2ft) high.

Y. gloriosa 'Variegata', or 'Aureovarie-gata', is the variegated form of Adam's needle. It is a small, tree-like species, slowly forming a branchless trunk 1.8-3m (6-10ft) high, topped by leaf rosettes. Its rigid, fiercely spine-tipped young leaves are glaucous grey, margined and striped with dull, creamy yellow and pink, fading to creamy white on older leaves. 'Medio-striata' is an old, rare form, with leaves centrally striped white. The flowers, on spikes up to 1.8cm (6ft) high, are creamy white with deep pink tinges.

The brightest variegated yucca is 'Garland's Gold', a compact, hybrid form, with golden-centred leaves. All variegated forms must be propagated from offsets.

INDEX